BARTH AND RATIONALITY

Barth and Rationality

Critical Realism in Theology

D. Paul La Montagne

CASCADE *Books* · Eugene, Oregon

BARTH AND RATIONALITY
Critical Realism in Theology

Cascade Books
An Imprint of Wipf and Stock Publishers
199 W. 8th Ave., Suite 3
Eugene, OR 97401

www.wipfandstock.com

Material from *The Retreat to Commitment* by W. W. Bartley, 1984, La Salle and London: Open Court Publishing, © 1962, 1964, 1982 and 1984 by William Warren Bartley, III, used with the kind permission of Open Court Publishing Company, a division of Carus Publishing.

Material from "Fate and Idea in Theology" by Karl Barth, translated by George Hunsinger, in *The Way of Theology in Karl Barth*, edited by H. Martin Rumscheidt, 1986, Allison Park, Pennsylvania: Pickwick Publications, © by Pickwick Publications, used with the kind permission of Wipf & Stock Publishers, Eugene Oregon.

Material from *Church Dogmatics: The Doctrine of the Word of God, volume I part 1* by Karl Barth, translated by G. W. Bromiley, 1975, Edinburgh: T. & T. Clark, © 1975 T. & T. Clark Limited, and *Church Dogmatics: The Doctrine of the Word of God, volume I part 2* by Karl Barth, translated by G. T. Thompson and Harold Knight, 1956, Edinburgh: T. & T. Clark, © 1956 T. & T. Clark Limited, and *Church Dogmatics: The Doctrine of God, volume II part 1* by Karl Barth, translated by T. H. L. Parker, W. B. Johnston, Harold Knight, and J. L. M. Haire, 1957, Edinburgh: T. & T. Clark, © 1957 T. & T. Clark Limited, used by the kind permission of Continuum International Publishing Group.

ISBN 13: 978-1-61097-656-5

Cataloging-in-Publication data:

La Montagne, D. Paul.

   Barth and rationality : critical realism in theology / D. Paul La Montagne, with a foreword by Bruce L. McCormack.

   xii + 236 p. ; 23 cm. Includes bibliographical references and index(es).

   ISBN 13: 978-1-61097-656-5

   1. Barth, Karl, 1886–1968. 2. Kant, Immanuel, 1724–1804. 3. Critical realism. 4. Knowledge, theory of (Religion). 5. Science and religion. I. McCormack, Bruce L. II. Title.

BX4827.B3 L125 2012

Manufactured in the U.S.A.

Contents

Foreword

For the great majority of Christian theologians, mathematics is at best an arcane discipline with little or no relevance to the work they do. At worst, it was a general education requirement or two taken in college, brushed up quickly in order to receive a barely acceptable score on a GRE, and then immediately forgotten. The truth is, however, that we will not attain to an adequate understanding of what it means to do theology "under the conditions of modernity" unless we know something about the revolutions that have taken place in this discipline, especially in the last century and a half. Revolutions in mathematics have an impact on the field of physics and physics is a field that those working in the fields of philosophy of religion and philosophical epistemology cannot afford to ignore—not to mention those Christian theologians working on the doctrine of creation.

But where is the theologian desirous of obtaining an overview of advances in mathematics and an understanding of their implications for philosophical and theological epistemology to turn? Scholars with advanced degrees in both mathematics and theology are virtually non-existent. A good many of those who participate in the current debates over the relation of theology and the natural sciences come to their task with serious training only in the latter disciplines. Where the field of Christian systematic theology is concerned, they are largely self-taught. It is the rare person who possesses an advanced degree in theology and a more than causal interest in physics and mathematics. D. Paul La Montagne is such a person.

La Montagne first came to my attention as a Masters of Divinity student at Princeton Theological Seminary. He came to us armed with an undergraduate degree in mathematics—and his interest in pure mathematics (that part of the field devoted to solving puzzles which often had no known applications) remained strong. When, later, as a PhD student working in the fields of theology and science and systematic theology, he found himself less than challenged by the regiment of seminars we required him to take, he took additional courses at Princeton University. I remember in particular two courses entitled "Intermediate Logic: The Incompleteness Theorems" and "Set Theory as a Foundation of Mathematics" in the Philosophy Department (cross-listed with the Mathematics Department) of that university that deeply engaged his attention. All of this is to say: Paul La Montagne is as well prepared to assess the implications of advances made in the field of mathematics for Christian theology as anyone now working in the various fields contributing to theology and science debates. Only a person possessed of advanced degrees in all the pertinent fields could be better prepared and, as I say, they are few, if any.

One of the things that La Montagne argues in this book is that there have been three developments in mathematics over the course of the last two hundred years that have exercised a considerable influence on philosophical epistemology: first, the discovery and elaboration of non-Euclidean geometries; second, the proof of the Gödel incompleteness theorems; and, third, the development of multi-valued and other alternative logics. Taken together, these developments have undermined the classical belief that there are universal and necessary rational standards to which the truth-claims made in any and every discipline must be subjected. Rigor in a particular scientific discipline is now understood to based (in part, at least) on certain axiomatic choices that are made in accordance with the needs of that discipline. And that has, in turn, made fallibilist epistemologies respectable.

La Montagne's goal in this study is show that a particular theological epistemology—*viz.* that of Karl Barth—is not only "scientific" when seen in the light of the subject-matter of the discipline within which he worked but also, and more importantly, closely akin to the *critical* versions of "scientific realism" now celebrated by a good many philosophers of science.

With the publication of La Montagne's book, a new day has dawned in which Barth's "post-Kantian" theological epistemology has to be taken seriously by those engaged in the theology and science debates. That Barth scholars, too, should take notice, goes without saying. Barth's theology is interpreted in the wrong frame of reference when it is subjected to the standards of a more ancient philosophical epistemology—which is what inevitably happens when that theology is interpreted in the light of those church fathers whose debt to ancient epistemologies was great. That Barth's theology represents a distinctive variant within so-called "*modern* theology" becomes very clear in the pages that follow.

My gratitude to Paul LaMontagne for what I have learned from him is profound. I now eagerly look forward to seeing what others will do with the hard-earned results of his inquiry.

Bruce L. McCormack
Charles Hodge Professor of Systematic Theology
Princeton Theological Seminary
September 26, 2011

Acknowledgments

This book is a revision and significant expansion of my dissertation at Princeton Theological Seminary, presented in 2001. Without the criticisms of my committee and the corrections and clarifications I have been able to make because of them, it would not be nearly so worthwhile as it may now be. Dr. Diogenes Allen's comments were particularly helpful (which means that I was in serious error on the points that he addressed). Dr. van Huyssteen deserves special thanks and great praise besides. He permitted me to write a dissertation that challenged directly a position he had taken in one of his early works. This bespeaks a confidence in his own work, coupled with a willingness to hear and encourage the challenging of that work, which ought to be both common and normative in scholarship. He is a gentleman and a scholar of the first water, and I give him my sincere gratitude.

The debt of gratitude and honor that I owe to Dr. Bruce McCormack for both his friendship and his instruction is one that cannot even be calculated, much less paid. Unfortunately this means that he who is owed most is least thanked here.

When I was an undergraduate majoring in both mathematics and religion, Howard Gage was chair of the mathematics department. He understood immediately why a theologian would want to study mathematics and supported my hopes with both encouragement and friendship. He also gave me practical help in the form of work tutoring mathematics and grading papers, and then later, found for me and recommended me for a job, writing software for an automated blood chemistry analyzer, that provided income that was of critical importance in bridging the gap between undergraduate and graduate studies. It is a sadness that he did not live to see this work.

It always seems maudlin to read a scholar dedicating their work to their spouse, and citing their sacrifices. But when one comes to write it one realizes that it is a matter of simple justice. Linda suffered as much for this work as I did.

My thanks to Nathan P. LaMontagne and Dan Padgett who provided reading, comments and proofing to late drafts of this text.

1

Introduction

1.1 GENESIS OF THIS STUDY

In the conclusion of *Karl Barth's Critically Realistic Dialectical Theology* Bruce McCormack says:

> The adjectival phrase "critically realistic" has been employed throughout the present work in an attempt to distinguish Barth's version of dialectical theology from all the alternative conceptions . . . It should be noted that the choice of the phrase "critically realistic" was not made out of a desire to establish a comparison between Barth's theology and those contemporary schools of philosophical reflection which have also found in the phrase something apt for describing their own epistemologies. No such comparison was intended, for it is doubtful that it can be made—for two reasons. First, as the phrase has been used here, it describes a strictly theological epistemology. Critical realism has the significance of a witness to the mystery of divine action in revelation . . . Second, as has been argued throughout the book, to the extent that Barth concerned himself with philosophical epistemology at all, he was an idealist (and more specifically, a Kantian).[1]

---

1. McCormack, *Barth's Critically Realistic Dialectical Theology*, 464–65.

It is the purpose of this book to establish a comparison between the form that critical realism takes in Barth's dialectical theology and those schools of philosophical reflection that find critical realism to be an apt description of their own epistemological reflections.[2] Doing so will clarify some points in the interpretation of Barth. Moreover, it may turn out that using critical realism to address Barth and the object of his discourse will increase the breadth of our understanding of critical realism as well. "Critically realistic" is an adjectival qualification chosen for its usefulness in distinguishing Barth's particular variety of dialectical theology from that of the other dialectical theologians. It will be necessary to use the term "dialectical" adjectivally to distinguish the particular form of Barth's critical realism from that which is current in the philosophy of science. Critical realism in the philosophy of science is a response *to* and an interpretation *of* the history of science. Critical realism in Barth's theology is a response *to* and an interpretation *of* the self-revelation of God in Jesus Christ.[3] There are structural similarities, but they have different roots.

Barth's theology cannot be justified by its similarities to a viable option in the philosophy of science. But it can be explained more clearly by mining those similarities for analogies and metaphors. The differences will then stand out clearly and serve to limit the range, meaning, and effectiveness of those analogies and metaphors.[4] (Establishing such limits *improves* the value of analogies and metaphors, not reduces it.) The differences also make clear the specific object to which Barth addresses his discourse. Many of the claims that Barth wishes to make about this object are counterintuitive and Barth expresses himself in complex and sometimes paradoxical language in order to make those claims. The comparison with critical realism in the philosophy of science will make it possible, on occasion, to explain *how* Barth is using dialectical language. He does not do so in order to promote contradictions, which would

2. In an article length review of McCormack's book Colin Gunton directed the question of such a comparison to McCormack and asserted the value of such a study. Gunton, "McCormack's Karl Barth Book," 488.

3. See Gunton's acknowledgement that McCormack has made his case for treating Barth's philosophical commitments as a reflex of material decisions in the field of theology. Gunton, "McCormack's Karl Barth Book," 483–84, 490–91.

4. "The work of critically realistic philosophers may well provide *parables* of Barth's critically realistic construal of the dialectic of veiling and unveiling in God's self-revelation in Jesus Christ. But unless that revelation becomes the concern of philosophers too, irreducible differences will remain which ought not to be papered over." McCormack, "Barth in Context," 493.

then permit saying anything else without further control, but rather, to point to an object that refuses to be confined to the categories of human thought, no matter how broadly or formally conceived.

The specific purpose of this study is to explain what sort of a model of rationality Barth is using. This explanation will then be used to answer some longstanding charges that have been filed against Barth's theology: that it is a form of revelational positivism, that it is inherently irrational, and that it is irreducibly subjective. Explaining the rationality of Barth's theological work and defending it against various charges that it is philosophically defective does not by any means establish that it is true. It only establishes that it is sufficiently rational to be counted as a reasonable candidate for a model of how we ought to speak when we talk of God. At the end, the critically realistic characterization of Barth's dialectical theology will make it possible to provide a valuable caution and a possible guide for evaluating recent postmodern readings of Barth.

1.2 SPECIFICATIONS OF TERMS RELATED TO FOUNDATIONALISM

A brief word of historiography is in order. Postmodernism is a late developing interpretive theory, although the phenomenon may be older. Except in architecture and art, little before 1960 is explicitly called "postmodern," though research finds adumbrations of postmodernity in much late modern thought. Karl Barth is a modern, not a postmodern, thinker. But there are elements in his thought that are amenable to a postmodern reading. One of these elements is that Barth's theology is, in an important sense, postfoundational.

Every developed and articulated position, whether in philosophy, science, theology, or any other human endeavor, is highly structured and possessed of organizational rules, values, procedures, and principles. These are usually called the foundation of the position. No prejudice applies at this point, for having some sort of relative foundation is necessary for orderly and rational human thinking. But when some subset of those rules and principles is regarded as certain, self-demonstrating, and necessary for the justification of all other epistemic claims, then the position is what we call foundationalism or foundationalist.[5] This distinction is narrow, but deep.

5. Thiel, *Nonfoundationalism*, 1.

Foundationalism absolutizes its foundations.[6] It may do so immediately, proclaiming that the present foundations of the position are final, or it may do so mediately, claiming that ultimate foundations do exist and the present set is a reasonable approximation of them. This imposes a necessity upon us to be very careful about language. We often have good reason to say X is foundational to Y, or X is a foundation for Y. When we do we have, so far, only asserted the relationship between X and Y. Not until we call X absolute or universally necessary or self-demonstrating or the final reference point for testing epistemic claims have we turned our foundation into foundationalism. Modern thought is usually counted as foundationalist from the time of the rationalism of the Enlightenment until the present. Actually though, there are modifications to foundationalism that take place within the boundaries of modern thought, which I will take up when I address the history of science.

Nonfoundationalism is a philosophical movement with one root in a branch of early American pragmatism, represented by the work of William James (1842–1910), Charles Sanders Peirce (1839–1914), and John Dewey (1859–1952), and another in the later work of Ludwig Wittgenstein (1889–1951). Its postmodern version is evident in the work such philosophers as Wilfrid Sellars (1912–89), Willard Van Orman Quine (1908–2000), Richard Rorty (1931–2007), and Donald Davidson (1917–2003).[7] It is based upon a critical insistence that no form of human thought in any language or by any logic has any foundation whatsoever in the sense that foundationalism would mean it. There are no certain, self-demonstrating, universal, necessary rules of thought. There are only the relative, conventional, organizing rules, and principles of whatever language or conceptual scheme is being used. Those who practice nonfoundationalism treat philosophy as an analytical, diagnostic, and critical tool, rather than as a constructive enterprise.[8] They seem now to be somewhat in the majority among working philosophers.[9] For

6. van Huyssteen, *Shaping of Rationality*, 62–63.

7. Thiel, *Nonfoundationalism*, 6–37. These are some of the figures who gave it form. A list of other and later figures who could rightly be called postmodern would be inconveniently long, and might include some who are more important (in a relative postmodern way) than those mentioned here, e.g., Derrida, Lyotard.

8. See, for instance, Rorty's description of philosophy as a therapeutic and edifying practice, rather than a constructive one. Rorty, *Philosophy and the Mirror of Nature*, 5–6, 367–72.

9. Thiel, *Nonfoundationalism*, 37.

the most part, nonfoundational philosophers seem to be anti-realists in epistemology.

Postfoundationalism is a critical realist position articulated in response to nonfoundational criticism in theology and in the philosophy of science.[10] Postfoundationalism agrees with nonfoundationalism about the status of foundations but disagrees with most nonfoundationalism about realism in epistemology.[11] As a critical realist position, postfoundationalism is willing to treat nonfoundationalism with respect as a valuable critical theory, but it also asserts the value of constructive work in philosophy, theology, and in science.[12]

Almost all of what we call knowledge exists in our minds in the form of models of something to which we attribute reality. Each of those models is constructed on some relative foundation or other in thought. Postfoundationalism, accepting that those foundations are only relative organizational rules and principles of thought, takes the freedom to change or modify the foundations in order to support and develop better models to serve as our knowledge of reality. About this knowledge postfoundationalism makes a realist claim in the qualified manner appropriate to a critical realism that accepts much of the nonfoundational critique.

---

10. See the essays "The Shaping of Rationality in Science and Religion," in van Huyssteen, *Postfoundational Theology*, 238–65, and van Huyssteen, "Postfoundationalism in Theology and Science." It is important to note that what is here called postfoundationalism would be regarded by some European writers as simply one of the varieties of nonfoundationalism. The division between realism and anti-realism is not entailed in the division between foundationalism and nonfoundationalism. For this reason it is necessary to carefully label this postfoundational position, which maintains its critical realism not merely in the face of the nonfoundational critique, but by making full and conscious use of it. See van Huyssteen, *Shaping of Rationality*, 40–41.

11. "It seems to me that the common mistake of postmodernism and social constructivism is their belief that anti-foundationalism about science entails anti-realism." Niiniluoto, *Critical Scientific Realism*, 249.

12. "One way to do this would be to try to find and identify a model of rationality that would . . . lure us to move beyond the epistemological dichotomy of foundationalist objectivism and non-foundationalist relativism . . . A postfoundationalist model of rationality will take seriously the challenge of much of postmodern thinking, but will carefully distinguish between constructive and deconstructive modes of postmodern thinking. A postfoundationalist model of rationality will therefore especially incorporate into our reasoning strategies the relentless criticism of foundationalist assumptions." van Huyssteen, *Shaping of Rationality*, 8.

One of the theses advanced in this book is that Karl Barth's theology is an anticipation of postfoundationalism in theology. Because Barth did not see or encounter nonfoundationalism his anticipation does not articulate itself as postfoundationalism does now. It is this anticipatory postfoundationalism that Bruce McCormack is trying to capture when he coins the term "transfoundational" to refer to Barth's theology.[13] McCormack is careful to point out that Barth is only transfoundational in theology, with respect to the knowledge of God, and not as a product of philosophical reflection upon the problem of foundations. Transfoundationalism in Barth's theology plays the role of a witness to the mystery of God's action in revelation. Barth has not applied his insight to the problem of human knowledge in general, because his doctrines of God and of creation make it clear that God is not the creation, not even in its eschatological summation. Therefore, there is no reason to suppose that what one learns about the nature of human knowledge by observing it in the case of the knowledge of God is immediately transferable to the realm of knowledge of the world. If further study should show that there are correspondences, then they are contingent correspondences, not necessary and intrinsic ones. God may well have made the world, or some parts of it, to resemble God in some way. But God need not have done so, and it is certain that in many ways the world does not resemble God at all. Because Barth supposes that God reveals by using and giving new content to our ordinary and normal knowing process, it is always proper to examine the human character of our knowledge in order to understand and explain what limits God transcends when becoming immanent in our knowledge. But because God transcends those limits in an act of revelation, the nature and character of that process, and of human knowledge as such, cannot be directly imputed to God. If further study of human knowing should show that there are correspondences to how we know God in self-revelation, then they are contingent correspondences created by God's grace in revelation, and not necessary and intrinsic ones.

Another anticipatory form of postfoundationalism occurred in the second half of the nineteenth century and at the beginning of the twentieth when discoveries in the physical sciences made it clear that some seemingly self-evident presuppositions were, in fact, not appropriate to the description of physical reality. The classic case is the relativity theory

13. McCormack, *Orthodox and Modern*, 124–27.

of Einstein in which absolute time and space as understood by Newton in terms of Euclidean geometry were put aside. The problem extends itself into quantum theory where apparently contradictory models, that light is a wave phenomenon and that light is a particulate phenomenon, are both necessary to describe the full range of behavior of the reality of light in the world, thus calling into question the presuppositions of the models. The contradiction is understood to lie in the system of thought in which we are attempting to describe the behavior of the world, not in reality itself, and the differing assumptions are used alternatively, according to what kind of statements need to be made, not simultaneously. But the self-evidence of our presuppositions is still impugned.

Once such considerations arise, once a system of thought that is committed to realistic description becomes aware that its own most basic rules are precisely that and not foundations sunk into the structure of reality itself, then I am willing to call it postfoundational, even if only by anticipation. Such a position may not have moved very far from foundationalism. Einstein himself considered one of the purposes of the theory of relativity to be to find invariants. He was looking for things that did not change when the frame of reference was changed. And he found some too, such as the speed of light. Often such positions, especially those to which I am giving credit for being postfoundational by anticipation, continue to construct large, complexly structured, rigorously founded bodies of knowledge in which being postfoundational is confined to an awareness that the basic rules of the system are not final foundations but conventional assumptions which can be changed or adjusted to produce a better description of reality. Most of modern science is, and has been since the late 1800s, postfoundational.

Large, highly structured, rigorously mathematical structures of knowledge are too valuable to be abandoned simply because we have abandoned foundationalist assumptions. Sometimes, in the history of thought, this anticipatory postfoundationalism is hard to detect because working scientists usually still hope to elaborate a system of theoretical commitments that is so much better than any of the alternatives that it can be treated in practical terms as though it were founded in the nature of reality itself. They are aware that their most basic rules and principles are not absolute foundations. But they are not about to change them until repeated and prominent behaviors in the world force them to do so by being very nearly impossible to describe and account for under the current rules and principles. Nonetheless, where such events, such major changes of theoretical commitments, do occur, and, moreover, are expected to occur in the course of a generations-long investigation into the unknown, it is still proper to call these positions postfoundational.

The danger is that such changes will be regarded as successive approximations to a real, correct, proper, and true foundation. But since the second half of the nineteenth century when mathematics reorganized and rigorized the foundations of the real number system, when non-Euclidean geometries were elucidated, when set theory was given its first formulations and its extension to transfinite sets led to paradoxical philosophical questions, mathematical truth has been understood to be hypothetical truth, not approximate truth or absolute truth.[14] This means that even a foundation is understood in mathematics to be a hypothesis. Since 1931, after the proof of the Gödel incompleteness theorems, mathematics has understood that even such a simple phenomenon as whole number arithmetic cannot be described completely by any finite system of assumptions, no matter how complex. Since mathematics and mathematical logic are the most basic rules and principles in most of the sciences, this means that where modern science is self-aware at all it is aware of being postfoundational.

1.3 CAUTIONS, LIMITS, AND POTENTIAL PROBLEMS

In his 1974 commencement address at Cal Tech, Richard Feynman said of the ethics of scientific theorizing:

> It's a kind of scientific integrity . . . If you are doing an experiment, you should report everything that you think might make it invalid—not only what you think is right about it . . . Details that could throw doubt on your interpretation must be given, if you know them . . . There is also a more subtle problem. When you put a lot of ideas together to make an elaborate theory, you want to make sure, when explaining what fits, that those things it fits

14. Boyer, *History of the Calculus*, 308. By this mathematicians mean that all truth is hypothecated upon the postulates or axioms of the system within which statements are being made. The status of the postulates and axioms themselves is very much in question. A great many working mathematicians are formalists. They believe that axioms and postulates are chosen freely and mathematics consists of the logical investigation of the relations and consequences of the axioms chosen. Thus their contention that mathematical truth is hypothetical truth is the equivalent of saying that mathematical truth is contingent truth, not necessary truth.

are not just the things that gave you the idea for the theory; but that the finished theory makes something else come out right, in addition. In summary, the idea is to give *all* of the information to help others judge the value of your contribution; not just the information that leads to judgment in one particular direction or another.[15]

In conformity with this standard several cautions must be issued right at the beginning of this work.

First, mathematics and the philosophy of science are being used in this work to explicate some difficult features of Barth's theology. Though I have reviewed the major dispute in the philosophy of science with an attempt at fairness to both sides, I have also made judgments about the various arguments and taken positions in the philosophy of mathematics and the philosophy of science on the basis of those judgments. The reader must always question whether I have thereby unconsciously let the ends of this study rather than the merits of the arguments control my judgments. A hermeneutic of suspicion is always appropriate, so long as it is not the only hermeneutical heuristic being employed and the possibility of an affirmative judgment is not precluded.

Second, concerning the mathematics used in this book: the great advantage of mathematics is that it is inherently simple and easy. Mathematicians are fond of saying things like, "I don't know any non-trivial mathematics."[16] This means that when a piece of mathematics is understood at all, it is understood in a way that makes the structures, relations, and inferences that it symbolizes obvious.[17] This allows it to be used to spread something out in an ordered fashion so that its various

---

15. Feynman, *The Pleasure of Finding Things Out*, 209–10.

16. Barrow, *Pi in the Sky*, 133–34. This is, of course, a simplification. But simplifying is precisely what mathematicians spend a great deal of their time and effort doing. New results are often complex, difficult, and specialized. Further work consists of finding simpler and more obvious solutions, or proofs that use more standard techniques, until the work can be understood by students as well as researchers. See ibid., 233–34.

17. Hilbert, speaking in praise of Dirichlet's work in 1905, enunciated a criterion for good mathematics: "to conquer the problems with a minimum of blind calculation, a maximum of clear-seeing thoughts." Cited in Stein, "Logos, Logic, and Logistiké," 239. See also 239–45 for the impact of this criterion on the arithmetization of analysis in the nineteenth century.

relations can be seen plainly and clearly.[18] For this reason it is often enormously helpful in making explanations and organizing knowledge.[19]

The mathematics that I use here is standard textbook stuff in advanced classes in set theory and mathematical logic. But remembering that mathematical truth is hypothetical, contingent truth, the reader is warned that the fact that some aspect of Barth's theology, or of critical realism, has been explained with a bit of mathematics in a clear and well ordered manner does not mean anything one way or another about its truth. As mathematics is the symbolic logic of possible relations, positions or theories that do not correspond to the world can also be described with mathematics in a clear and well ordered manner.

Mathematics is only productive of knowledge of the world,
$\qquad\qquad\qquad\qquad\qquad\qquad\qquad$ of external reality,
when the clarity and order that it brings to explanations
$\qquad$ can be used to facilitate an understanding
$\qquad\qquad$ of the basic rules and principles of a body of knowledge,
$\qquad\qquad\qquad$ the way those rules and principles work together,
$\qquad\qquad\qquad\qquad$ and the implications of the knowledge founded
$\qquad\qquad\qquad\qquad\qquad$ (hypothetically) upon those principles and rules,
so that the knowledge may be used in an ongoing investigation of reality
$\qquad$ in which conflicts and anomalies may arise
$\qquad\qquad$ such that we will find it necessary to exercise our judgment
$\qquad\qquad\qquad$ to make new rules, or change the rules,
$\qquad\qquad\qquad\qquad$ or adopt new axioms or postulates.

Third, one of the difficulties in explaining why Barth's dialectical theology is critically realistic is accounting for his commitment to Kantian philosophy, a strictly foundationalist option. Kant's philosophy is strongly idealistic, yet I will be arguing that Barth uses it in a critically realistic way. Moreover, Barth never describes himself as a critical realist, although that is, in part, because the term was not readily available to him. In order to demonstrate why Barth's use of Kant is critically realistic it is necessary to look at some issues in the history of idealist philosophy

18. Stein, "Logos, Logic, and Logistiké," 252, attributes to C. S. Peirce and G. F. B. Riemann the idea that mathematics, though not specifically empirical itself, provides "the means of *formulating* hypotheses or theories for the empirical sciences." (My emphasis.)

19. Kurt Gödel seems to have held a similar opinion of the way that mathematics is valuable in philosophy. Wang, *Reflections on Kurt Gödel*, 64.

in Germany from the time of Kant to that of Barth, even though I am not a specialist in this history. Idealism, realism, and critical realism are not absolute markers. They are to be found on a spectrum and the value we give to each of these positions may depend upon what part of the spectrum we transit in order to reach one of these positions. The historical argument is necessary in order to identify where on the spectrum Barth starts (with Cohen's neo-Kantian critical idealism) and why, relative to that starting point, Kant is a critically realistic option. In this history we also see what options and presuppositions Barth is turning his back on when he moves out of Cohen's neo-Kantianism to a version that reads Kant more plainly. The soundness of my argument here is confined to the broad outlines of the history and their relevance for Barth's background. It is all too likely that I have made a multitude of lesser errors in characterizing this history.

Fourth, the first part of this work is designed to acquaint systematic theologians and Barth specialists with sufficient material from mathematics and the philosophy of science to be able to better explain Barth. Mathematicians, philosophers of science, and theologians familiar with the science and theology dialogue may well find the exposition of critical realism slow, simple, and lacking nuance. Moreover, I am attempting to combine applied mathematics, the philosophy of science and systematic theology in a unified endeavor. The possibility of confusion will always lurk in the shadows preparing an ambush.[20]

1.4 ENDS

This book is based immediately upon the work of Bruce McCormack in *Karl Barth's Critically Realistic Dialectical Theology*. That work is taken largely for granted here. But I now start where McCormack left off, and here attempt the task that McCormack declined, and indeed doubted could be done: comparing the form that critical realism takes in Karl Barth's dialectical theology with those schools of philosophical thought that also use the term "critical realism" to describe their own epistemological thought.[21] The end result of this study should be a much

20. I am very much indebted to professor Diogenes Allen for pointing out several errors of exposition and calling attention to some of the potential confusions.

21. Also, McCormack's own researches have not led him to a direct engagement of these issues.

clearer understanding of what it means to be critically realistic in theology. In making this attempt I am trying to show that one element of McCormack's thesis, that Barth is critically realistic, fulfills one of the conditions for a good theory set out by Feynman above. It not only fits the things that gave him the idea for the theory, problems in describing and periodizing Barth's development, but also makes something else come out right in addition, by answering certain philosophical charges that have been lodged against Barth.

But most of all, this work should promote valuable conversation. Karl Barth exhibited a longstanding commitment to carrying on extended and serious conversation with precisely those theologians with whom he was in greatest disagreement: the liberal school from Schleiermacher through the Ritschlians to his own time when he broke with them. This can be seen throughout his own theological work in the *Church Dogmatics* and in *Protestant Theology in the Nineteenth Century*. But notice: his break with the liberals was a break in substance, *not* a break in the conversation. Unfortunately, for a long time it appeared that the heirs of Barth and the heirs of the liberal theologians had each decided independently that there was no compelling reason to carry on any conversation with the other school. There are signs that the critically realistic reading of Barth's dialectical theology may help us past this impasse. It is to be hoped that the present work will contribute to that conversation. Theology on both sides has much to gain.

Barth was not consciously a critical realist. Dialectical critical realism is here a description of the implications of the position to which Barth is forced by interaction with the object of his discourse, God in the act of self-revelation. Barth uses a foundationalist epistemology, Kant's, in a postfoundational way because he finds it necessary if he is to remain faithful to the object of his discourse. But once we have identified and understood how and why Barth is being critically realistic in his dialectical theology, we may well be able to find ways to say what Barth was saying using an epistemological theory that is critically realistic from the beginning.[22] That will be a task for a future work, to which this is only prolegomenon. But when that work has been taken in hand, then we will not merely have understood Barth, but also used what we understand in

---

22. In various different places T. F. Torrance, Colin Gunton, and Bruce McCormack have suggested that of Michael Polanyi as a possible candidate. As best I can tell, no one has yet followed up on this suggestion in detail.

him to go further and deeper into the subject than Barth himself. And this is only what Barth would have desired. The church which has been reformed according to the Word of God nevertheless always needs to be reformed in the light of further encounter with the Word of God.

2

Critical Realism

Critical realism is a philosophical attitude toward the relationship between knowledge and reality.[1] It is usually found in close company with
some particular epistemology, but different epistemological theories
may be viewed in a critically realistic way. Moreover, the same epistemology, Kant's for instance, may be viewed anti-realistically, idealistically (the classic interpretation), or even (as will be argued in chapter 5)
in a critically realistic way. As it is the burden of this book to describe the
particular form that critical realism takes in Karl Barth's theology and to
argue that this form of critical realism supports a defense of his theology
against charges that it is philosophically deficient, it is important to begin with a broad statement of what makes a position critically realistic.
Particular forms will require further specification. But discerning the
broad pattern is a necessary preliminary to arguing that Barth's theology
qualifies as one of them.

2.1 TYPOLOGY

Unsurprisingly, critical realism has two constitutive ingredients: (I) a
realistic element and (II) a critical element. The realistic element must

1. In van Kooten Niekerk, "Critical Realist Perspective," 51, van Kooten Niekerk
says that "critical realism is a philosophical view of the nature of knowledge." This
seems to treat critical realism as first order epistemology. I consider it to be *second*
order epistemology.

have two essential features. First (I-a), it must assert the existence of an other that is at least more than and different than the knowing subject, usually the world as a whole, conceived of as an independent external reality. The knowing subject may be a subset of the world to be known, but if so it must be a proper subset thereof. The knowing subject is not identified with an ultimate reason by which the world is created and maintained, as in absolute idealism. In critical realism that which is known is truly other than the knowing subject.

Secondly (I-b), it must assert that the knowing subject can have real knowledge of the world. The first feature is not sufficient by itself to constitute the realistic element in a critically realistic position.[2] In fact, most forms of anti-realism accept the notion that there is an independent external reality, arguing that its independence and externality are precisely why there is no real knowledge of it.[3] At a minimum, a claim that there is such a thing as real knowledge of the world must assert that knowledgeable statements truly refer. This minimum is not necessarily sufficient, as it is possible to describe reference in sociological and semantic terms without making any realistic commitment.[4] But this minimum constitutes a starting point, and particular forms of critical realism will go on to describe how and why knowledgeable statements refer, and to discuss why they constitute knowledge over and above mere semantic reference.

The critical element also has two essential features. First (II-a), knowledge is understood to be *mediated*. This means that it is neither

2. Kees van Kooten Niekerk expresses the same thing when he argues that critical realism affirms both metaphysical realism and epistemological realism. Ibid., 58.

3. This must be noted, because some in the modern discussion of the philosophy of science have argued against the anti-realists as though their claim were that the physical world does not exist as realists imagine it or that the concept of an independent physical world was indefensible. Trigg, *Reality at Risk* seems to be making this error. Devitt, *Realism and Truth* is better, as he distinguishes between metaphysical realism and epistemological realism. But he seems to think that settling the issue of metaphysical realism first—though it was never under attack, except in Berkeleyian and Absolute Idealism—will accomplish something towards addressing the issue of epistemological realism. For maximum clarity see Niiniluoto, *Critical Scientific Realism*, 3–4.

4. As in the strong program in the sociology of knowledge. Philosophical argumentation for this understanding of reference can be found in Rorty, *Philosophy and the Mirror of Nature*, 284–94. Rorty there refers to the later position of Hilary Putnam as also being an abandonment of any attempt to maintain a metaphysical or transcendent grounding for a theory of reference.

direct and intuitive, as in naïve realism or the sensory theory of neo-realism, nor is it identical with the known, as in scholastic Aristoteleanism, in which the mind knows by conforming itself to the inherent intelligibility of the object known.[5] Second (II-b), and almost as a consequence of the first, there must be some sort of critical theory about the nature and limits of reason or of knowledge, which is used to make judgments about the character of the mediation. Different critical theories can be used with realistic intention and often the most distinctive thing about a particular form of critical realism is the critical theory that it employs. Moreover, the same critical theory can sometimes be used with either realistic or anti-realistic intention.

In all cases the great problem in arguing for a form of critical realism is to explain how and why knowledge that is admitted to be mediated and fallible is nonetheless asserted to be real knowledge of a truly other. This problem never goes away because it is inherent in critical realism. But it is not necessary to make the problem go away; it is only necessary to address it in a manner that does not pretend to have thereby disposed of it. I will later produce a suggestion of why the inherency of this problem constitutes an argument for, rather than against, critical realism.[6]

An alternative typology can be found in Ilkka Niiniluoto's work, *Critical Scientific Realism*. It is specifically designed for the current discussion of scientific realism and is less useful for my purpose than the more general scheme I have offered here. But it is of the highest quality, making possible the most careful distinctions and should be held in mind as an important contrast and possible corrective to what I have proposed.

Niiniluoto lists several forms of realism: ontological, semantic, epistemological, axiological, methodological, and ethical.[7] He then proposes a hierarchy of five theses about them which characterize scientific realism and its alternatives.[8] First is (R0) ontological realism, corresponding to my I-a, which distinguishes critical realism from subjective idealism and phenomenalism. Second (R1), semantic realism, which distinguishes critical realism from pragmatism and anarchism. Niiniluoto accepts

5. A highly developed form of this can be found in Lonergan, *Insight*. Lonergan develops this understanding of knowledge in a much more modern manner than in Aquinas, with full and careful attention to the empirical sciences and an awareness of Kant.

6. See 6.1.3 of this work.

7. Niiniluoto, *Critical Scientific Realism*, 1–2.

8. Ibid., 10–13.

Tarski's "model-theoretic definition [of semantics] as an adequate explication of the classical correspondence theory of truth."[9] He also offers a significant enhancement of this theory with a carefully formalized definition of the truthlikeness of statements that cannot be properly asserted as true in a strict bivalent language under two-valued logic.[10] Third (R2), theoretical realism, which distinguishes critical realism from descriptive empiricism and instrumentalism. It also serves to distinguish half-realisms like entity realism and structural realism, which might possibly fall under a broader definition of critical realism (such as mine). R1 and R2 together are the basis for epistemological realism and would fall under my I-b. Fourth (R3), axiological realism, which distinguishes critical realism from methodological non-realism and constructive empiricism. This falls partly under my I-b and partly under II-b. Fifth (R4), fallible realism, which modifies and conditions epistemological realism and distinguishes critical realism from naive realism.[11] This thesis falls partly under my II-a and partly under II-b. Finally (R5), critical realism, which is distinguished at this final step from a skepticism that may accept all the previous theses. The success of science is taken here as an argument for the truth of this thesis over against those positions from which critical realism has been distinguished. R5, along with the evidence for it and the arguments that support it falls under my II-b.

Niiniluoto's typology, and especially the chapter-length arguments that he makes for its theses (replete with useful formalisms), is by far the best I have seen for the discussion of current issues in the philosophy of science.[12]

I have taken the trouble to generalize on the nature of critical realism because the modern discussion is almost completely focused upon that particular form of critical realism that is called scientific realism. If that were the only defensible form of critical realism there would be no point in arguing that Karl Barth's theology is critically realistic. For this reason I have offered a broader typology and will start with a brief

9. Ibid., 42. See also Hooker, *A Realistic Theory of Science*, 33.

10. Niiniluoto, *Critical Scientific Realism*, 64–78.

11. "Realism in epistemology should employ the fallibilist conceptions of probable, conjectural, and truthlike knowledge—and thereby avoid the Scylla of infallibilism and the Charybdis of scepticism." Ibid., 85.

12. Another typology of critical realism and characterization of scientific realism can be found in Hooker, *A Realistic Theory of Science*, 88–92, 181.

examination of the earliest developed form of critical realism in order to illustrate the use of the broader typology.

2.2 EARLY CRITICAL REALISM

Critical Realism first appears in a distinct self-conscious form after World War I. The distant background for critical realism is the medieval discussion of the problem of universals, whether they were real and independently existing things, or merely names for the characteristics that were common to a class. The immediate background for critical realism is Kant. Kant argued strongly that the universality and necessity that we find in the objects of our experience are due to the structure of our intuition (both sensible and pure) and the categories of reason by which our understanding organizes experience into objects. What things may be in *themselves* is beyond our knowledge. The success of his philosophy and of the even more speculative absolute idealism that succeeded it gave rise to a reaction in the direction of realism. The first flush of that reaction was little more than naïve realism in philosophical clothing (commonly called Neo-Realism). But after the First World War there were arguments for a more considered realism that was not naïve, but in some way critical.

In 1920 a group of Americans, mostly pragmatists,[13] Durant Drake, Arthur O. Lovejoy, James Bisset Pratt, Arthur K. Rogers, George Santayana, Roy Wood Sellars, and C. A. Strong, published *Essays in Critical Realism: A Co-Operative Study of the Problem of Knowledge*. This co-operative work followed upon Sellars's 1916 work, *Critical Realism*. There had been passing uses of the phrase "critical realism" before this,[14] but this is one of the first two independent self-conscious uses of the term "critical realism" to describe an epistemological theory.[15] It is probably the seminal one.

13. Sellars says that he is not a pragmatist. Sellars, *Critical Realism*, 256.

14. Some of the neo-Kantians, in an attempt to turn in a realistic direction without leaving Kant behind, made use of phrases close to critical realism. See Köhnke, *The Rise of Neo-Kantianism*, 108–14, 245. I am not attempting a comprehensive history of critical realism here, and have therefore ignored these early precursors, as well as the development of critical realism in the period from 1930 through 1960.

15. The other was Hicks, *Critical Realism*. He collected essays he had previously published and public lectures he had given, beginning in 1917. He claimed priority of the Americans both in time, and also in the logical sense that he was using the term "critical" in a legitimate Kantian sense. He adopted a perceptual theory very much like that of the Americans in which the object of perception is itself the cause of the pattern

For the Americans it seemed obvious that philosophy should return to a more realistic epistemology. The growing success of the sciences was seen as significant reason for regarding speculative idealism, which followed Kant, as excessive.[16] For them, the "critical" ingredient in critical realism was most emphatically *not* the critical philosophy of Kant.[17] Their use of the term "critical" is meant to reflect two things. First, that they are critical of both the natural realism of common people (but not pejoratively)[18] and of the Neo-Realist school (pejoratively) that preceded them in reaction against speculative idealism.[19] Most specifically, they are critical of the theory of perception offered by the Neo-Realists because it asserted that real objects were *directly* experienced in perception. The pragmatists understand perception and conception to be *mediated* reference to reality, not direct and immediate.[20] Second, they affirm that the investigative and theory testing procedures of science criticize the knowledge we have initially in perception so as to discern the character or essence of the object of perception in a way that can be referred to the object itself.[21]

The main features of critical realism as it is advanced by the American pragmatists are these:

(1) The reality of the physical world, an external and independent world of objects, is taken for granted. They admit that the existence of the external world cannot be deduced directly from the data of sense. It is an assumption that is to be justified on the pragmatic grounds that it works.[22] Moreover, as the common sense assumption of almost all human

that is grasped in the act of perception. The act of knowledge is then no longer one of synthesizing, but rather one of discriminating, distinguishing, and comparing (see ibid., 6–7). It is difficult to understand, after such a radical move, how his epistemology is still Kantian, except perhaps by historical descent. The problem with basing critical realism upon such a theory of perception, for the Americans as well as for Dawes, is that it begs the question critical realism is supposed to address. It simply is not critical enough.

16. Drake, et al., *Essays in Critical Realism*, 187.

17. Ibid., iv, "Needless to say, the word 'critical' has no reference to the Kantian philosophy." Throughout the book the authors make clear their distance from Kant; see, for instance, ibid., 86–88, 110, 173, 211.

18. Sellars, *Critical Realism*, 7–21, 27.

19. Drake, et al., *Essays in Critical Realism*, vi, 3–4, 7–11, 12–15, 20 fn. 1, 88–89, 188–89.

20. Ibid., 48, 96–97.

21. Ibid., 110, 191, 203.

22. Ibid., 5–6.

beings, it does not need to be established before we can begin to do philosophy, but only defended against contrary notions. And knowledge, to be real, does not have to achieve the necessity and universality that Kant required of theoretical knowledge. It simply has to work, as knowledge of the world.[23] This is where we see these authors at their most pragmatic.

This feature corresponds directly to my I-a.

(2) The knowledge that we have of the world in perception and conception is not immediate, but is mediated. It is not directly identical with the object in the world.[24] Indeed, it could not be so and yet still be *our* knowledge, for our knowledge is a psychical entity in our minds, while the object is a physical object in the world.[25] This means that critical realism regards knowledge as an achievement of the mind rather than as a gift given to the mind by external reality. In this respect it acknowledges the contribution of idealism to philosophy.[26]

This feature corresponds directly to my II-a.

---

23. Ibid., 77, 105.

24. Ibid., 48. See also p. 76, Arthur O. Lovejoy, "Pragmatism *Versus* the Pragmatist:" "*A consistent pragmatism must recognize:*

(a) That all 'instrumental' knowledge is, or at least includes and requires, 'presentative' knowledge, a representation of not-present existents by present data;

(b) That, pragmatically considered, knowledge is thus necessarily and constantly conversant with entities which are existentially 'transcendent' of the knowing experience, and frequently with entities which transcend the total experience of the knower;

(c) That, if a real physical world having the characteristics set forth by natural science is assumed, certain of the contents of experience, and specifically the contents of anticipation and retrospection, cannot be assigned to that world, and must therefore be called 'psychical' (i.e., experienced but not physical) entities;

(d) That knowledge is mediated through such psychical existences, and would be impossible without them." (Emphasis belongs to original author.)

25. Ibid., 76. Also ibid., 165, George Santayana, "Three Proofs of Realism": "Now there is obviously no contradiction in maintaining both that knowledge is something added to its subject-matter, previously unknown, and at the same time that this acquired knowledge describes that subject matter correctly. Indeed, how could there be any description, correct or incorrect, if it were not in existence something new, and in deliverance and intent something relevant. A portrait, to be a portrait, must be distinct from the sitter, and must at the same time somehow resemble or be referred to him; the question how good a portrait it is, or what are the best methods of portraiture would not otherwise arise. So knowledge could not be knowledge at all unless it were a fresh fact, not identical in existence with its object; and it could not be true knowledge unless, in its deliverance, it specified some of the qualities or relations which really belong to that object."

26. Sellars, *Critical Realism*, 143.

The dualism of the mind and the world is accepted because attempts to eliminate dualism produce unsatisfactory results. Eliminating dualism in the direction of realism produces a theory of perception that is inadequate to deal with the problem of error and a theory of conception that is inadequate to deal with the history of progress in the natural sciences. Eliminating the dualism in the direction of idealism produces a denial of the known reality and independence of the physical world, contrary to the initial hypothesis of critical realism.[27] Critical realism is to be understood as a middle way between objectivism and subjectivism,[28] or between realism and idealism. Sellars wrote in 1916:

> While the pressure of my reflection was evidently toward realism, I was dissatisfied with current realisms and felt that idealism had the better of the argument so far as generally accepted principles were concerned . . . The problem which was formulating itself was to reach a position which would do justice to both the idealistic motives in experience and the realistic structure and meanings . . . My thesis is, then, that idealism and realism have had essentially the same view of knowledge . . . Philosophy limited itself to a controversial study of the subject-object duality and did not lift its eyes to the triad consisting of subject, idea-object (in science analyzable into propositions), and physical existent. It is to this triad that Critical Realism calls attention. It is my persuasion that this more complex form of realism does justice to the truth contained on both sides in the old antithesis.[29]

(3) The mediated knowledge that we have of the world in perception and conception does actually refer to the world and the objects in it. It refers to the world for three reasons. One, objects in the world are the physical cause of the sensations of which perception is constituted.[30] They are active entities that affect the knower and so prompt the knower to attribute perceived qualities to an active entity in the world.[31] Two, the nature of the objects in the world is the logical cause of the patterns that we intuit in perception as character-complexes or the essences

27. Drake, et al., *Essays in Critical Realism*, 32, 86–89.

28. Ibid., 3–4.

29. Sellars, *Critical Realism*, xiii–xv.

30. Ibid., 136–38. "Not only must there be direct or indirect causal relations between the subject and the object, but the knowledge obtained thereby is correlative to the object, rather than presentational of the object."

31. Drake, et al., *Essays in Critical Realism*, 95–97, 110.

of things.[32] Three, it is in the nature of our perception and conception that we project our perceptions and conceptions outward, immediately and unreflectively affirming them of some existing thing in the external world.[33]

This corresponds directly to my I-b.

(4) Our use of science to test and revise the mediated knowledge we have in perception and conception permits us to claim some conformity between our knowledge and the things that it is knowledge of.

> The logic of science emphasizes the critical interplay of data of observation and theory. Ideas and methods become objects of reflection. This setting and tested responsibility of the knowledge-content allow us to claim a genuine conformity between it and the physical existents known, a conformity which justifies the thought of the existent in terms of the content . . . The knower is confined to the datum, and can never literally inspect the existent which he affirms and claims to know . . . Knowledge rests upon the use of data as revelations of objects because of what may, I think, be rightly called a logical identity between them. No term can, however, be a substitute for an appreciation of the actual situation. Physical being is determinate, and knowledge-content is a function of factors so connected therewith that it reflects it and has cognitive value with respect to it.[34]

This tested mediated knowledge is sufficient for us to know *what* we refer to even though we cannot pretend to have exhaustive knowledge of its inner nature.[35] Again, the claim is pragmatic, but it is not pragmatic to the point of reducing knowledge to an instrument for working our will in the world, as in the pragmatism of Dewey.[36] A real claim is made that the objects which we know because they "affect us and are affected by us through real causal relations, which are quite independent of our

---

32. Ibid., 19–20, 28–29, 117. Roy Wood Sellars, in the 1969 preface to the reissue of *Critical Realism*, claims to have been skeptical from the beginning about the resort to essences or character-complexes, but admits that it took him some time to clarify his analysis. Sellars, *Critical Realism*, ix.

33. Drake, et al., *Essays in Critical Realism*, 92.

34. Ibid., 203.

35. Ibid., 110. Sellars makes it clear that critically realistic knowledge is not and cannot be an image or a faithful copy of the physical world. It is rather fallibly justified propositional *knowledge* of the physical world. Sellars, *Critical Realism*, xiv–xv.

36. Lovejoy, "Pragmatism versus the Pragmatist," especially p. 70, in Drake, et al., *Essays in Critical Realism*, 35–80.

knowledge . . . are therefore the objects of physical science. The laws of their activities and the relations they bear to each other and to us are perfectly capable of investigation, and the conclusions of science are to be regarded as true knowledge of reality."[37] In this respect, the critical realists sound much like the scientific realists that we will encounter later.

This corresponds directly to my II-b. Of course, my discernment of the main features of this form of critical realism has been controlled by my typology. However, this is not a pernicious circle because the test of the typology is whether the discernment of the main features of a form of critical realism under the control of that typology produces a cogent and compelling explication of the nature and character of that form of critical realism.

The characteristic move of this early form of critical realism lies in the way that the second and third features are combined. Knowledge is acknowledged to be mediated; it is even admitted (without taking the consequences as seriously as is currently common) that the psychical entities in and through which knowledge is mediated are our own constructions, which we imagine and take as our data.[38] But the reference value of knowledge is asserted and defended and taken as the basic ground upon which to claim that we can investigate the world and correct our perceptions and conceptions of it so that we make truth claims for our knowledge.[39] Dualism is hereby accepted, but not permitted to become grounds for skepticism, because knowledge is affirmed to be both transitive and relevant. Its transitivity and relevance have to be balanced, and neither permitted to be lost, nor to become absolute.[40]

Against the charge that critical realism leads to skepticism, perhaps of the Kantian sort, it is contended that critical realism recognizes the fact of transcendence in knowledge, both in conception and in perception. Transcendence is here precisely the reference value of perception and conception. This means that critical realism acknowledges the chasm between the knower and the known, between the percept and the object

37. Ibid., 110.

38. Ibid., 23.

39. Critical realism takes issue here with what it understands to be the basic assumptions of idealism: (1) that objects must actually be in the field of experience to be known; (2) that everything in the field of experience is mental; and (3) that the knowledge of what is non-mental cannot be mediated by what is mental. Sellars, *Critical Realism*, 184–88.

40. Drake, et al., *Essays in Critical Realism*, 168–69.

of perception, but it regards this chasm as bridged, as transcended, by the reference value of the perception or the conception. It differs from neo-realism in regarding all knowledge, all conception, and even all perception, as mediated and not direct. But it differs from Kantianism in regarding the mediation as having real reference value, that real reference value being established and refined by the present process of intersubjective testing and the future process of continuing learning.[41]

The critical realism of the American pragmatists has four important weaknesses. First, it often seems that these people have not truly understood Kant. They deny his conclusions, and so do not take his arguments seriously.[42] Second, many of their arguments are of the form: if there is such a thing as knowledge, then this is what it must be like.[43] Our common understanding of the everyday world, and our scientific investigation of the physical world are assumed to be acknowledged as knowledge, and thus to justify their description of its nature. Third, their theory of perception borders closely upon naïve realism or scholastic Aristotelianism.[44] The patterns, character-complexes, or essences that we have in perception are claimed to be *given to us by the things themselves*, so that we do not construct them, but rather discern them. Fourth, they do not really understand the history of science. But then, no one else did in those days.

The pragmatic critical realism of the American writers, despite its deficiencies, is of value to us in this investigation because it exhibits a broader perspective upon critical realism than the later discussions of

41. Ibid., 99–103.

42. At least in *Essays*. Sellars, *Critical Realism* (see chapter VI), takes Kant more seriously and evidences more understanding and appreciation than do his colleagues in *Essays in Critical Realism*.

43. Drake, et al., *Essays in Critical Realism*, 166,169. This argument has the form, if A exists, then it is like B. A exists. Therefore, it is like B. In form this is, of course, a perfectly valid form of *modus ponens*. The difficulty with it lies in the initial premise. The premise that if A, realistic knowledge, exists, then it must be like B, the critically realistic characterization of it being offered here, conceals the fact that what we are really dealing with is an abduction, an inference to the best explanation. The validity of abduction, as will be seen later in chapter 4, is entirely in question.

44. This is the substance of Sellars's later objection to the reliance upon essences or character-complexes in the theory of perception. He suggests that a constructive, information-processing model of the interplay between stimulus and response is better. This is much more in accord with advances in scientific realism's theory of perception since 1920. Sellars, *Critical Realism*, ix.

scientific realism. The American pragmatists considered that their description of critical realism served as a reasonable justification for being realistic about the ordinary observable objects of everyday life, such as tables, chairs, trees, and such, as well as for the less directly observable objects of the sciences, such as atoms and forces. It is seminal for the later forms of critical realism; it already possesses, or at least adumbrates, almost all of the characteristics of the more developed forms of critical realism that followed it.

2.3 CRITICAL REALISM IN GENERAL

Though it could be adapted to common sense uses, it can be seen how the early critical realism of the American pragmatists was already aimed in the direction of scientific practice and scientific knowledge. The advantage of the typology of critical realism that I have introduced here is that it can be adapted with reasonable effort to a critically realistic understanding of music theory, or the art of housekeeping, or the study of marketing. It might productively be applied to the field of literary criticism, where critical theory combined with realism could distinguish between interpretation as the art of finding and elucidating the author's intentions and interpretation as the art of responding to and elaborating upon the text regardless of the author's intentions, while also investigating the relation between the two rather than treating them as disjoint alternatives.

Let us consider this for a moment. We have literature, a reality in the world, at least as pieces of paper with printing upon them. Their reality as literature, as communications in human language in the form of narrative or description or poetry or other communication with aesthetic value, must be assumed. It is a reality external to the reader, though internalized in the act of appreciation. This is critically realistic characteristic I-a. The practice of literary criticism asserts that there is or can be knowledge of this literature, both knowledge about it (in social and historical criticism) and knowledge of it (in aesthetic apprehension of it). This is characteristic I-b. This knowledge is mediated in and through language. Sometimes it is mediated in and through more than one language, if the literature is translated. It is also mediated in and by the act of reading, which does not merely place the words on the page into the mind of the reader, but requires readers to draw upon their experience in order to receive those words as sentences, as thoughts of a mind, as stories or as poetry, as meaning. Moreover, the literature is not truly apprehended without also being interpreted. However much or little the interpretation may be like or unlike, true or untrue to the text, the interpretation is, nonetheless and indisputably, a text that is different from the original text being interpreted. This is critically realistic characteristic II-a. Finally, characteristic II-b, the critical theory being used to criticize the interpretation and thus to interpret the interpretation as knowledge of the text is the particular hermeneutics of the interpreter.

A case for a critical realism between that of literary criticism and scientific realism might be elucidated for the practice of history. It is in these fields that are less technical and in which access to the object of knowledge is more indirect and non-linear than in the physical sciences that the typology I have offered here should show its value. Its breadth and its simplicity permit it to be used productively in fields that are difficult to reduce to a rigorously structured form.

In broad uses of the term "critical realism" it will be necessary to consider and address the question of whether a particular variety of critical realism is good or bad, useful or useless, or even obfuscatory. But it is better to use broad definitions and then address the matter of quality than to attempt to define a thing so closely that bad examples are defined as not being the thing at all. It is often attempted to define art or music in such a way that bad art or poor music is treated as not being art at all. We see how this procedure often fails when the creative ability of artists proves the beauty of objects and compositions that were once not even accepted as art. In more intellectual fields this practice often takes the form of alleging that certain arguments or discourse are not rational. Sometimes this is necessary, as life and scholarship are too short to spend on flying saucers. But it is also often an attempt to dismiss a position or argument without having to consider its substance or address its putative object.

Scientific realism,[45] to which we will now turn, offers a much more complex and nuanced understanding of the realistic character of scientific knowledge, one that seriously attempts to address severe difficulties raised by other philosophers of science. But in order to do so it focuses upon well-developed scientific theories and often makes no commitment

---

45. Sellars used the term "scientific realism" to denote the reflective critical realism of working scientists, rather than the philosophical position that it now denotes. Sellars, *Critical Realism*, 22–30.

whatsoever about the realism of other forms of knowledge.[46] It is more thoroughly critical than these early forms of critical realism, and it develops a less naïve theory of perception. But it is still involved in a difficult and ongoing controversy with anti-realistic philosophers of science and has not yet taken time or effort to extend its gains to other forms and fields of knowledge. This book will discuss the attempt to extend the meaning of critical realism into the realm of theology.

46. Ernan McMullin makes it a part of his definition of what scientific realism means that it asserts a realism of knowledge only for theories that have exhibited long term success. McMullin, "A Case for Scientific Realism," 26.

3

Scientific Realism

3.1 THE GENESIS OF SCIENTIFIC REALISM

Critical realism, in its early form, did not become a major movement in the philosophy of the twentieth century.[1] It was taken up in the analytic philosophy of science in the 1950s and appears in a new form in discussions of the history and philosophy of science in the 1970s and 80s.[2] In order to understand the character that it took at that time, we will have to consider how the history and philosophy of science developed towards a particular crisis in the 1960s.

Vaughn R. McKim in the foreword to *Construction and Constraint* says:

> The idea that science as it has evolved in Western culture acquired a unique, and uniquely effective, mode of knowing and explaining is one that still exerts a powerful attraction. As recently as thirty years ago [1960], philosophers of science were nearly

1. Roy Wood Sellars continued to publish on the subject of critical realism and his son, Wilfred Sellars, also continued to advocate this position, although in a different context and using different language. Eventually his position approaches that of the scientific realists. Sellars, *Philosophical Perspectives*, 185.

2. The extent to which critical realism was a continuing element in the analytic philosophy of the middle years of the century would require an historical study that I do not wish to pursue here, as my purpose is to examine the form that it took in response to the nonfoundationalist critique.

unanimous in holding that the mature physical sciences embody powerful principles of method and reasoning which virtually guarantee that knowledge claims receiving the endorsement of a scientific community are free from any taint of personal bias, ideology, or gratuitous metaphysical prejudice. Thus, the task such philosophers set for themselves was not that of *criticizing* scientific rationality, but rather that of seeking to *understand* its precise nature in a more transparent way.[3]

This means that the history and philosophy of science throughout the first half of the twentieth century were largely positivist in character. There were several developments along the way. The positivism of Comte gave way in the 1920s to the more developed and specific logical positivism of the Vienna circle. Logical positivism collapsed because of the inadequacy of its verification criterion as an intelligible demarcation between science and non-science, between propositional statements with truth-value and non-propositional statements.[4] In more detail:

> The chief objections to the positivist theory of science are (1) theories are not definitionally reducible to finitely, observationally verifiable assertions; (2) scientific method is not rationally confinable to entailment from the facts; (3) observation is not a transparent category but a complex anthromorphic process, itself investigated by science; (4) historical intertheory relations do not fit in the accumulative model; (5) accepted observationally-based facts do not belong to an eternal, theory-free category but are theory-laden and subject to theoretical criticism. To these I would especially add the criticism that (6,7) science is not isolated from the individual and from society in the manner presupposed by positivism; (8) that method is not rationally universal either across scientists at a time or across history; (9) that logic does not have the privileged status given it by positivism but is itself open to broadly empirical investigation; and (10) that there is not the gulf between the normative and the descriptive presupposed by positivism.[5]

One of the important replacements for logical positivism was the critical rationalism of Karl Popper (indeed, Popper's work solidified and confirmed the collapse of logical positivism).[6] Popper's insight, that

3. Ernan McMullin, *Construction and Constraint*, vii.

4. Niiniluoto, *Critical Scientific Realism*, 6.

5. Hooker, *A Realistic Theory of Science*, 156.

6. Bartley, *Retreat to Commitment*, 56.

science often proceeds not by the verification of theories, but rather through their *dis*confirmation by experimental and observational fact, is of critical importance for understanding the subsequent discussion.[7] But Popper's attempt to make the logical use of *modus tollens*, denying the consequent, the criterion for the demarcation of science from non-science, and the single universal form of rationality by which science works and advances, still had many weaknesses.[8]

The received view of the nature and structure of scientific theories and of the historical development of the physical sciences was subjected to a devastating critique beginning in 1962 with the publication of Thomas S. Kuhn's *The Structure of Scientific Revolutions*.[9] This was an historical and sociological investigation with philosophical consequences. The underlying assumptions of the received view were either a naïve realism or a positivistic phenomenalism, the reliance upon a universal scientific language embodied in mathematics and logic, and the correspondence theory of truth.[10] All these assumptions have come under critique as well, especially in the work of Paul Feyerabend, who also started with an historical and sociological investigation of the sciences, but took a much more radical view of the philosophical consequences of that investigation than did Kuhn.[11]

The history of science has been marked by a number of major revolutions: the Copernican Model of the solar system overturning the Ptolemaic, the atomic theory of chemistry overturning the phlogiston theory of combustion, the theory of relativity overturning the Newtonian physics of absolute space and absolute time, and the quantum theory

7. Popper, *Logic of Scientific Discovery*, translated by Karl Popper from his *Logik der Forschung*, published in Vienna in 1934, 40ff.

8. Kolakowski, *The Alienation of Reason*, 184–86 treats Popper as a positivist both in historical descent and in character. Hooker, *A Realistic Theory of Science*, 81–82, also identifies the metaphilosophy of Popper as very nearly identical with the metaphilosophy of positivism and empiricism.

9. Peacocke, *Intimations of Reality*, 16–17; Kuhn, *The Structure of Scientific Revolutions*.

10. Thus the received view was positivistic. See Hooker, *A Realistic Theory of Science*, 62–63.

11. Feyerabend, *Against Method*. Feyerabend is a self-described anarchist. He takes in a more radical sense than Kuhn the incommensurability of competing theories. He also works with the idea that all theories have some legitimate ground for being considered in the discussion of the nature and character of the world, and that all theories are false to fact if tested in the rigorous way that is usually claimed to be a *sine non qua* of scientific reasoning.

overturning the classical physics of determinate causation. Kuhn undertook to study these events historically. The teaching of science in the schools tends to obliterate the history of these revolutions because the purpose of scientific education is indoctrination into the current paradigm of how to practice a particular science in order to qualify its students for their profession.[12] What Kuhn discovered was that scientific revolutions had a strong element of discontinuity to them.

In times of normal science seminal accomplishments, along with their associated theoretical structures, are taken as paradigms that define the proper practice of science, and the kinds of puzzles and problems that scientists should be working on, along with the nature of what will constitute acceptable solutions to those puzzles.[13] During periods of normal science theoretical commitments are taken for granted, and it is this relief from the need to begin every investigation from first principles that in large part makes possible the normal progress of science. In times of crisis anomalies accumulate, that is, puzzles and problems that resist solution despite concentrated effort. In response, scientists begin to consider ontological questions in their scientific discussions. Eventually a new paradigm emerges—with its own theoretical structures—that resolves the anomaly and initiates a new period of normal puzzle-solving science.[14]

What is significant is that the new paradigm is usually incommensurable with the old one. It often appeals to a different set of metaphysical entities. The atomic theory of chemistry introduced atoms and denied the reality of phlogiston. Relativity theory introduced four-dimensional space-time and denied the absolute and separate space and time of Newtonian Physics. It also denied the existence of the ether as

12. Kuhn, *The Structure of Scientific Revolutions*, 136–43, chapter xi, "The Invisibility of Revolutions." See also Feyerabend, *Against Method*, 11.

13. Kuhn, *The Structure of Scientific Revolutions*, 23–42, chapters iii and iv, "The Nature of Normal Science," and "Normal Science as Puzzle Solving." The nature and character of the paradigm, that is the combination of actual achievements, theoretical commitments, accepted theoretical practices, and projected questions for investigation, required some questioning by scholars and clarification by Kuhn before it was understood to bind together these different elements which had often been treated separately. See the "Postscript," 174–91, and also Thomas S. Kuhn, "Second Thoughts on Paradigms," in Kuhn, *The Essential Tension*, 293–319.

14. Kuhn, *The Structure of Scientific Revolutions*, 52–76, chapters vi and vii, "Anomaly and the Emergence of Scientific Discoveries," and "Crisis and the Emergence of Scientific Theories."

a medium for the propagation of light and other electromagnetic radiation. Quantum physics, in the standard interpretation, denied the determinate causality of classical physics and introduced some very strange entities as well as accepting random events as legitimate causes. Field theory replaced the notion of action at a distance and gave a much different meaning to the term "force." Kuhn and Feyerabend argued that the incommensurability of competing paradigms in a time of crisis and revolution in a scientific field meant two things. First, there was no direct rational way of comparing and evaluating competing paradigms and theories to determine which was more adequate. Nor did the experimental and observational facts by themselves serve to determine which of two theories was correct. Second, a change of paradigms in a scientific revolution was like a change of worldview and was often experienced by the scientists in the midst of the revolution like a religious conversion.[15]

This means that scientific theories are not adopted solely for rational reasons, nor are they specifically determined by the facts to which they refer.[16] In most cases the new theories and paradigms that are adopted do not actually offer a better or more complete explanation of the facts at the time they are first adopted. What they do offer is a solution to persistent anomalies and the hope of *eventually* providing a more complete explanation of phenomena, along with an attractive new set of puzzles and problems to be solved. The recovery of explanations for phenomena explained by the previous paradigm or theory and the resolution of any contradictions present in the new paradigm are some of the puzzles that the new paradigm sets for the period of normal science that follows its acceptance.[17]

15. Ibid., 92–135, chapters ix and x, "The Nature and Necessity of Scientific Revolutions," and "Revolutions as Changes of Worldview."

16. Feyerabend, *Against Method*, 226. "Incommensurable theories, then, can be *refuted* by reference to their own respective kinds of experience; i.e., by discovering the *internal contradictions* from which they are suffering . . . Their *contents* cannot be compared. Nor is it possible to make a judgment of verisimilitude except within the confines of a particular theory . . . None of the methods which Carnap, Hempel, Nagel, Popper, or even Lakatos want to use for rationalizing scientific changes can be applied, and the one that *can* be applied, refutation, is greatly reduced in strength. What remains are aesthetic judgments, judgments of taste, metaphysical prejudices, religious desires, in short, *what remains are our subjective wishes.*" (Emphasis Feyerabend.)

17. Kuhn, *The Structure of Scientific Revolutions*, 144–73, chapters xii and xiii, "The Resolution of Revolutions," and "Progress through Revolutions." See also Ernan McMullin, *Construction and Constraint*, 2 "What he [Kuhn] wanted to underline was

The immediate effect of Kuhn's work was to greatly enhance the importance of the sociology of science. This led to the development of what was usually called the strong program in the sociology of science. M. Mulkay gives a brief and clear statement of that program in *Science and the Sociology of Knowledge*:

> Scientific knowledge . . . offers an account of the physical world which is mediated through available cultural resources; and these resources are in no way definitive . . . The physical world could be analyzed perfectly adequately by means of language and presuppositions quite different from those employed in the modern scientific community. *There is, therefore, nothing in the physical world which uniquely determines the conclusions of that community* . . . There is no alternative but to regard the products of science as social constructions like all other cultural products . . . One of the central claims of the revised view is that scientific assertions are socially created and not directly given by the physical world as was previously supposed.[18]

It was in reaction to the strong program in the sociology of science that critical realism was recast in a form that is usually called scientific realism.[19] Despite the reality of scientific revolutions and the discontinuity of theoretical structures involved in changes of paradigm, it has seemed to many philosophers and historians of science that (1) the long term success of science, (2) its progress, even through revolutions, (3) its history of discovering new observable entities, (4) its commitment to rational explanation, even though the standards of what counts as rational scientific explanation may change, (5) its development of structural explanations of the world, and, most of all, (6) its willingness to change its theoretical structures when confronted with the actual behavior of the world, all work together to justify "the basic claim made by scientific realism . . . that the long term success of a scientific theory gives reason

---

that the transition from one paradigm to another could not be brought about by force of logic alone. Though reasons played a part, even a crucial part, in motivating such transitions, they were not coercive; some would be persuaded by them, others would not be."

18. Mulkay, *Science and the Sociology of Knowledge*, 60–62. Cited in Peacocke, *Intimations of Reality*, 20.

19. Peacocke, *Intimations of Reality*, 18–19. See also McMullin, "The Shaping of Scientific Rationality," 2; McMullin, "A Case for Scientific Realism," 17–18; and Sellars, *Philosophical Perspectives*, 337–69.

to believe that something like the entities and structure postulated in the theory actually exist."[20]

3.2 THE CHARACTER OF SCIENTIFIC REALISM

This form of critical realism, scientific realism, has several significant characteristics.

3.2.1 The Reality of Knowledge

Scientific Realism takes the external existence of the physical world for granted. So too do most of the opponents of this view. The question between them is not whether there is an actual physical world, but rather, whether we have *real knowledge* of that world. What real knowledge is, or would be if we had it, is an issue that is difficult to address. In the classical view real knowledge was knowledge according to causes, reached by universal and necessary rational means.[21] Real knowledge could be partial, but it could not be fallible. This picture has been abandoned by both anti-realists and critical realists in the philosophy of science. The difference between them lies in what they each claim is entailed by this abandonment.

Anti-realists sometimes talk as if the abandonment of this concept meant precisely that human beings have no real knowledge of the world,[22] and that scientific realism must be committed to the classical concept of the nature of knowledge.[23] So Bas van Fraasen says: "Science

20. McMullin, "A Case for Scientific Realism," 26. See similar statements in Devitt, *Realism and Truth*, 108–9; van Huyssteen, *Postfoundational Theology*, 51, and Trigg, *Rationality and Science*, 96–98.

21. Brown, *Rationality*, 3–16.

22. Levin, "What Kind of an Explanation is Truth?," 125, mentions such anti-realism: "The antirealism that interests me does not regard theories as possibly false despite all evidence; it regards them as devoid of truth value. The committed instrumentalist— Duhem, for example—wants to say that even 'true' scientific theories, theories that give the best account of the world that it is possible to give, are not really *true*."

23. Couvalis, *The Philosophy of Science*, 9, takes note of this problem and the surprising agreement between positivist defenders of science and anti-realist critics. "The first problem is the critics [of science] are working with the false idea that the only kind of knowledge worthy of the name is knowledge that uses and is based on precise distinctions and statements, is absolutely unchallengeable, and is established by methods that conform to formal, law-like, patterns. This idea has caused endless mischief throughout the history of western philosophy. It occurs in Descartes' famous *Discourse*

aims to give us, in its theories, a literally true story of what the world is like; and acceptance of a scientific theory involves the belief that it is true. This is the correct statement of scientific realism."[24]

Scientific realists refuse this interpretation of what the correct statement of their position is.[25] The word "literally" must be omitted because scientific realists are critical realists and do not think that even a true theory is a "literal" picture of the world.[26] All knowledge is mediated, even true knowledge. The scientific realist is committed to constructing an understanding of what true referential knowledge means, even though the classical concept has been abandoned. The problem lies in an understanding of what is meant by correspondence truth. Many anti-realists claim that there is no meaningful or interesting way to understand the idea of correspondence truth.[27] Scientific realists claim that the success of science demonstrates that there is something to the idea of correspondence, even if the history of science demonstrates that correspondence can no longer be understood in the classical manner.

The correct statement of scientific realism is like McMullin's:

> The basic claim made by scientific realism, once again, is that the long term success of a scientific theory gives reason to believe that something like the entities and structure postulated by the theory actually exist. There are four important qualifications built into this: (1) the theory must be successful over a significant period of time; (2) the explanatory success of the theory gives some reason, though not a conclusive warrant, to believe it; (3) what is believed is that the theoretical structures are *something like* the structure of the real world; (4) no claim is made for a special, more basic, privileged form of existence for the postulated entities.[28]

---

on Method, and was revived in this century because enormous advances in formal logic mesmerized philosophers by seeming to offer them the possibility that they would be able to give a precise account of the basis and nature of all types of justifiable reasoning. The idea underlies the work of the critics of science in the same way as it underlies the arguments of the most dogmatic defenders of science."

24. Van Fraasen, *The Scientific Image*, 8. Van Fraasen admits that this is almost too naive a picture of scientific realism (ibid., 6–7), but uses it nonetheless.

25. McMullin, "A Case for Scientific Realism," 35; Niiniluoto, *Critical Scientific Realism*, 117.

26. Niiniluoto, *Critical Scientific Realism*, 117.

27. So Richard Rorty and the later Hilary Putnam. McMullin, "A Case for Scientific Realism," 23–26.

28. Ibid., 26.

This statement shows all the basic features of critical realism.[29] It asserts the existence of an other when it says that the "entities and structure postulated by the theory actually exist." It emphasizes that this other is truly other when it qualifies this claim by saying that "the theoretical structures are *something* like the structure of the real world," which is to admit that they are not identical to the real world (my I-a). But the same statement that qualifies theoretical structures also asserts that they are "something *like*" the structure of the real world, and thus qualify as real knowledge of it (my I-b). In that only likeness is postulated, the entities and structures of theory are admitted to be only mediated knowledge of the world (my II-a) and it is their character as mediating constructions that prompts the qualification that "no claim is made for a special, more basic, privileged form of existence for the postulated entities."[30] Finally, the critical theory to be used is a philosophical understanding of the history of science as shown in the reservation that claims are only made for theories that are "successful over a significant period of time" (my II-b). All four qualifications serve to emphasize that a philosophical understanding of the history of science is a critical theory because it works to specify the inherent limitations of scientific knowledge and recognize it as a fallible enterprise requiring on-going correction.[31] But again, these are all regarded as qualifications *of* knowledge that is real, rather than as demonstrations that *no* knowledge is real.

29. Boyd, "The Current Status of Scientific Realism," in Leplin, *Scientific Realism*, 41–42, defines scientific realism in four central theses, somewhat different than McMullin's, the first, third, and fourth of which are framed so as to support the contention that scientific realism is a form of critical realism.

30. Van Huyssteen, *Postfoundational Theology*, 166–67, makes the same judgment: "The success of a theory in scientific realism does not therefore warrant the claim that something exactly corresponding to this construct exists. The success of a theory can, at best, warrant a claim that an entity exists that possesses *among others* the properties attributed to it by the theory. This not only accounts for the notion of *approximate truth* in realism but also for the central role of *metaphors* in scientific theorizing. Theories—and their metaphors—thus provide epistemic access to entities that could not have been known otherwise."

31. See Feyerabend, *Against Method*, 24, for a discussion of how the history of science acts as a critical theory which points out the limitations of scientific knowledge and methodology. Feyerabend is himself an anarchist rather than a critical realist, but his point about the history of science serving as a critical theory still applies. Moreover, as I will suggest shortly, even Feyerabend can be given a critically realistic reading if one is prepared to be sufficiently critical.

3.2.2 Postfoundationalism

Scientific realism is postfoundational. It accepts that there is no single universally valid form of rationality. Historical studies show that the form of scientific rationality changes over time and scientific realism accepts this.[32] "Scientific change is not merely a successive alteration of substantive beliefs occasioned by new discoveries about the world; scientific change and innovation extend also to the methods, rules of reasoning, and concepts employed in science and in talking about science. Even the criteria of what it is to be a scientific 'theory' or 'explanation' change; and thus the notion that *theory* or *explanation* are 'metascientific concepts' with meanings independent of scientific beliefs, is rejected."[33]

What scientific realism rejects is the supposition that there are no constraints upon such changes. Three constraints seem to have persisted, even through some radical revolutions. First, that scientific theories shall be empirically adequate; that they shall save the appearances, that they shall account for what we actually find in the laboratory and in the field. Second, that theories should enjoy predictive success. Third, that theories should provide causal explanations.[34] The first constraint, that theories shall be empirically adequate, is an application of the general attitude of scientific realism, and of most working scientists for that matter, that theory is secondary to reality, and where they conflict, theory must adjust.[35] In this the scientific realist claims that the provisionality of scientific theory, the fact that it is subject to change, is no bar to the reference value of those theories.[36] Indeed, the fact that theory does change in response to reality is a positive reason for claiming that it has reference value. The second constraint requires that theories do more than account for such things as are presently known and requires them to predict things not presently known. This means that the requirement to make progress is built into scientific practice at the level of goals and values. It also requires that scientific theories not be *ad hoc* constructions.[37]

32. McMullin, *Construction and Constraint*, 22.

33. Shapere, "The Character of Scientific Change," cited in McMullin, *Construction and Constraint*, 17.

34. McMullin, *Construction and Constraint*, 41.

35. On conformity with experience see also van Kooten Niekerk, "Critical Realist Perspective," 59–60.

36. Peacocke, *Intimations of Reality*, 25.

37. Van Kooten Niekerk, "Critical Realist Perspective," 59, "An important demand

The third constraint holds even where the notion of what constitutes a cause or an explanation changes in the course of the development of a science. Causality in quantum physics is radically different than in classical physics, but causal explanations are still expected.

Scientific realism recognizes that these constraints operate at a high level. They have to do with our understanding of how theories in general are to be constructed so as to have a relationship to reality that can be characterized as knowledge. They do not operate as constraints at a lower level determining what sorts of things we must find when we use particular theories to investigate the world. At that level scientific realism is capable of being as nonfoundationalist as is Feyerabend when he asserts that "anything goes."

> The idea of a method that contains firm, unchanging, and absolutely binding principles for conducting the business of science meets considerable difficulty when confronted with the results of historical research . . . [T]here is not a single rule, however plausible, and however firmly grounded in epistemology, that is not violated at some time or other . . . [S]uch violations are not accidental events, . . . they are necessary for progress. Indeed, one of the most striking features of recent discussions in the history and philosophy of science is the realization that events and developments . . . occurred only because some thinkers either *decided* not to be bound by certain 'obvious' methodological rules, or because they *unwittingly broke* them . . . This liberal practice, I repeat, is not just a *fact* of the history of science. It is both reasonable and *absolutely necessary* for the growth of knowledge.[38]

This is a statement about the history of science and its implications for the philosophy of science with which scientific realism is prepared to agree,[39] but for a *critically realistic reason*. If the other to be known is truly other, then there can be no guarantee ahead of time that any particular method, technique, theory, or philosophical standpoint will be adequate for constructing knowledge of the other. And, as Feyerabend, Kuhn, Laudan, and others have pointed out at length, there have been numerous examples in the history of science where what seemed to be

here is that proposed theories be tested on their ability to account for data that do not belong to the basis of their formulation."

38. Feyerabend, *Against Method*, 14.

39. See McMullin, *Construction and Constraint*, 7–10, to see how far he is prepared to go in accepting Feyerabend's conclusions.

the only possible way of thinking about something turned out to be inadequate, and new and seemingly outrageous ways of thinking had to be invented to cope with it. The liberal practice of anything goes is both reasonable and necessary because it is a truly unknown, truly other, that we are investigating in the sciences.[40]

Moreover, the mediated nature of human knowledge means that even true and corresponding knowledge is not identical with the reality known. Not being identical it is, in its turn, fallible. But despite the fallibility of all human knowledge the critical realist still maintains that we have real referential knowledge of an other precisely because this other demonstrates repeatedly in the history of science an ability to confound our expectations and suppositions. At the very least we know that there is something other than our own ideas and conceptions that is capable of being an independent cause. The business of science, demonstrated repeatedly in its history, is to pursue our present theoretical commitments with such vigor and rigor that reality is forced to show itself by proving that we have understood it wrongly once again. This positive knowledge that is present along with the negative knowledge when science is forced once again to seek and find new ideas and new descriptions is why the critical realist insists that the history of science does not merely prove that we cannot know anything at all.[41] But it is this same positive knowledge that also forces the critical realist to abandon classical foundationalism.

---

40. Feyerabend cites Albert Einstein from Einstein, *Albert Einstein, Philosopher Scientist*, 683–84, in support of this: "The external conditions which are set for [the scientist] by the facts of experience do not permit him to let himself be too much restricted, in the construction of his conceptual world, by the adherence to an epistemological system. He, therefore, must appear to the systematic epistemologist as a type of unscrupulous opportunist." See his own discussion of this in Feyerabend, *Against Method*, 11–14.

41. Couvalis, while appreciating Popper's insight, also recognizes that it is deficient in that it fails to explain the value of the positive knowledge that accompanies the negative demonstration. Couvalis, *The Philosophy of Science*, 75: "Falsificationism has considerable merits. It makes clear that some theories cannot be arrived at through enumerative induction, and it rightly stresses the importance in theoretical science of producing bold conjectures which can be ruthlessly tested. However, it fails to present a cogent account of why it is rational to act on well corroborated theories, and also fails to explain why we should prefer well corroborated theories if we want to arrive at the truth. It thus fails to show that preferring well-corroborated theories is rational. It needs to be supplemented by a hypothesis that well-corroborated theories are more likely to be true."

3.2.3 Critical Issues and Limitations

Scientific realism accepts every available criticism and does not rule any-thing out *a priori*.[42] Thus it accepts, in large part, the historical work of Kuhn and Feyerabend, though it differs, with Feyerabend at least, about the significance of that history. Scientific realism is willing to accept from the sociologists of knowledge that science is a social product and that scientific theories are socially constructed. But it claims that social construction is not the sole determination of scientific theory. Any dis-tortive influences that social or personal factors may have are limited in their effects by the complex test methods characteristic of science.[43] This means that scientific realism claims that the facts are co-determinative with social construction of scientific theory.

Olaf Pederson describes as a fundamental scientific experience the repeated human discovery of unanticipated relations in our experience of the world that persist through theoretic changes and resist reduction to *a priori* structures of human thought. After examining biographic and philosophical statements by several scientists he says: "The fundamen-tal scientific experience is so strong because something from a world beyond the human mind is fed into it in some way which is difficult to explain and communicate. The mind is certainly full of operations and bustling with activity; but what it really has to work upon is something not provided by itself."[44]

Of course, that upon which the mind has to work, which is not provided by itself, might well be merely the occasion and stimulus for the mind to construct the objects of its knowledge without thereby be-ing any constituent part of that knowledge. But the *manner* in which the world beyond the human mind stimulates it to construct knowledge suggests that it is indeed a constituent part of that knowledge.

This claim of co-determination is made despite the fact that scien-tific realism accepts the underdetermination of theory by fact and the theory-laden character of scientific fact. That scientific fact is theory-laden means that it is scientific theory and practice that determine what

42. McMullin, *Construction and Constraint*, 22, accepts, at the methodological level, Paul Feyerabend's claim that in the sciences "anything goes." See Feyerabend, *Against Method*, 19.

43. Peacocke, *Intimations of Reality*, 21; Niiniluoto, *Critical Scientific Realism*, 300.

44. Pedersen, "Christian Belief and the Fascination of Science," 129–33. My atten-tion was called to this interesting article by van Kooten Niekerk in "A Critical Realist Perspective."

shall be recognized and accepted as fact. George Couvalis characterizes the theory-ladenness of observation as follows:

> These three claims are:
>
> 1. all experience is permeated by theories;
> 2. theories direct our observations, tell us which observations are significant, and indicate how they are significant;
> 3. all statements about what we observe are theoretical and cannot be derived from experience.[45]

These claims arise out of Kuhn's study of the role of paradigms in the practice of normal science and are amplified by Feyerabend and others working in the sociology of science.[46] All parties to the dispute seem to accept claims 1, 2, and the first half of claim 3. But scientific realism disputes the second half of claim 3, admitting that observation statements cannot be derived *solely* from experience, but insisting that experience is *one* of the determinants of observation statements. Scientific realism takes note of the historical fact that anomalies do arise in the practice of normal science. Despite the theory-laden character of fact, facts appear which are an embarrassment to theory. Indeed, it is also an element of Kuhn's work that normal science works in such a way as to promote the discovery of anomalies that lead to crisis.[47] Scientific realism takes this to mean that the social construction of science is not sufficiently powerful to blind scientists permanently to facts that cannot be conformed to current theory.

The underdetermination of theory by fact means that the facts available in any given case of making a choice between theories are not sufficient to determine conclusively and uniquely which theory best fits those facts. This is actually nothing new. Henri Poincaré, the French mathematician, called attention to this as long ago as 1901. On the basis of his studies of the new systems of non-Euclidian geometry and his consequent understanding of the power of mathematics to generate new alternative sets of axioms whose properties could be investigated, Poincaré asserted that any finite phenomenon which could be explained

---

45. Couvalis, *The Philosophy of Science*, 11.

46. Feyerabend, *Against Method*, 22–23, 26–29, 61–62, 229.

47. Kuhn, *The Structure of Scientific Revolutions*, 152, 166. This is one of the reasons why Kuhn does not wish to be categorized as a total relativist. See Kuhn, *The Essential Tension*, 320–44.

at all could be explained equally well in an infinite number of different ways.[48] However, there would also be an infinite number of explanations that did not suit the phenomenon at all. Poincaré advocated a kind of modified Kantianism. The forms of intuition and the categories of reason were not fixed, universal, and necessary, but were, rather, conventions. They were subject to change and variation. But they still served, as in Kant, as the conditions that make experience possible at all. They are chosen for convenience in describing the world. But experience itself guides us in choosing what axioms will be most convenient.[49]

In the traditional view of the development of science the facts would eventually determine a unique set of conventions that is most convenient. Modern anti-realists would say that the convenience in question is personal, individual, and idiosyncratic. Critical realists argue that neither does the behavior of the world produce a unique set of the most convenient assumptions, nor are assumptions totally idiosyncratic, but rather that the behavior of the world is sometimes sufficient to judge one set of assumptions more convenient than another in particular cases. Other cases are imaginable in which different sets of assumptions are equally convenient. But where a given set of conventions proves most convenient over an increasing range of cases and despite comparison to a number of different alternatives, then scientific realism argues that there is warrant for believing that set of conventions to correspond in some way to what is actually the case.

Scientific realism applies this insight of Poincaré to the problem of the underdetermination of theory by fact. Reality does not *uniquely* determine what theoretical structures can truly refer to it.[50] But it does determinately separate our ideas into two infinite classes: those that are an adequate understanding of the data of experience and those that are not. There are an infinite number of different ways of thinking about

48. Poincaré, *The Foundations of Science*, x.

49. Ibid., 17, 28–31.

50. In this respect it agrees with the statement of the strong program in the sociology of science. But in its strongest form the sociology of science has often been taken to mean that if the world does not uniquely determine our theoretical structures, then it does not determine them *at all*. It is this stronger understanding with which scientific realism differs. See also Boyd, "The Current Status of Scientific Realism," 77–78: "Similarly, it is *not* a thesis of the version of scientific realism defended here that there is one completely true theory which would be the 'asymptotic limit' of scientific theorizing if science were pursued long enough."

reality which are true, but that does not mean that there is no such thing as falsehood.[51] Moreover, even though both sets may well be infinite, it seems likely from the history of science that theories which are adequate, convenient, and true, or highly truthlike, are as rare among all possible theories as the prime numbers are among all possible numbers. Moreover, they may be as hard to find and identify as the prime numbers.[52] All our theoretical structures are social constructions, and social and historical factors may well determine which of an infinite variety of ways of thinking about reality will be actual in any given community at any given time. But the facts are co-determinative of our theories, forcing us to reject those that do not work and to construct others, out of an infinite variety of possibilities, to take their place.[53]

3.2.4 Reference Value

Scientific realism maintains that scientific theories truly refer. Scientific theories are full of invisible entities such as quarks, fields, virtual particles, dark matter, and the like. Claiming reference for such objects is not easy. But these theories have led to the discovery of a great variety of observable, though previously hidden, entities and phenomena, such as bacteria, viruses, the planet Neptune, and the bending of light in the gravitational field of the sun. The success of scientific theories in discovering hidden structures that account causally for observed phenomena is taken as a

51. Compare Niiniluoto, *Critical Scientific Realism*, 205, "Semantic realism is compatible with ontological pluralism: the non-epistemic correspondence theory of truth can be combined with the idea that objects can be individuated and identified in alternative ways through different conceptual systems."

52. Mathematicians have been able to prove that the number of prime numbers smaller than n is approximately equal to $n/\ln(n)$. This means that the prime numbers become rarer as we go to higher and higher numbers. They comprise about 1/4 of the first hundred numbers, but only about 1/13 of the first million. Nonetheless, the prime numbers are just as infinite as the natural numbers among whom they are found. Also, no one has ever been able to demonstrate a formula that will always and only produce prime numbers, and it is doubted that there is or can be such a formula (unless and until the Riemann hypothesis is proved and its consequences investigated).

53. Van Kooten Niekerk makes a similar point in his discussion of Putnam's later anti-realism (or internal realism, as Putnam calls it). "That 'too many correspondences exist'—because of different possibilities of conceptualization—is no good argument. For this does not alter the importance of being able, on the basis of different conceptual possibilities, to separate statements that correspond with (conceptualized) experience from statements which notoriously do not (and therefore must be considered as false)." Van Kooten Niekerk, "Critical Realist Perspective," 57.

warrant for the belief that something like the entities and structure postulated in scientific theories do actually exist.[54]

One of the problems in claiming reference value for our theories is that, measured by the standards of current theories, many key terms in past and/or supplanted theories are now thought not to refer. As Putnam put it (and as many others have quoted it, either to affirm or deny): "Eventually the following metainduction becomes overwhelmingly compelling: *just as no term used in the science of more than fifty (or whatever) years ago referred, so it will turn out that no term used now refers* (except maybe observational terms, if there are such)."[55]

But because critical realism regards even true referential knowledge as indirect and mediated (see 3.2.5 following) it does not accept the premise of this metainduction.[56] No term that refers does so perfectly and with no excess beyond the actual behavior of the world that it attempts to refer to. For that reason reference must be construed with some charity.[57] Some terms no longer refer because we have abandoned the ontological commitments that were embodied in them. For instance, we no longer believe in the electro-magnetic ether. But that does not mean that such terms did not ever refer. Indeed, Saul Kripke points out that reference can be successful even though the descriptive content of the referring statement is false.[58]

Ether was once used to refer to the medium of the wave properties of electro-magnetic radiation, and those wave properties are still regarded as real, but are now understood as taking place in, or constituting significant characteristics of a packaged unit of energy travelling through space as a photon (or as a dynamic knot in an electromagnetic field). Perhaps better, but more esoteric: the wave properties of electromagnetic radiation subsist in the mathematical description of the integral that

54. McMullin, "A Case for Scientific Realism," 27–28; Boyd, "The Current Status of Scientific Realism," 58–60.

55. Putnam, "What is Realism?," 146, emphasis Putnam's.

56. Niiniluoto, *Critical Scientific Realism*, 130.

57. Putnam, "What is Realism?," 146. See also Laudan, "A Confutation of Convergent Realism," 221–24, for a discussion and criticism of Putnam's principle of charity in the concept of reference.

58. This interesting point of Kripke's was called to my attention in van Kooten Niekerk, "Critical Realist Perspective," 63. Niiniluoto also supports the idea that reference invariance is possible in spite of meaning variance. Niiniluoto, *Critical Scientific Realism*, 109, 124–32.

sums the various possible quantum states and their related probabilities for the particle of mass/energy commonly called a photon. In either case, the wave *properties* still exist, and are still properties of electro-magnetic radiation. The ether hypothesis presumed that the medium of those wave properties was some extraordinary kind of physical substance. Quantum Electrodynamics presumes the medium to be either the behavior of the mathematical descriptions necessary to represent the actual behavior of photons and electrons or the electromagnetic field in its entirety. For the critical realist reality is other than the terms that are used to refer to it. The fact that some terms are abandoned as misleading does not mean that they never referred. In many cases they referred well enough to lead us into the experimental interaction with the reality in question that forced us to abandon the term being used as inadequate and misleading.[59]

This referential value, even though it is expressed in metaphorical terms, even though the knowledge that refers is indirect and mediated, is demonstrated also by the fertility of successful scientific theories.[60]

> This kind of fertility is a persistent feature of structural explanations in the natural sciences over the last three centuries and especially during the last century. How can it best be understood? . . . What best explains it is the supposition that the model approximates sufficiently well the structures of the world that are causally responsible for the phenomena to be explained to make it profitable for the scientist to take the model's metaphoric extensions seriously . . . Here, as so often in science, theoretical entities previously unobserved, or in some cases even thought to be unobservable, are in fact observed and the expectations of theory are borne out, to no one's surprise. The separation between observable and unobservable postulated by many anti-realists in regard to ontological status does not seem to stand up.[61]

It will be remembered that the original form of critical realism was marred by a naïve and inadequate theory of perception. Scientific realism has a theory of perception that is not a built-in part of its epistemology,

---

59. McMullin, "A Case for Scientific Realism," 22; Couvalis, *The Philosophy of Science*, 105–7.

60. "A theoretical realist interprets theories as speaking of the *same unknown entities*, identified indirectly through their causal role and influences, so that successive theories may give conjectural but increasingly accurate descriptions of the nature of things." Niiniluoto, *Critical Scientific Realism*, 276.

61. McMullin, "A Case for Scientific Realism," 33.

but a product of studies in the sociology of knowledge, the psychology of childhood development, a study of the working of the nerves and brain in sensory perception, and the history of science. The relation of that theory of perception to the problem of the reference value of our perceptions and consequent conceptualizations can be put like this:

Our perceptions of the world and its objects are our own constructions, learned with great effort in early childhood and become so automatic as to be sub-conscious. This occurs as we are socialized to the use of language and the underlying idea of consensus reality that makes language an instrument of communication. It is part of the construction of these perceptions that they refer. We have constructed them to refer. We have been forced to construct them to refer not only by our social environment and cultural training but also by a world that constantly from our earliest youth has refused to be what we want it to be, what we expect it to be, what we mistakenly think we know it to be.[62] Our attempts to construct mental objects that successfully refer have been stimulated from the beginning by this activity of the world and by our desire to know it in order to anticipate, appreciate, and use it. The very thing that proves that our constructions are not perfectly successful in referring, which is the continuing power of the world to surprise us, is, paradoxically enough, precisely the justification for the claim that our constructions do refer. They refer because they have not been constructed once and for all either in an idealist sense or as a cultural product, but because they have been continuously reconstructed in response to the constant surprise that is the real world. The power to refer, despite the fact that the quality of reference is a quality that we have constructed for our perceptions, is not bestowed upon our perceptions by ourselves. We constructed the idea or the quality of reference, but the power or actuality of reference is bestowed upon our perceptions by reality itself when it forces us to reconstruct our ideas, our theories, and our objects. We are who we are, and believe what we believe, and think what we think, and see and hear what we see and hear because reality has refused to leave us unchanged, has refused to condone any tendency we may have towards solipsism. This awareness of the effect that reality has had upon us while we have been constructing knowledge of it is the justification

62. "The realist instead gives emphasis to the factuality (Peircean 'secondness') of the world, i.e., its ability to resist our will." Niiniluoto, *Critical Scientific Realism*, 286.

for believing that reality has bestowed the power of reference upon our constructions.[63]

3.2.5 Mediated, Indirect, Fallible Knowledge

Scientific realism regards knowledge as *mediated* and *indirect*. All scientific knowledge is admitted to be a social construction. It is only one of an infinity of possible forms that true knowledge of the world might take. Thus our knowledge of the world is not directly identical with the world that we know. Our knowledge of the world is mediated through our own social conventions for knowing it. But because some of those social conventions are a ruthless demand for empirical adequacy, a willingness to accommodate theory to fact, and an urge for exploration that constantly discovers new entities and structures in the world that test the predictive and descriptive limits of our theories, our knowledge is constructed from the beginning to refer.

This means that our knowledge is not *just* a social construction. It refers because reality as well as social construction is a constitutive causal agent in producing our knowledge. The social constructions we call knowledge are as much a product of how the world behaves as they are of cultural contexts and social pressures. Nancey Murphy makes this same point, saying: "While concepts are human contrivances and not pictures or representations, they are shaped by a real world. And *given* a stable set of concepts, we can go on to formulate sentences, most of whose criteria for acceptance (or acceptance as true) can best be described as a combination of coherence and empirical adequacy . . . Given a stable conceptual system, truth is, in part, a function of the way the world is."[64]

Because our knowledge of the world is indirect and mediated, it is *fallible*. It is subject to the present process of inter-subjective testing and the future process of continued learning. But fallible does not mean false.

---

63. "The justification of a belief crucially depends upon our interaction with the object of the belief. This is an essential feature of knowledge seeking in science." Ibid., 261. Also "Interaction is the critical element in the development of human cognition, since it makes possible the transmission of information about reality to the human mind." Ibid., 206.

64. Murphy, "The Limits of Pragmatism and the Limits of Realism," 354. Niiniluoto concurs in this judgment calling it a game theoretical way of understanding the relation between our choice of language and nature's choice of the structure of the world in that language. He offers this as a way of interpreting Kuhn as a critical realist. Niiniluoto, *Critical Scientific Realism*, 224.

Even though new theories are often incommensurable with the theories they replace, most of the knowledge content of the old theory survives the transition.[65] Newton's theory of gravitation does not survive the transition to Einstein's theory of General Relativity, because the underlying metaphysical structures change. Gravity ceases to be a force acting at a distance, and becomes a shape in the structure of space-time. But the mathematical relationships between entities in Newton's theory of gravity do survive in General Relativity as special cases and as approximations that hold good, except in the most extreme circumstances.[66] Moreover, the planet Neptune was discovered by an application of Newton's theory of gravity to the problem of the orbit of Uranus. The discovery remains valid even though the theory of gravity changes. The electrons of modern quantum physics are not the electrons of classical atomic theory. But there is historical continuity between them, even though the theoretical understanding of their nature and character has changed.[67]

3.2.6 Hypothetical Method

Scientific realism continues to regard hypothetical method as characteristic of the sciences.[68] It is not taken to be a criterion of demarcation between science and all else, for scientific realism is not looking for such a criterion as the positivists were. Nor is it regarded as a foundational form of universally valid rationality that guarantees true knowledge of reality. But it is considered to be the characteristic form of an investigation into the unknown.

Karl Popper's work in *The Logic of Scientific Discovery* and *Conjectures and Refutations* made clear the importance and essential character of hypothetical method in science. The postfoundational stance of critical realism also emphasizes its importance. If the foundations of our theories are not the foundations of reality itself, then deductions from that theory may well have no correspondence to reality and must, necessarily, be treated as hypotheses.

65. Kuhn, *The Structure of Scientific Revolutions*, 169.

66. "No fairer destiny could be allotted to any physical theory, than that it should of itself point out the way to the introduction of a more comprehensive theory, in which it lives as a limiting case." Einstein, *Relativity*, 86.

67. Peacocke, *Intimations of Reality*, 27.

68. See McMullin, *The Inference That Makes Science*, for an extended defense of this thesis. He argues for a continuity extending all the way from Aristotelean science to modern science.

Moreover, hypothetical method is amenable to the insights, imagination, genius, and daring of scientists. Under its protections wild ideas, compatible with no present theory, may be advanced for consideration and testing. Where anomalies in present theories do not exist such ideas will receive scant attention. But when anomalies have accumulated and a change of theory is probably necessary, hypothetical method enables new proposals to be considered. If the power of the world to surprise us is taken for granted, then hypothetical method is the best way to respond to such surprises.

3.3 SUMMARY

Scientific realism, as a modern form of critical realism, has developed these characteristics because of the observed fact in the history of science that reality does have the power to surprise us, to refuse to be what we think we know it to be, even in the face of strongly held and deeply socialized beliefs. This does not mean that we expect to achieve knowledge that is purified of social construction. The new theories we construct to accommodate reality when we are forced to change our ideas and our theories are just as thoroughly social products as the old ones. But they are constructions that arise out of a new encounter with reality; they are a response to something that is other than and more than our own social constructions. They are as much determined by the way things are as by the structure of our minds and the character of our theories.

These characteristics of scientific realism fit well under my more general typology for critical realisms. The reality of knowledge (3.2.1) corresponds to I-a, reference value (3.2.4) corresponds to I-b, the scientific realist response to the critical issues of underdetermination and theory-ladenness (3.2.3) contribute to I-b, while the issues themselves come under II-a. The mediated character of scientific knowledge (3.2.5) corresponds to II-a, and the postfoundational character of the practice of science (3.2.2) and the significance of hypothetical method (3.2.6), along with the limitations and critical issues (3.2.3), correspond to II-b. The importance of the general typology is its applicability to fields other than the natural sciences. But its validity can be tested (not for justification but for denial according *modus tollens*) by its ability to encompass the description of scientific realism, a well developed, widely recognized, and reasonably rigorous form of critical realism.

4

Rationality and Critical Realism

4.1 MULTIDIMENSIONAL KNOWLEDGE

Jarrett Leplin, in the introduction to *Scientific Realism*, says: "Most of the parties to the dispute tend to suppose that insofar as realism is an empirical thesis, the facts needed to assess it are in. Realism is either warranted by the impressive record of scientific success, or refuted by the discontinuities of theory change or the substantive findings of quantum mechanics."[1] This is largely borne out in the writings of various parties to the dispute.[2] However, this is an inadequate view of the question. Scientific realism is not directly a *scientific* thesis about the world, but rather a *philosophical* thesis about the relationship between scientific theory and practice and the world.[3] Therefore, it has empirical elements

1. Leplin, *Scientific Realism*, 7.

2. McMullin, "A Case for Scientific Realism," 29–30; Boyd, "The Current Status of Scientific Realism," 58–59, 65; Putnam, "What is Realism?," 141; Laudan, "A Confutation of Convergent Realism," 218; Sellars, *Critical Realism*, xiii.

3. McMullin seems to understand this, saying: "realism as I have defined it is *in part* an empirical thesis. There could well be a universe in which observable regularities would *not* be explainable in terms of hidden structures, that is, a world in which retroduction would not work." (Emphasis added.) McMullin, "A Case for Scientific Realism," 29. But he admits that "the doctrine itself [scientific realism] is still a philosophical one." See also van Huyssteen, *Theology and the Justification of Faith*, 149: "As we shall see, scientific realism is so called because it makes a proposal about the reliability of scientific knowledge as such, and is therefore basically a philosophical position."

and an examination of empirical considerations are a part of evaluating this thesis. Scientific disputes over theories are usually disputes over which postulates will generate theories that are in some way better for describing particular physical and/or empirical realities. But scientific realism is a dispute at a second level about (1) what postulates will generate a metatheory that is better for describing the process of scientific disputes, (2) the meaning of scientific theories, and (3) the meaning of the word "better" when it is used to describe why one theory supplants another. This makes it a philosophical thesis.

Not only is this a dispute over a philosophical thesis, but it is also one in which the choice of postulates seems to be open, at least as the discussion is currently posed. An open choice of postulates is one in which two or more different and inconsistent postulates can each reasonably be adopted and a self-consistent theory developed from them. The classic case of this is the parallel postulate in geometry. For 2,000 years it was taken for granted in Geometry that exactly one line parallel to a given line could be drawn through any given point. But in the late 1800s it was shown that complete and self consistent geometries could be developed on the assumption that either no parallel lines could be drawn through the given point, or alternatively that an infinite number of parallel lines could be drawn through the given point.[4] At first this seemed to be but an interesting intellectual game, but under Einstein's general theory of relativity it turned out that one of these odd new geometries was actually more useful for describing the behavior of the world than traditional Euclidean geometry.

Both the antirealists and the scientific realists in this debate elaborate their positions with articulateness and self-consistency. They each find ways to account for almost everything interesting and accurate about the history and character of science that the other side adduces in

---

4. Boyer and Merzbach, *A History of Mathematics*, 519–22, 545–46, 610–11. A more modern example is the continuum hypothesis. Cantor proved that the cardinality of the continuum is greater than the cardinality of the counting numbers. But the question remained and was posed by David Hilbert at the mathematical congress in Paris in 1901 whether there were any infinite numbers with cardinality greater than that of the counting numbers and less than that of the continuum. In 1940 Kurt Gödel proved that the continuum hypothesis was consistent with the axioms of set theory. In 1963 Paul Cohen proved that it was independent. This means that there is an open choice of postulates that will either affirm or deny the continuum hypothesis. Two different versions of set theory, both interesting, can be developed thereby. See also Poincaré, *The Foundations of Science*, 55–60, 65.

defense of its own position. Neither has produced an irrefutable argument. Not merely is there not yet sufficient empirical evidence to decide between them, but more importantly, empirical evidence cannot, in the nature of the dispute, ever be sufficient to decide the issue. A choice between antirealism and critical realism will be the result of a judgment, not a calculation.

Under the anti-realist postulate all the evidence from the history and practice of science to which scientific realists point in making the assertion that there is such a thing as real knowledge of the world only constitutes evidence that the social pressures in science work in the direction of ever more complex and articulate theories about the world. Scientists make their careers by establishing new descriptions of the world or promoting a change in the theoretical commitments from which our descriptions of the world spring. This creates the impression that our knowledge is changing because of the behavior of the world, when it is actually the behavior of scientists that changes it. The only thing that can be meaningfully supposed about the world on this account is that it is sufficiently complex and inaccessible to give endless opportunities for scientists to argue with other scientists, make their reputations, and justify their research by articulating and complexifying the knowledge that is called science.

Under the scientific realist postulate all the evidence of the human and socially constructed character of knowledge is no more than a contribution to the critical theory by which scientific realism distinguishes knowledge of the world from the language and symbols we use in our knowledge of it. Since scientific knowledge is not regarded as solely determined by the nature of the world, but co-determined by the behavior of the world and the social constructions of working scientists, all the criticisms of the anti-realists only serve to specify more closely one set of the co-determinants of scientific knowledge. The power of the world to be another set of co-determinants is not affected thereby.[5]

5. Poincaré, whom I have earlier cited in support of this idea that social construction and the actual behavior of reality are co-determinate of the structure and character of our knowledge, is usually counted as a conventionalist, and thus a mild sort of anti-realist. But Royce, "Introduction," 17, gives him a critically realistic reading: "But it is experience itself which points out to us what lines of interpretation will prove most convenient. Instead of Kant's rigid list of a priori 'forms,' we consequently have in M. Poincaré's account a set of conventions, neither wholly subjective and arbitrary, nor yet imposed upon us unambiguously by the external compulsion of experience

Critical realism supposes that our knowledge is a function of a great many independent variables. Some of them are variables that represent real physical causes of our knowledge. Because it is so hard to deal with many variables at the same time, we usually only take account of a few. Indeed, one of the major criteria for good experimental work is reducing the number of free variables by means of adequate controls. Others of the variables in our knowledge represent socially constructed, interpersonal, historical, and cultural causes of our knowledge. Again, because it is difficult to deal with many variables at once, works of history or sociology or even philosophy seldom take account of more than a few at a time.

The question remains whether these variables are all independent. It is part of the ongoing exploratory process of both the sciences and philosophy that sometimes variables previously taken to be independent are reduced to functions of other variables already in hand. A positivistic reductionism would even assert that the social, historical, psychological, and interpersonal variables that are primarily concerned in the determination of the sorts of social constructs that we use for knowledge of the world are nonetheless ultimately products of physical causes. But critical realism does not accept such radical reductionism and examines carefully lesser reductionisms.

For instance, there does not appear to be any way to derive the rules of organization in a complex multicellular organism from a consideration of the laws of physics, chemistry, and biochemistry. At most

---

. . . Characteristic remains, however, for our author, as, in his own contrasting way, for Kant, the thought that *without principles which at every stage transcend precise confirmation through such experience as is then accessible the organization of experience is impossible.*" (Emphasis Royce.) Cf. Poincaré, *The Foundations of Science*, 28–29: "The last [conventions] are met with above all in mathematics and the related sciences. Thence precisely it is that these sciences get their rigor; these conventions are the work of the free activity of our mind, which, in this domain, recognizes no obstacle. Here our mind can affirm, since it decrees; but let us understand that while these decrees are imposed upon *our* science, which, without them, would be impossible, they are not imposed upon nature. Are they then arbitrary? No, else they were sterile. Experiment leaves us our freedom of choice, but it guides us by aiding us to discern the easiest way . . . Now every day we see it [science] work under our very eyes. That could not be if it taught us nothing of reality . . . [T]his frame into which we wish to force everything is of our own construction; but we have not made it at random. We have made it, so to speak, by measure and therefore we can make the facts fit into it without changing what is essential in them." Einstein articulates a similar attitude. See the quote cited in Wang, *Reflections on Kurt Gödel*, 153.

these determine the structure of the DNA molecule and the inherent freedom and variability of the base pairs that constitute its coding. They determine the way that certain sequences of base pairs code for certain proteins. But what order the base pairs come in, what proteins they do actually code out of the many, many possible proteins, and how those proteins function together to compose a complex organism are not derivable from chemistry alone. They are not independent in the sense that the organism can exist apart from the reality of the underlying biochemistry, but rather in the sense that they cannot be reduced to it. They are an emergent level of organization not reducible to the laws that govern the underlying levels.[6]

Because our knowledge is a function of a great many variables, some physical and some social, a complete mathematical description of that function would require as many dimensions as there are independent variables, that is, at least several dozen, and probably several hundred or several thousand. An attempt to reduce knowledge to a function of just the physical variables, as in a positivistic practice of science, or to just the social variables, as in the strong program in the sociology of science, amounts to an attempt to take a cross section in fewer dimensions of the larger object. Such a cross-section will be a valid picture of the whole object *as found in a space of those fewer dimensions*. It will be self-consistent and with respect to the dimensions in which it is found it will be reasonably complete. This is why reductionism almost always seems to work.

This is much like partial differentiation in multi-variable calculus. By holding other variables constant one can differentiate with respect to a single variable. Partial derivatives can be obtained for each variable in this way. The derivative of the whole multi-variable function is a matrix composed of partial derivatives. Thus, if we hold the physical variables constant (presuming thereby that the physical world is the same for all observers, whatever the perceived world may be), then we may investigate how knowledge changes relative to its social variables. Similarly, if we hold the social variables constant (as when scientists investigating

6. Barbour, *Religion in an Age of Science*, 162–72, discusses the information theory and systems analysis understanding of the meaning of levels of organization both concretely, in a discussion of molecular genetics, and more abstractly, in a discussion of the problems of reductionism. All this discussion of emergent levels of order is based upon the work of Ilya Prigogine in the field of nonequilibrium thermodynamics. See ibid., 113.

any given field of phenomena form a single community with a shared paradigm), then we may investigate how knowledge changes with respect to the physical variables.

The scientific effort to reduce our knowledge to those variables that are independent of human social and mental structures seems to be as successful (more so, considered quantitatively) as the sociological and philosophical effort to reduce our knowledge to those variables that spring from human construction. Critical realism refuses to make either of these reductions and attempts to deal with the difficulties of describing our knowledge in as many dimensions as are necessary to represent both the physical and the social variables of which it is a function.[7] Critical realism attempts to treat social constructions in the same critically realistic way as it does the behavior of mass/energy which gives rise to the complex physical theories of the sciences.[8]

4.2 RATIONALITY

It is in a dispute over a choice of postulates that the failure of the classical model of rationality is seen most clearly. Under the classical theory of rationality postulates were supposed to be rock-bottom self-evident propositions over which there could be little dispute because it was assumed that their necessity and universality and the rules that followed from them would eventually force all rational agents to choose the same ones or their equivalents.[9] But a dispute over a choice of postulates is one in which it is necessary to either choose between competing rules, or else to develop new rules. Moreover, such disputes arise because the rules with which we are already familiar have failed in some way. In such cases the classical model of rationality is no help.[10]

---

7. Niiniluoto also resists reductionism while appreciating and appropriating many of the results of reductionist analysis. Niiniluoto, *Critical Scientific Realism*, 14–15.

8. See van Huyssteen, *Theology and the Justification of Faith*, 154: "It should now be clear why scientific realism has developed into one of the most important positions in the current philosophy of science debate: it not only highlights the role of metaphoric reference in scientific theory formation while honoring the provisionality and socio-historical character of all knowledge, but it also enables us to retain the ideals of truth, objectivity, rationality, and scientific progress in an exciting and reinterpreted way."

9. Brown, *Rationality*, 19.

10. Ibid., 139.

The failure of the classical model of rationality does not mean that rules are inappropriate to the reasoning process, nor that theoretical structures using rules should not be elaborated.[11] It only means that such rules are the products of rational thought, rather than its foundations. Harold I. Brown has argued extensively and carefully for an understanding of rationality that focuses on the underlying act of judgment by which rational thinking produces and chooses its rules, as well as recognizes which cases come under which rules. For Brown, "judgment is the ability to evaluate a situation, assess evidence, and come to a reasonable decision without following rules."[12] Brown's understanding of the nature of judgment is an approach to the problem of rationality that is well suited to critical realism.[13] Wentzel van Huyssteen interprets the importance of Brown's concept for critical realism as follows: "Brown's notion of the role of judgment in rational decision making is exciting because in the end it frees us from the idea that only infallibility or perfectibility counts in epistemic matters. When at any point in time we make a decision for something in the light of the best reasons available to us, there need be no incompatibility between accepting a set of fallible claims for a substantial period of time and being prepared to reconsider them when we have good reasons for doing so."[14]

11. Feyerabend, *Against Method*, 249: "The limitation of all rules and standards is recognized by *naïve anarchism*. A naïve anarchist says (a) that both absolute rules and context dependent rules have their limits and infers (b) that all rules and standards are worthless and should be given up . . . Thus while I agree with (a) I do not agree with (b). I argue that all rules have their limits and that there is no comprehensive rationality. I do not argue that we should proceed without rules and standards."

12. Brown, *Rationality*, 137. For the whole discussion of judgment and its role at the root of rationality see ibid., 137–65.

13. Couvalis, *The Philosophy of Science*, 91, describes the nature of Kuhn's claims about how scientific revolutions take place in a manner that emphasizes the place of judgment in a situation in which precise rules cannot be followed. His description of Kuhn implies that scientific practice is often rational in the manner described by Brown, rather than in a traditionally rationalist manner. "He [Kuhn] claims that psychological and historical research show that our methods for using concepts and for judging theories are things which we extrapolate by analogy from important instances and which we only usefully extrapolate by adapting our judgments to particular contexts. They cannot be usefully articulated as precise and general rules. As an argument for his claim, he points out it is a striking feature of scientific research that scientists radically disagree about the nature of the standards for judging the merits of scientific hypotheses, even though they agree in their judgments about the merits of [particular] hypotheses."

14. van Huyssteen, *Postfoundational Theology*, 247–48.

Critical realism must avoid the foundationalism of the classical theory of rationality for two reasons. First, because foundationalism lends itself to the reductionism that critical realism refuses to make in examining the variables, both physical and social, of which our knowledge is a function. Second, if the other that we are seeking to know is truly other, then there can be no guarantee ahead of time that any one form of thought will be appropriate for describing it, even if that form of thought is the only one we can imagine. At the same time, critical realism has no intention of abandoning rational thought. But rational thought will have to be conceived in a manner that makes it responsive to the realities that it is employed to know, rather than as a standard that determines what is real and what is not. Critical realism insists upon combining the reality of our knowledge of the world with a critical awareness of the manner in which we construct that knowledge.

> To the critical realist science is discovery and exploration as well as construction and invention. Unlike the naïve realist, and along with the instrumentalist, the critical realist model of rationality recognizes the importance of human imagination in the formation of theories. In this way critical realists try to acknowledge both the creativity of their thought and the existence of structures in reality not created by the human mind. Concerning the role of models in scientific theory, critical realism will be defending a position between literalism, on the one hand, and fictionalism, on the other. In this sense theoretical models now become valid but provisional and limited ways of imagining what otherwise can never be truly observable.[15]

Brown understands judgment as something that can work without rules, but that is not incompatible with rules. Judgment is used in making up new rules, in applying existing rules, and in choosing between competing rules. Moreover judgment is understood to be fallible without being regarded as baseless or impotent. The fact that a judgment may ultimately need to be revised does not mean that it must be revised immediately. The immediate context may well be one in which the judgment at issue holds and need not be revised at this time. Whether this is so is itself a matter of judgment, and that judgment depends upon meaningful knowledge of a body of information that is relevant to whatever issue is under consideration. That is to say, judgment is not simply

---

15. van Huyssteen, *Theology and the Justification of Faith*, 157.

the ability to make up rules out of nothing, nor is it fallible because no judgment has any grounds whatsoever. Rules are made up, or chosen, or applied, with respect to some reality. Judgments are recognized as fallible with respect to some reality. Meaningful knowledge of a body of relevant information, despite the fallible character of that information, is a prerequisite for making good judgments.[16]

The nature of rationality and its relation to these questions cannot be ignored. In chapter 7 we will attempt to use a critically realistic understanding of Barth's theology to answer criticisms against it stemming primarily from Wolfhart Pannenberg and W. W. Bartley. The main thrust of these criticisms is that Barth's theology is either inherently irrational, or else fails to apply necessary universal rational standards. A large part of the reply to those criticisms depends upon the judgment that critical realism requires a more broadly conceived understanding of what constitutes a rational act than either of those gentlemen will acknowledge.

Kees van Kooten Niekerk, in his valuable article on "A Critical Realist Perspective on the Dialogue between Theology and Science," defines critical realism in part by saying: "On the one hand, it [critical realism] holds that it is possible to acquire knowledge about the external or physical world as it really is, independent of the human mind or subjectivity. That is why it is called *realism*."[17] I have tried to argue in this chapter that this definition is simply not critical enough. The correct statement would be that critical realism holds that it is possible to acquire knowledge about things as they really are. Period.

Such knowledge is *not* independent of the human mind or subjectivity for two reasons. First, because even those features of knowledge that seem most independent of the human mind and subjectivity, mathematical relations, are not.[18] The things that we use as numbers—and most especially the real numbers as they are used in the physical sciences—are human constructions. This is shown by the hundreds of

16. Brown, *Rationality*, 139–49. See also the discussion of the work of Michael Polanyi, 159–65.

17. van Kooten Niekerk, "Critical Realist Perspective," 51.

18. It is mathematical relations that are most often seen as likely to represent the independent reality of the external world. See Ibid., 68: "But within the body of scientific knowledge it seems that the nonfigurative mathematical statements of primary relations, somewhat paradoxically, bring us most closely to a precise picture of the real world!" And yet van Kooten Niekerk also seems to understand that even mathematics does not give us direct access to the external world.

years of mathematical development that were necessary to clarify the foundations of the real number system, and which led to the development of new definitions of number in set theory taken as a foundation of mathematics.[19] Numbers may well be external realities to which our constructed mathematical concepts refer, but if so, they are certainly not physical realities. In any case the numbers that we use to do physics and the other sciences are our own conceptually constructed numbers.

Second, because knowledge is by its nature something in our human minds. It is a product of our human subjectivity. Knowledge is a pattern in the mind that refers to external reality, but knowledge itself is internal to the mind and to subjectivity. It is the external or physical world to which knowledge refers that is independent, not the knowledge itself.[20] Critical realism accepts that knowledge is a psychical structure in our own minds, and thereby not identical with the known, wherever the known is something other than the mind itself. This means that knowledge, *realistic* knowledge, is never independent or apodictically certain.

4.3 THE MODEL THEORY OF KNOWLEDGE

Sallie McFague calls attention to the importance of models in both theology and science, and indeed, for all knowledge that can be considered critically realistic:

> A form of critical realism can be defended as appropriate for both fields. While some might hold that scientific models are concerned only with "experimentation" and theological models only with "imagination," a metaphorical sensibility will insist that neither is the case. "Discovery" and "creation" are both involved in models of whatever field, and all knowledge is dependent, in some fashion and in varying degrees, on models, which both "are and are not" what they model. The tension of metaphorical

19. Not easily or clearly, as it takes a study of the history of mathematics, as well as courses in mathematical logic and set theory to see it. But the definitions given to the real numbers or even the natural numbers in set theory are strange enough that most engineering students taking calculus think them weird. The oddity arises, of course, from attempting a definition that produces all the familiar characteristics of numbers in the most parsimonious and rigorous way.

20. "For a theoretical realist, laws of nature are linguistic expressions of *regularities* or *invariances* which exist 'out there' in nature. Laws as statements are human constructions, but causal and other regularities are mind independent aspects of reality." Niiniluoto, *Critical Scientific Realism*, 133.

thinking, its insistence on relativity and partiality while still supporting the possibility that some models "fit" reality better than others, appears to be at the heart of science, as it should also be at the heart of theology.[21]

Human knowledge is usually some sort of a model of the object known. Most precisely, a model is a pattern of programming in the mind, an algorithm, with an associated data set, which is used to do three things. First it represents the reality to which our knowledge refers in the processes of our minds, where it interacts with other knowledge and other ideas. It is not an image in a mirror, but an abstract and symbolic representation. Moreover, it is an active process, rather than a static object. Second, it mimics the behavior of the reality to which it refers. When it does this well it interacts with other knowledge and ideas in our minds in a manner that can be mapped onto the interactions of that reality with other realities in the world. Third, it reduces the reality to a smaller and more manageable set of ideas (of algorithms and programming patterns) which can be used to recreate details of the reality referred to without requiring a massive storage of empirical data which would clog the mind with real, but in that form useless, information.

These characteristics account for the "is and is not" relationship of models to the realities they are models of. They are why critical realism has to take account of both negative ("we found evidence against this") and positive ("we found evidence to support this") knowledge in the act of knowing. The fact that human knowledge is some sort of model that is usually an algorithmic compression accounts for both the partiality and relativity of our knowledge, as well as for the possibility that some models do fit reality better than others. The presumption that there is some set of universal and necessary rules that can be used to determine how good a fit a given model has to a given reality cannot be upheld if we admit that we are investigating an unknown reality. It is necessary to bring the model into interaction with the reality to which it refers and to check it regularly.

Most of the rules and presumptions that we use to construct our models have been invented or selected to produce a wide variety of possible models, but that does not constitute a guarantee that the flexibility of our models will match the variability of the realities they are being

21. McFague, *Metaphoric Theology*, 101.

used to know. The ongoing process of inquiry will require the rules to be re-evaluated and changed from time to time in order to improve the fit of our models to the world. This does not mean that the rules are either impotent or arbitrary. They are chosen in a rational act of judgment in a situation that is not totally without rules, but that is beyond rules in the sense that in this situation it is the rules themselves that are being mooted. But, as Brown points out, the rule-choosing situation is still one in which a rational agent can act, and act rationally, despite the fact that it is the rules of rationality itself that are in question. The rational agent acts with a great deal of freedom, yet is not totally arbitrary. First, the rules are not abandoned wholesale and formed anew from out of nothing, but are rather reformed piecemeal, checking at each stage what effect the new or variant rule may have. Second, choosing new rules is done with regard to some relevant body of information.[22]

In mathematical terms, a model is a set that satisfies—or elements of which satisfy—the formulas of a theory, or the conditions of statements in a theory, making those statements true. Thus, the mathematical and the ordinary usage of the term "model" are converse of one another. In mathematics a model is a model of a theory. In ordinary usage, a model is a model of the object. When a model of a theory can be mapped onto an object or reality in the world—that is, when a correspondence can be set up between the model of the theory and the object in the world—then we gain confidence that the theory makes true statements about the object and call the model of the theory a model of the object in the world as well.[23]

It is this duality in the meaning of the term model that is responsible for the initial confusion over the meaning of Kuhn's term "paradigm." A paradigm, if it is to be a scientific instrument for knowledge of the world, must necessarily include not just a well-defined theory but also a model of that theory, an interpretation function for relating the statements of the theory to its model, and a mapping of the model onto the behavior of the world. The interpretation function is usually mathematical, but the function for mapping the model onto the world is usually a collection of judgments (not classically rational rules) about how to apply the model

22. Brown, *Rationality*, 150–65.

23. "Further, it is by now well established and accepted that the study of theories and scientific change can successfully employ concepts borrowed from set theory and logical model theory." Niiniluoto, *Critical Scientific Realism*, 14.

to the world and how to extend (and correct) the mapping by appropriate experimentation. Moreover, in many cases the model can be used to show why one theory supplants another.[24]

Models are used in science and the humanities to make explanations about the objects of knowledge.[25] The model as a model of knowledge can be used to explain in a critically realistic way why knowledge has characteristics that can be used in both realistic and anti-realistic arguments about the nature and character of knowledge.[26] Models are constructions *by* and *in* the mind, conditioned by the nature of the minds in which they reside and conditioned by the social processes in which human beings cooperate together to formulate them. But as constructions that are used to represent and mimic realities, that are mapped onto the world, and that are brought into interaction with the realities of the world to test and correct the constructed models, they have the essential features of real knowledge. They refer to and correspond to the objects they are constructed to represent. Reference is not identity and correspondence can usually never be known to be complete or consistent (except in some cases where both the object and the model are abstract mathematical entities). But the whole argument of critical realism is that the history of science shows that reference does not need to be identity, nor does correspondence need to be complete or provably consistent in order for knowledge to be real.

Moreover, the use of models applies in a critical way to the whole problem of foundations, because even in mathematics, where the correspondence in modeling can sometimes be handled in the most rigorous way, there is an essential incompleteness in every systematic theory complex enough to be worthy of being used.

4.3.1 Correspondence Truth

The idea of correspondence truth is important to critical realism, despite the suggestion that no meaningful idea of correspondence can

24. "A powerful theory can model in its modeling resources the models of another theory (thereby explaining why they broke down and the degree of the failure)." Hooker, *A Realistic Theory of Science*, 57.

25. Van Huyssteen, *Theology and the Justification of Faith*, xv.

26. Dedekind considered that the capacity to envisage mappings, without which the model theory of knowledge is impotent, is one "without which no thinking at all is possible." Stein, "Logos, Logic, and Logistiké," 246.

be elaborated.[27] The argument has sometimes seemed to proceed as if correspondence had to be total and complete or else it would be nothing more than empirical adequacy. But this is expecting too much. The elaboration of a meaningful idea of correspondence requires a simple approach that does not attempt more than it can accomplish, nor fall prey to the "all or nothing" fallacy. Correspondence does *not* mean that the knowledge in question is a literal image of the reality known such that every feature of the reality either is or can be found in the image. Neither does it mean that every feature of the image or model that constitutes knowledge of the object is to be found in the object. To this extent Rorty's criticisms of the mind and its knowledge as a "mirror of nature" are correct. But the supposition that this is what correspondence truth means is only an instance of the "all or nothing" fallacy that Niiniluoto identifies and argues against.[28]

First of all, correspondence (or a mapping, in more general mathematical terms) simply means that there is a function, relation, method, pattern, or algorithm for assigning members of one field, model, or set to those of another. A correspondence is not necessarily one-to-one, although that might well be a criterion for a good correspondence in modeling knowledge of an object. Because a correspondence is an assignment there is no necessary or organic reason that one field or set should resemble the other. Whatever resemblance there may be lies in the function or algorithm for making assignments.

Because knowledge is usually found in our minds as a model, both of a theory and of an object, correspondence in knowledge usually means at least two different things. First, there must be a correspondence between the elements of the model and the statements of the theory. In this correspondence the elements of the model fulfill the truth conditions of the statements in the theory. This is merely Tarskian semantics. The correspondence here is not necessarily one-to-one. There may be many statements whose truth conditions are fulfilled by a given set of elements in the model. There may well be different sets of elements in the model that fulfill the truth conditions of any given statement.

---

27. "The central question before us is whether the realist's assertions about the interrelations between truth, reference, and success are sound." Laudan, "A Confutation of Convergent Realism," 221.

28. Niiniluoto, *Critical Scientific Realism*, 81, 93.

Second, there must be a mapping of the model onto the world, or objects in the world. This is the more difficult correspondence. Its algorithms often include experiments, techniques, procedures, and methods that do not seem strictly mathematical. This mapping is practically never one-to-one. The model as knowledge is an algorithmic compression of our experience of the world. Were it not it would not be knowledge, for the world appears to be both inexhaustible and irreducibly complex, whereas our minds are finite, or, at most, denumerably infinite.[29]

Both correspondences are fallible, but the first kind does not usually fail, as both parts of the correspondence are under our control. The fallibility of the second sort, the mapping of our models onto the world, is only too well known. But fallibility should not mean that the idea of correspondence truth needs to be abandoned. When a correspondence fails, it does not fail to have ever been any kind of correspondence at all. It may fail to map newly discovered objects or events that were not taken into account in constructing the model in the first place. Sometimes normal science can extend the model to cover them. It may be presumed to map all of a certain set of objects or events, and turn out to map only some of them. Usually normal science can determine how to limit the domain of the mapping so as to restore the correspondence.[30] It is in the nature of a model, as an algorithmic compression, to purport to cover all of the objects or events that fall in the range of the mapping from its domain. But the failure to cover all does not mean that the model never mapped any. Even when the practices of normal science fail, and a new theory or a new paradigm with a new model of a theory become necessary, not all of the old correspondences become void, indeed, not even most of them do.

The inexhaustibility and irreducible complexity of the world mean, first, that there are always objects and events yet to be discovered that are not and cannot be mapped by our current models. But where our theories and models do turn out to map objects and events that were not taken into account when they were invented they demonstrate that they are more than merely empirically adequate. When they work in such a manner as to enable research to discover objects and events that they themselves *cannot* map, then even in that failure they prove the value

29. The Gödel incompleteness theorems prove and define the inexhaustibility of mathematics at least. Wang, *Reflections on Kurt Gödel*, 146.

30. Kuhn, *The Structure of Scientific Revolutions*, chapters iii and iv.

of the correspondence they did provide. Now, random searching would also eventually discover such things. But when a paradigm focuses research so as to discover them at a higher rate than random searching would, it may be presumed that its correspondences are meaningful. Since the unknown is unknown it is not possible to *determine* ahead of time whether the use of theories and models that have been constructed to correspond discovers new things of new complexity faster than random searching. But it may be possible to make a judgment.

Second, the complexity of the world is such that it cannot be completely captured by any finite or denumerably infinite theory or model.[31] Since the Skolem-Löwenheim theorem demonstrates that any theory that has a model at all has a denumerable model,[32] an irreducibly complex world has no model at all. Or rather, no theory that describes it completely has a model. Not only is the set of possible true statements about the world bigger than the set that can be produced by any theory, but also, the complexity of the world is such that any finitistic theory must produce false statements as the world is discovered and exposed in greater and greater detail. This means that *no* theory is formally true, in the strict two-valued sense of the word.[33] But this does not mean that no theory corresponds to the world, nor that a given theory that fails to correspond *completely* thereby fails to correspond at all. It only means that it is one of the functions of continuing research to determine the limits to the domain of the theory in which its statements do correspond.

Because the complexity of the world is probably irreducible—that is, infinite of an order greater than the denumerable infinity of possible statements from a theory—it cannot properly be said that one theory or statement is closer to the truth than another. The distance from *any* finite number to infinity is always the same and always infinite. But it

31. Isaac Asimov, in answer to a question about whether science would ever get all the answers and be left with nothing to do, once said: "It is my belief that the universe possesses, in its essence, fractal properties of a very complex sort and that the pursuit of science shares these properties. It follows that any part of the universe that remains ununderstood, and any part of scientific investigation that remains unresolved, contains within it all the complexity of the original. Therefore we'll never finish. No matter how far we go, the road ahead will be as long as it was at the start, and that's the secret of the universe." Asimov, *The Secret of the Universe*, 181.

32. Boulos and Jeffrey, *Computability and Logic*, 141–44.

33. Niiniluoto, *Critical Scientific Realism*, 139: "As we have repeatedly emphasized, it is not a surprise to critical scientific realists that scientific theories are typically speaking strictly false."

can, and very properly, be said that one theory is better than another if the range of its statements that correspond is greater than that of another (most easily judged when the better theory includes the entire range of the lesser theory within its own range). It can also be very properly said that one statement is more truthlike than another.[34] For though two different numbers are the same distance from infinity, nevertheless one is greater than the other and they are capable of comparison.[35]

Correspondence truth only becomes untenable when it is defined under a classical two-valued logic model of rationality. In critical realism, where multi-valued logics are a useful tool for dealing with statements that do not conform to the law of the excluded middle or the principle of bivalence,[36] correspondence truth is not taken for granted, but it is nonetheless the object of good theoretical and interpretive work. It is perfectly tenable and gives us the most useful understanding of the relation in which knowledge is both of the mind and of the object.

4.4 MATHEMATICS

4.4.1 Historical Perspectives and the Limits of Mathematics

The Greeks invented postulational thinking in mathematics. At first different mathematicians utilized different postulates as starting points, with the result that occasionally one mathematician would prove what another had taken as a postulate, but only by taking as a postulate what someone else had proved. It was Euclid who first put together, in his *Elements*, a parsimonious set of postulates from which it was possible to derive the whole of plane geometry. This example stood for almost 2,000 years as the paradigm act of mathematical system building.[37]

When the calculus was invented in the second half of the seventeenth century by Newton and Leibniz, it was not built upon a thorough and rigorous postulational base. But for nearly 200 years mathematicians were so enchanted with the power and fertility of analytic methods that

34. Ibid., 203, defines progress as increasing truthlikeness, not increasing certainty.

35. This is why Laudan, "A Confutation of Convergent Realism" can be largely correct, and yet not amount to a compelling critique of critical realism. The idea of truthlikeness is developed in much greater detail and with much more rigorous formalism in Niiniluoto, *Critical Scientific Realism*, 64–78.

36. Zinov'ev, *Philosophical Problems of Many Valued Logic*, 4–7, 16–19, 23–41.

37. Eves, *An Introduction to the History of Mathematics*, 112–15.

they rather contributed to the fertility than cleaned out the basement. In the second half of the nineteenth century a concern for the rigorous postulational foundations of analysis became one of the key concerns of mathematicians. This resulted in a program known as "the arithmetization of analysis" that not only put analysis on a sounder footing, but also, through the work of such mathematicians as Peano and Dedekind, put the real number system itself onto much sounder footing. Parsimonious sets of postulates were exhibited from which it was possible to generate all of what we know as arithmetic and analysis.[38]

Throughout most of mathematical history it had been assumed that postulates were merely statements of what was, at its heart, self-evident necessary truth. Kant certainly assumed this when he undertook to construct an epistemology that had as a primary purpose explaining how such knowledge as that obtained in Euclidean geometry was possible, and when he considered that the necessity and certainty of mathematics were the archetypical case of good theoretical knowledge. But the work that was done in non-Euclidean geometries made it clear that different sets of postulates with different sets of consequences could be elaborated in a manner that was consistent with mathematical reasoning. It was Poincaré, as previously mentioned, who made the clearest statement that postulates were chosen by convention, not by self evidence, for the sake of the consequences that could be derived from them.[39]

By this time it had long been recognized that the Elements of Euclid were full of unstated assumptions and meaningless definitions. In 1899, in his *Grundlagen der Geometrie*, David Hilbert put geometry upon a sound postulational basis. In doing so he formulated twenty-one explicit axioms, as opposed to Euclid's ten, and accepted as well three terms and six relationships as undefined. In this work Hilbert became the leading

---

38. Boyer, *History of the Calculus*, 267–99.

39. The status of Poincaré's conventionalism is a problem. His invocation of mathematical intuition in arguments against the logicists and his belief that what he is doing is compatible with Kant suggests that, in some sense, mathematics has a content. But his arguments about the vicious circle principle imply the opposite. See Goldfarb, "Poincaré Against the Logicists," 63–65. But Poincaré's view is still widely held: "to a large extent mathematicians have accepted axiom systems on the basis of the ability of those axioms to bring order and intelligibility to a field and/or to generate interesting and fruitful conclusions. In an important sense, what legitimized the calculus in the eyes of its creators was that by means of its methods they attained conclusions that were recognized as correct and meaningful." Crowe, "Ten Misconceptions About Mathematics and Its History," 272.

figure in the axiomatic and formalist school of thought, which maintained that undefined terms had no referents and no meaning other than that given to them in the axioms of the system. This makes mathematics to be solely formal with no external content and has been the source of the fertility of modern mathematics, for it made it possible for mathematicians to create new branches of mathematics simply by creating new sets of axioms and exploring their consequences.

For those who followed Hilbert the problem of consistency became critical. Where axioms may be chosen at will, with respect only to the conclusions that follow from them, it is of critical importance that the systems derived from the axioms be consistent; that is, incapable of ever proving a contradiction. Hilbert had managed to prove that his axiomatization of geometry would be both complete and consistent if it could be proved that arithmetic was complete and consistent. At the famous Mathematical Congress at Paris in 1900 Hilbert proposed as one of his twenty-one problems to be solved in the coming century the proof of the completeness and consistency of arithmetic.

Bertrand Russell and Alfred North Whitehead very shortly thereafter began the publication of their massive *Principia Mathematica*. They took a position close to but not exactly congruent with Hilbert's. It was their contention that though many of the axioms of mathematics were matters of choice, all of them stood upon a core foundation in the axioms of logic. In great detail and with explicit and painstaking rigor they demonstrated that the entirety of arithmetic could be derived from simple axioms. This was an incredible and impressive piece of work, but it did not yet demonstrate that arithmetic was complete and consistent.[40]

Arithmetic would be complete if it could be shown that every true statement in arithmetic was capable of being proved. It was not necessary to actually exhibit the proofs, for some of them were certain to be so complicated as to require more steps than could be completed in any probable lifetime. It was only necessary to demonstrate the possibility of proof in a finite number of steps. In 1930 Kurt Gödel made the first step towards such a proof with what is called the completeness theorem. This theorem did not demonstrate that every true statement in arithmetic could be proved, but only that every statement in arithmetic that could

---

40. For the previous three paragraphs see Boyer and Merzbach, *A History of Mathematics*, 609–14.

be proved at all could be proved using the system that was then current, that of the *Principia Mathematica*. It seemed like a good first step.

But when he attempted to make the next step Gödel proved two very surprising things. The first was that no theory of arithmetic can ever be complete. He did this by exhibiting a method for constructing true statements about arithmetic that were incapable of being proved within the theory of arithmetic. Moreover, he showed that even if the theory of arithmetic was strengthened by adding postulates to dispose of the undecidable statements it would still be possible to construct further undecidable statements. Next, he showed that it was impossible, within the theory of arithmetic, to prove that arithmetic was consistent. Arithmetic might be consistent, indeed, in his proof it was necessary for him to assume that it was consistent, but it could not be proved to be so from out of its own postulates. All of these results were proved to hold true for any larger system of thought that contained integer arithmetic as a subset.[41]

These unexpected results changed the character of the Hilbertian program for the axiomatization of mathematics.[42] They also killed the hope of the Vienna Circle Logical Positivists that a set of mathematical postulates could be chosen from which all of modern science would be derivable by logic.[43]

Several interesting mathematical consequences followed. The first was that logic *itself* came to be regarded as an axiomatized field of mathematics where alternative choices of postulates were possible. Three-valued, many-valued, and even infinite-valued logics were invented.

41. An excellent popular exposition of Gödel's completeness and incompleteness theorems can be found in Hofstadter, *Gödel, Escher, Bach*. Briefer, but more technical expositions are in the appendices of Wang, *Reflections on Kurt Gödel*. They can be approached without compromise in a textbook such as Boolos and Jeffrey, *Computability and Logic*. English translations of the original papers can be found in van Heijenoort, *A Sourcebook in Mathematical Logic*, 582–91, 596–616.

42. Wang, *Reflections on Kurt Gödel*, 276. There are those who claim that the Hilbertian program is not damaged in the least by the incompleteness theorems of Gödel. Detlefson, *Hilbert's Program*, xi, makes this claim. But in supporting his claim he says that in Hilbert's program we must distinguish between formal mathematical proofs, which are ideal in nature and constructed from terms that have no referent and take their meaning from their associated axioms, and the metamathematical evaluation of those proofs as having content. But this is the step that Hilbert did not take, and that his program for the formalization and axiomatization of mathematics did not envisage.

43. Eves, *An Introduction to the History of Mathematics*, 483.

Second of all, even within traditional two-valued logic, consequences began to flow from Gödel's theorem. Perhaps the most famous is Tarski's theorem on the indefinability of truth, which states that arithmetical truth cannot be defined with the confines of arithmetic. This does not mean that there is no such thing as arithmetical truth, for Tarski's theorem assumes that there are true statements in arithmetic. It means that there is no process within arithmetic that can either produce, or even identify, *all* true statements.[44]

At this point I must offer some cautions about how to understand the implications of the incompleteness theorems and how to apply them.

First of all, the incompleteness theorems are a very specialized piece of mathematical reasoning. They constitute what was and continues to be a very surprising discovery about the limits of mathematical theories accomplished by rigorous mathematical demonstration. But their rigor limits their *direct* application to systems of thought and proof that include the integers and the operations of addition and multiplication. Since all of the sciences make use of mathematics, the incompleteness theorems are legitimately used to understand the limits of formal reasoning in any philosophy of science. But systems of thought that do not use the integers and their arithmetic are affected by the incompleteness theorems only by a speculative conjecture derived from them but lacking any rigorous demonstration. It is not clear that we can formalize all systems of thought by the use of arithmetic.

A second caution is that the incompleteness theorems must not be over-interpreted. The first incompleteness theorem does clearly state that every possible system of formal proofs in the field of integer arithmetic, and any larger system that includes integer arithmetic, is necessarily incomplete. But this is in no way an indication that such systems of formal proofs are weak. It is, in fact, a characteristic of the first incompleteness theorem that it requires a very powerful system of formal proofs for its proof. In mathematics, this is a measure of how strong a system of formal proofs is. A system that cannot prove the equivalent of

---

44. I learned mathematical logic in classes at Princeton University on "Mathematical Logic" and "Set Theory as a Foundation for Mathematics," taught by John Burgess and using Boulos and Jeffrey, *Computability and Logic* and Hrbacek and Jech, *Introduction to Set Theory* as textbooks. See Boulos and Jeffrey chapter 19 for this material on Tarksi's theorem. See Moore, "The Emergence of First Order Logic," 95–135, for an excellent history of the developments in logic leading to Gödel, and the effect of his work on the axiomatization of logics.

the first incompleteness theorem is very weak indeed, and is also unable to prove a great deal else about integer arithmetic that we are used to thinking of as demonstrable.

Another problem of over-interpretation arises with the second incompleteness theorem, which is corollary to the first and also requires a strong system of formal proofs. This theorem clearly states that no possible system of formal proofs about integer arithmetic, and no larger system that includes integer arithmetic, is able to prove itself to be consistent. This does not mean that the system of formal proofs *is* inconsistent. In fact, the proof that a system cannot prove its own consistency involves the assumption that the system is consistent. A system that is inconsistent can be used to prove anything, even its own consistency. Precisely by the fact that we can prove in a system of formal proofs about integer arithmetic that the system cannot prove that it is consistent we see that the system is, at least, not disqualified from being consistent. But this insight is not something that can be proved in the system.

It is, in fact, possible to formulate a subset of arithmetic small enough for it to be proved that this particular subset is consistent and complete, that is, that every true statement which can be made at all in that subset can be proved in that subset. The problem is that all such subsets are very limited. The propositional logic of statements can, for instance, be proven to be consistent.[45] But this only applies to the formal framework, in which statements are empty variables. As soon as a field of discourse is designated about which statements are being made, so that statements are no longer empty place-holders but content containing references to a designated field, consistency becomes a matter which may not be susceptible to proof, even if it is a necessary assumption. So also the problem of incompleteness arises when a system of formal proofs is made to refer to some field of objects other than its own formal statements.

This is the ultimate importance of the Gödel incompleteness theorems. By forcing us to see the truth of things which they prove cannot be proved they demonstrate that rationality is certainly a larger thing than can ever possibly be formalized in mathematical proof.[46] Rationality

45. So can arithmetic with the operation of addition alone. Wang, *Reflections on Kurt Gödel*, 173.

46. Penrose, *The Emperor's New Mind*, 405 ff, takes this as part of the evidence that neither consciousness nor true intelligence can be achieved by artificial intelligence and that there is more to the human mind than can be coded in a set of algorithms. I am not

must include the judgment that works without rules of which Brown speaks. The incompleteness theorems *suggest* that rationality is a larger thing than can be contained in any system of thought. Indeed, and this is the point, the incompleteness theorems suggest that all forms of mathematical logic or philosophical logic are themselves *models* of logic, rather than some necessary foundational logic. This justifies the critically realistic practice of treating all theoretical structures, even those that seem to be logically necessary, as models that may have to be revised in the course of continuing encounter with the reality of the world.[47] Moreover, the incompleteness theorems give no great comfort to anti-realism. They are one of the most important evidences against foundationalism, but not against critical realism. The consistency of arithmetic must be assumed in order to prove that arithmetic is incomplete. The truth value of statements in arithmetic must be assumed in order to prove that truth cannot be defined. This means that the incompleteness theorems and Tarski's theorem do not support an anti-realistic understanding of the nature and character of knowledge, at least, not of mathematical knowledge. Of course, neither do they support a realistic understanding.

4.4.2 The Unreasonable Effectiveness of Mathematics

Since Eugene Wigner called attention to the matter, there has been some discussion of why mathematics seems to be so unaccountably effective in describing the world.[48] It is no particular surprise that mathematics should be effective in counting sheep or keeping track of money. But that the most complex and intricate details of the physical world and its most mysterious and counter-intuitive characteristics, such as are found in quantum physics, should be amenable to mathematical description seems at first glance to be unreasonable. Why should the world behave in such a way that mathematics is effective in describing, explaining, and

---

yet satisfied with this, as it seems certain that the actions of the brain, viewed neurologically, can (theoretically, since it is a rather large job) be coded in a set of algorithms. Nor did Gödel himself consider that his theorem settled the question of mind surpassing matter. Wang, *Reflections on Kurt Gödel*, 146, 197. Neither does Douglas Hofstadter agree with Penrose. See Hofstadter, *Gödel, Escher, Bach*, 641–80.

47. This also applies to theological models. van Huyssteen, *Theology and the Justification of Faith*, 144.

48. Wigner, "The Unreasonable Effectiveness of Mathematics."

exploring it? Or is the effectiveness of mathematics simply a fortunate coincidence?

The most obvious explanation is that there is an ontological connection between mathematics and the secret inner nature of reality.[49] This suggestion goes back, at least, to the Pythagoreans and was a strong part of the Platonic system. Where it has not been so regarded mathematics has nevertheless often been taken as an essential ingredient of thought or reason. In differing ways both Kant and the logical positivists took this position. Mathematics has often been regarded as the archetype of good reasoning. "Its very structure forms a model for all other searches after absolute truth."[50]

But there is no such thing as absolute truth, at least not the way that people usually mean it. Absolute truth is truth that holds no matter what (or in all possible worlds). But that means that if there is any such thing as absolute truth, it is not semantic truth, because semantic truth depends precisely upon what is the case in the world. That is what makes it semantic. Only a logical tautology can be absolutely true because it is true no matter what the truth values of the statements of which it is composed may be; its truth value is solely the product of its logical form. Because what is the case in the world affects the truth value of the tautology not at all, a tautology necessarily says nothing whatsoever about what is or is not the case in the world.

The sentential logic has only to do with the preservation of truth in the combination and manipulation of statements. The statements themselves must first have truth value. Logic, in and of itself, says nothing about the world. The statements that are the variables of logic say something about the world. Their truth value is not determined by logic, but rather by what is the case in the world. Therefore, the truth value of statements about the world is always relative truth, not absolute truth. It is relative to the presuppositions and structures of the language in which the statements are made, and it is relative to the actual state of the world about which the statements are made. This means, counter-intuitively, that although relative truth is less certain than absolute truth, it is more important, more significant, and more valuable than absolute truth.[51]

49. "By translating the actual into the numerical we have found the secret to the structure and workings of the universe." Barrow, *Pi in the Sky*, vii. See also ibid., 1.

50. Ibid., 4.

51. "The weakest true statement is a tautology. In our formulation of cognitive problems, tautology is the disjunction of all complete answers, and thus it represents

The Cartesian search for what cannot be doubted is a retreat from the world.

Furthermore, since logic is itself an axiomatizable field with different forms under different axioms, even tautology is relative, not absolute, truth. It is relative to the axioms of the system rather than to what is the case in the world. But all this is only to be expected, since the very word "truth" denotes a relation between a statement and the world that the statement is about. As it denotes a relation, calling a statement true already implies that it is relative. "Absolute truth" is an oxymoron.[52]

The unreasonable effectiveness of mathematics is not unreasonable at all. Indeed, it is rather to be expected, not because mathematics is the secret inner nature of reality, but rather because it is not. Nor is mathematics effective because it is the necessary shape of rational thought. It is very close to the nature of rational thought, but reason and its formalization, rationality, come first and mathematics arises from them.

Mathematics in actual practice is an interplay between intuition, axiomatic thinking, formalization, and demonstrated insight, or proof.[53] Producing refined formalisms and axiomatic systems is often a specialist's task, but every pure mathematician strives to embody intuitions and insights in appropriate axioms and proofs. Insight into already established structures and mathematical objects and intuition of consequences and implications, all demonstrated in proof, compose the majority of working mathematics. Axiomatic systems, especially of logics (which are of primary interest for a consideration of the relation of mathematics to rationality), consist of symbols and axioms that institute relations among those symbols and give rules for manipulating the symbols in order to produce sentences to be affirmed. The relations among the symbols instituted by the axioms constitute the mathematical objects

---

the suspension of judgment. In other words, tautology is the answer 'I don't know.' False answers may be better than a tautology, if they are sufficiently close to the truth—therefore, some false statements may be more truthlike than some true ones." Niiniluoto, *Critical Scientific Realism*, 74.

52. According to Wang this was also the opinion of Kurt Gödel. Wang, *Reflections on Kurt Gödel*, 285. Friedman indicates that Carnap also held this opinion, Friedman, "Logical Truth and Analycity in Carnap," 86. Not only does mathematical proof not produce absolute truth, but it is not even unproblematical in its own field. In the same collection see Crowe, "Ten Misconceptions About Mathematics and Its History," 267–69.

53. My position is compatible with the mixed mathematics understanding that was common up through the nineteenth century. See Daston, "Fitting Numbers to the World," 221–24.

of which the system speaks. There well may be ultimate references for mathematical objects with independent platonic or ideal reality. But even if so, we are not in *direct* contact with them.[54] Our formalizations and axiomatizations are but hypotheses about them.

The immediate objects of mathematics are the implications and consequences of the hypotheses we have chosen. The consequences of our hypothetical postulates and axioms (in which we symbolize possible relations) have ideal existence. But the search for those hypothetical postulates and axioms that will have ultimate ideal mathematical objects as their consequences is a fallible quasi-empirical investigation.[55] The critically realistic way to put this would be: the ideal reality of the objects of mathematics is precisely what forces us in our practice of mathematics to be both formalists and intuitionists, and to pursue the consequences of the formalizations of our intuitions in a fallible search.

The content of pure mathematics is possible relations. But because that content is indefinite, universal, and ideal, mathematics in general often seems to be formal and empty. As its field is *all* possible relations, no *particular* relation or set of relations constitute its distinctive content. It is only in application that it has substantial, rather than formal, content. But this is precisely why mathematics is so effective.[56] Having no particular and substantial content of its own, its interference with the realities to which it is applied is minimized. The mathematics we are currently using to symbolize some reality in the world is not the only one that will work (although it may be the only one we have been able to formulate so far). Whenever we find the mathematics we are using to

---

54. It is occasionally claimed that mathematical intuition *is* direct contact with the ultimate references of mathematical objects. But I take the critical realist position that even intuition is held or embodied in the mind as some kind of psychical structure, and is therefore mediated rather than direct contact.

55. This is my own horseback ballpark conclusion from years of doing mathematics. Imre Lakatoš, having studied these matters in much greater extent, detail, and depth comes to much the same conclusion. Niiniluoto, *Critical Scientific Realism*, 262, also considers that it is possible to be both a constructivist and a realist in mathematics.

56. The idealizing character of mathematical description of the world can then be dealt with as a second iteration of the process of describing the world with mathematics. "The problem of idealization should be solved by a theory of measurement (metrization) which shows precisely under what conditions empirical relations (e.g., is heavier than, is longer than) can be represented isomorphically by means of relations between real numbers. Such representation theorems give a license to a realist to explain how and why mathematics is applicable to the representation of reality." Ibid., 135.

be inadequate because reality exhibits some relation that is not captured in our current mathematics it is usually possible to find some variation that will work.[57] Whatever relations can be imagined or hypothesized about the world can be given symbolic representation and the logic of those relations formalized for those symbols by appropriate axioms. It is, of course, always in question whether the formalization in hand is the best for the relation in question. Where several interrelated relations are considered, it may well be at issue whether the formalization is even adequate, much less best.[58]

It is the incredible variety and flexibility of mathematics that make it so effective in describing the world. They arise from its refusal to be treated as the inner nature of reality, but rather as the art of imagination made rigorous and exhibited in formal demonstration so as to communicate itself as public knowledge and not private inspiration. For this reason large portions of mathematics have not yet been, and may never be, given practical application to some aspect of the world around us. Only a mathematics with no intrinsic connection to the nature of the world can be so well suited to the investigation of the unknown.

Moreover, the unreasonable effectiveness of mathematics may be somewhat of an illusion. Simple characteristics of the world can be represented by simple mathematics. The integers and their operations are sufficient for accounting. More difficult characteristics of the world require more difficult mathematics. Ballistics and economic theory require the calculus. The most abstruse and hard to conceive aspects of the physical world, such as general relativity or quantum theory, require mathematics that is notoriously difficult. Were it the case that the most difficult to understand behaviors of the world could be captured in relatively simple mathematics, then we might consider its effectiveness to be amazing or unreasonable. But as things stand it is no more unreasonable that mathematics is effective in describing, explaining, and exploring the world than it is that human thought is effective in doing these things.

57. Turing did prove that there are uncomputable functions, and it is probable that some relations in reality can only be represented by such. "Kronecker's concession to geometry and mechanics of freedom from this requirement [that mathematics be reducible to calculation] is tacit recognition that there is no reason to assume a priori that structural relationships in nature are necessarily all of an effectively computable kind." Stein, "Logos, Logic, and Logistiké," 252.

58. Kitcher and Aspray, "An Opinionated Introduction," 4–8 for the difficulties involved in formalizing even so basic a matter as the foundations of arithmetic.

Of course, it *is* quite amazing that human thought is effective. But it is not unreasonable when viewed by a critical realist. The reality of the world is constantly criticizing our understanding of it, and we are forced thereby into a critical awareness of the limits of our knowledge, as well as of its substance and reality. It is our awareness of the unknown character of what we do not (yet) know that makes the effectiveness of our thought so very reasonable. In a critically realistic view of the nature and character of human knowledge, it makes perfect sense that human thought is effective at knowing what it knows. No advance claims are made for its effectiveness in knowing the unknown. But we do hold a faithful hope that the world will force us to enlarge the realm of human thought, and that we will thereby enlarge the realm of the known (even if the unknown remains infinite).

4.5 CRITICALLY REALISTIC KNOWLEDGE

To acquire knowledge of external reality or the physical world as it really is means to acquire knowledge that cannot be *reduced* to the human mind or human subjectivity. It means that the thing known is a *necessary* cause of the knowledge that knows it. This is the realistic component. But the thing known is not a sufficient cause of the knowledge that knows it. This is the critical component. It is possible to acquire knowledge in which the human mind and subjectivity, which cannot be separated out from the knowledge, acknowledge and attempt to highlight and clarify the ways in which external reality or the physical world are some of the causes of that knowledge. Such knowledge, when it exists, corresponds in some ways to the nature and structure of the mind, in some ways to the social processes by which it is constructed, and in some ways to the external reality to which it refers. It has often been true that elements of our knowledge that correspond to our social constructions have been mistaken for correspondences to external reality. But since external reality remains a necessary cause of our knowledge, some of the features of that knowledge will correspond to external reality. Whether we ever actually have such knowledge, and which features of our knowledge correspond to external reality, is always a matter that must be judged on a case-by-case basis.

Critical realism as I have described it here is a broader and a more critical position than scientific realism. It is broader in that it can be understood to apply to all our knowledge,[59] not just our knowledge of the physical world. It is more critical in that it recognizes that even knowledge of the physical world as it really is cannot be independent of the human mind and subjectivity. Scientific realism is a special case of critical realism, so conceived. It is this broader and more critical conception of critical realism that I intend to use to examine the theology of Karl Barth.

Critical realism has not been here defended for the idealistic reason that it is the only, the necessary, or the universal form of possible human thought about the nature and character of whatever external realities we might or might not encounter and how we know them. Rather it is an *a posteriori* theoretical construction with which we attempt to model the complex relationship between our knowledge and the reality to which we refer. It is a second order, rather than a first order hypothesis, but it is still an hypothesis about how and what our knowledge *may* be. What our knowledge *actually* is can only be found by attempting to use the hypothesis to examine the things we are doing when we claim to have knowledge.

59. Niiniluoto, *Critical Scientific Realism*, 144, discusses how the concept of truth-likeness can be used to make common sense realism compatible with scientific realism. Many of the points Niiniluoto makes are broadly critically realistic even though he is arguing for scientific realism specifically.

5

Barth and Kant

The form that idealism takes in Kant's philosophy has elements that make it more amenable to a critically realistic reading than the speculative idealism that followed. Barth understood Kant as an idealist, but one who could be given a critically realistic reading and whose epistemology could thereby be used in his own theology.[1] The history of German idealism after Kant made Barth's turn to a plainer reading of Kant a realistic move.

Many of the important developments in post-Kantian philosophy in the nineteenth century involve an extension of the techniques of transcendental inquiry into an idealist metaphysics untrammeled by realist constraints. The notion of the thing-in-itself as a realist limitation upon the possible extension of theoretical knowledge is abandoned as quickly as possible. Kant's tool for critiquing metaphysics, transcendental inquiry, becomes a tool for constructing an absolute idealist metaphysics. Post-Kantian philosophy developed in an un-Kantian way because it ignored the realist element in his thought.

The significance of this history for my thesis lies in Barth's own development. The Neo-Kantian background of Barth's early liberalism has been well documented by Simon Fisher, Bruce McCormack, Johann

---

1. He reads Kant in close conjunction with Plato. See Barth, *Romans*, 4, and the amplification of this point by Barth in his comments in the biographical sketch he wrote while at Münster as cited in McCormack, *Barth's Critically Realistic Dialectical Theology*, 216–17, n 26.

Friedrich Lohmann, and Clifford Blake Anderson, among others.[2] Barth's break with liberalism and his development of a dialectical theology included what Bruce McCormack has called "a turn in the direction of a more classically Kantian view."[3] Clifford Anderson and Friedrich Lohmann have demonstrated that this more classical Kantian view was available to Barth in the spectrum of Neo-Kantianism in the early twentieth century[4] and offered evidence that even during his student years Barth was slightly more inclined to it than to the more radical interpretation of his teachers in Marburg.[5] Seen in the light of the history of post-Kantian philosophy and the particular form of Neo-Kantian philosophy at Marburg, Barth's reading of Kant is critically realistic, especially as seen in Barth's chapter on Kant in *Protestant Theology in the Nineteenth Century*.

5.1 REALISTIC ELEMENTS IN KANT

I specified in section 2.1 that forms of critical realism have a realistic element and a critical element. Kant's critical epistemology recognizes that all our knowledge is constructed, and is so radical that he has often been read as an anti-realist. Kant at least accepts mere realism and is not a subjective idealist, which can be seen in his own direct refutation of subjective idealism incorporated into the *Critique of Pure Reason*.[6] His retention of the notion of the thing-in-itself, in spite of his denial of the possibility of theoretical knowledge of it, stands firmly at the edge of realism. He denies that it is the cause of our sensory awareness, because causation is one of the categories and only applies to the objects of experience.[7] But things in themselves are somehow implicated in the material conditions of experience, making possible the judgment of actuality.[8]

2. Fisher, *Revelatory Positivism*; McCormack, *Barth's Critically Realistic Dialectical Theology*; Lohmann, *Karl Barth und der Neukantianismus*; Anderson, "The Crisis of Theological Science."

3. McCormack, *Barth's Critically Realistic Dialectical Theology*, 207, n 1.

4. Anderson, "The Crisis of Theological Science" and Lohmann, *Karl Barth und der Neukantianismus*.

5. Anderson, "The Crisis of Theological Science," 216, 219.

6. Kant, *Critique of Pure Reason*, 244–47.

7. Ibid., 111–15, 184–87. Rescher, *Kant and the Reach of Reason*, 23–27, says that in Kant the causality of appearances by things-in-themselves is a product of the principle of sufficient reason, not of the categorical concept of causality. Things-in themselves are the *ground* rather than the *cause* of appearances.

8. von Rintelen, *Contemporary German Philosophy*, 10, 15.

The critically realistic function of the thing-in-itself is two-fold. First, it acknowledges something that is not bound to the structures of our thought. However it may be related to them it is not determined by them. The concept of the thing-in-itself asserts the reality of a mind-independent world. But at the same time it supports the critique of our faculties. By asserting that the objects of our experience are not things as they may be in themselves, it forces us to recognize them as appearances, the result of a constructive interaction between the mind and the world (rather than a total construct of the mind).[9] The realism of our knowledge is severely minimized, but the fact of something other than what we know is emphasized, making the transition from Kant to a fully realized critical realism possible.[10]

More important, for our purpose here, is Kant's argument in the *Foundations of the Metaphysics of Morals* and the *Critique of Practical*

9. Nicholas Rescher also reads the significance of the thing-in-itself this way. "To keep a pre-critical dogmatism in check we must stipulate the unknowability of noumena: to keep feckless idealism in check we must postulate their existence . . . A thing-in-itself whose nature is brought within the reach of the categories of understanding is ipso facto unable to do the job of endowing appearances with the intentionality of indicating something that stands altogether outside the phenomenal order, and thus to ensure that appearances are appearances *of* something. A cognitively domesticated thing-in-itself would (*ex hypothesi*) not be able to accomplish the important mission assigned to such things in the Kantian framework—namely, that of providing a basis of *mind externalilty* for the objects at issue in our knowledge." Rescher, *Kant and the Reach of Reason*, 13.

10. Buchdahl, *Kant and the Dynamics of Reason*, disputes this reading of Kant and the function of the things-in-themselves entirely. He considers that the problem of affection cannot be used to view Kant as a realist (ibid., 163). "What is thus absolutely central is that the affection and receptivity of sensibility expresses something ultimate, simply 'given'–not pointing to any 'external cause;' precisely 'corresponding' to that 'ultimacy' which is already expressed by the notion of the transcendental matter" (ibid., 131). "On the other hand, the notion that *Sachheit* stands for the fact that sensibility finds itself *determined* in respect of 'this or that' particular sensation, may in a loose manner of speech be said to designate its 'affection by the object'—i.e., the 'that'-aspect of the object" (ibid., 132). He interprets the transcendental object and the thing-in-itself as stages in a reduction-realization process by which the mind makes a transition from one sort of object to another (ibid., 13–15). This interpretation treats everything in Kant as completely and unambiguously idealistic. "What has become clear from the above is that the Kantian world is entirely 'enclosed' within its transcendental framework; the confines of the understanding and sensibility, of thought and intuition, at one or the other of our two 'corresponding' levels, reduction and realization, respectively" (ibid., 146). The only kind of realism he will allow in Kant is one that resembles Putnam's internal realism (ibid., 104). All his work is done with great care and turns upon points that are technical beyond my expertise. He is a specialist in the field, as I am not, but there are other specialists who support the judgments that I have made here.

Reason for freedom, God, and immortality as necessary postulates of pure reason in its practical application. It is both possible and necessary to refer to God and immortality even though we cannot have theoretical knowledge of them. It is not the case that the postulates of practical reason can be treated as mere structurally necessary fictions of thought.[11] Kant is not abandoning his previous position in this ascription of objectivity to these concepts, for even while asserting that practical reason justifies referring to them, he also reaffirms that the categories of the understanding, confined as they are in their application to the objects of experience, rather than things-in-themselves, cannot be used to further our knowledge of these realities.[12]

Giving Kant a critically realistic reading requires a recognition that the second critique was in mind from the beginning of the first and that the two critiques are intimately related and mutually necessary.[13] The habit of treating the first critique as Kant's epistemology and the second as his ethics is inadequate. Moreover, when read together the two critiques exhibit the manner in which Kant considers himself to have triumphed over both the British empiricism represented by Hume, and the dogmatic metaphysics represented by Wolff.[14] The same analysis of the nature of pure reason that demonstrates the possibility of synthetic *a priori* knowledge, over against the empiricists, also demonstrates the inherent limits of what can be known theoretically, over against the metaphysicians. But the demonstration of theoretical limits also functions to prevent a theoretical critique of what can be known by reason in its practical application, leaving room for a different, limited, but nonetheless real and referential metaphysics of freedom.

The interesting historical and philosophical question is how Kant's philosophy, which constituted a rejection of all previous metaphysics and a severe limitation on all future metaphysics, could be the source of the

11. Copleston, *Kant*, 132–35 argues this point most carefully.

12. Kant, *Critique of Practical Reason*, 139–42.

13. As Kant himself says in the introduction to the second edition of Kant, *Critique of Pure Reason*, 26–27, 29.

14. There is, of course, a third critique, *The Critique of Judgment*. It serves a crucial mediating function between the first two critiques, at least in the opinion of Copleston, *Fichte to Hegel*, 141–70. Cassirer, *Kant's Life and Thought*, 271–77, spends a long chapter on it, detailing its development from a consideration of the logical problem of subsuming particulars under a universal to the articulation of a theory of teleology. Considering the significance for Kant of logical considerations in both critiques it is clearly important, but I have not yet read it.

thoroughly developed metaphysics of speculative idealism. For Kant, the only possible metaphysics was one that consisted of a critique of reason.[15] Only in this way could the elements of experience that were not merely empirical be brought to light. Kant's own *Critique of Pure Reason* and *Critique of Practical Reason* are the best examples of what Kant thought that metaphysics could and should be. That the non-empirical elements of experience are contributed by the subject and do not give theoretical knowledge of the thing-in-itself is itself a metaphysical assertion.

Kant leaves the thing-in-itself in a very difficult position. One of the obvious ways out of the difficulty is to eliminate the thing-in-itself. It seemed to the speculative idealists who followed Kant to be an inconsistent remnant of the kind of metaphysics that Kant was criticizing. Once the thing-in-itself is eliminated the objects of knowledge will remain as subjective constructions. But these, along with the subject itself, will now be regarded as the primary reality (or perhaps the whole of it). As in Kant's own work the proper business of metaphysics becomes an investigation of the subject. In this way epistemology becomes metaphysics. In constructing metaphysics from a critique of reason and an analysis of the subject, speculative idealism is in continuity with Kant, but it distinguishes itself from him by referring this analysis to an absolute subject.

5.2 THE FATE OF THE THING-IN-ITSELF

In 1794 Johann Gottlieb Fichte, in his first year as Professor of Philosophy at Jena, published *The Science of Knowledge*, an attempt to turn Kantian criticism into a full fledged system.[16] For Fichte philosophy is, or ought to be, a science, a body of propositions that form a systematic whole and in which each proposition has a specific place that is dictated by strict logical dependence. Every science must have a single foundational proposition, true and certain, from which all else is derived deductively.[17] The science that investigates how the sciences are derived from their fundamental principles is philosophy, the science of science generally.[18]

15. Kant, *Prolegomena to any Future Metaphysics*, 105–10.

16. Fichte, *The Science of Knowledge.*

17. Fichte was certainly a foundationalist in the strongest sense of the term. As an absolute idealist, he considered that when a foundation had been identified or an item understood as foundational it meant that it was also certain, self-demonstrating, and the ground of all other epistemic claims.

18. Ibid., 11–19.

In later explanations of *The Science of Knowledge* Fichte says that there are two directions the search for the fundamental proposition of philosophy can lead. Some of our experiences are accompanied by a feeling of necessity, and some by a feeling of freedom. But in both cases experience is consciousness of an object by a subject. The search can go in the direction of the object, and attempt to explain experience as an effect of the thing-in-itself, or in the direction of the subject, and attempt to explain experience as an effect of the subject. The first leads to materialism and determinism, the second to idealism.[19] Fichte was convinced that Kant had mistakenly tried to have things both ways. In his analysis of freedom Kant went in the direction that Fichte is convinced that philosophy must go. But Kant's analysis of the understanding is limited by his refusal to abandon the notion of the thing-in-itself.

In the search for a fundamental principle of philosophy Fichte was convinced that nothing could be found by going down the road of empiricism, for all empirical philosophy would be unable to explain freedom. Idealism, however, may well be able to explain the feeling of necessity that accompanies certain experiences. The attempt by Kant to keep a foot in empirical philosophy while elucidating a basically idealist philosophy must have seemed to Fichte like a failure to be a single science because of attempting to have more than one fundamental principle.[20]

Kant began his philosophical work seeking the conditions of the possibility of experience. The result of this seeking was the categories of the understanding, and space and time as the forms of sensible intuition. In both cases logic was a critical ingredient of the seeking. Indeed, the categories are all derived from logical judgments.[21] Fichte begins by seeking the condition for the possibility of logical judgment, since logical judgment is the means of connecting the system of knowledge of every science with its fundamental principle.[22] The condition for the possibility of logical judgment is the self-positing reality of the ego. This means that before all positing, before all judgment, before all empirical

---

19. Copleston, *Fichte to Hegel*, 57–58.

20. Whatever criticisms Fichte may have had of Kant, he recognized the priority of the practical over the theoretical reason in Kant, and considered Kant to be an idealist. He considered his own philosophy to be a purification of Kant, not a refutation. See ibid., 19–20.

21. Kant, *Critique of Pure Reason*, 108–18.

22. Fichte, *Foundations of Transcendental Philosophy*, 90–91.

consciousness, the ego must be posited through itself.[23] "The Ego posits originally its own being."[24] For Fichte this is the fundamental principle of philosophy from which the fundamental principle of logic can be derived by deduction.

In this way Fichte has eliminated the Kantian thing-in-itself. But it is clearly a metaphysical assertion that Kant would have considered to be beyond the bounds of what pure reason could know. For Kant the transcendental unity of apperception was a condition of the possibility of experience, but the identification of this unity with an ego that lay behind the sensing and reasoning activity that constituted experience was an illegitimate use of the categories.[25] Fichte understands his analysis to escape from this objection by having derived his basic metaphysical statement from an analysis of the conditions of the possibility of logical judgment and prior to the deduction of the categories. It is a fundamental principle, not theoretical knowledge. Just as Kant considers freedom a reality to which thought can refer, even though it is a presupposition rather than theoretical knowledge, so Fichte thinks himself justified in asserting the self-positing Ego.

This self-positing Ego must clearly be an absolute Ego, else it would not posit its own being.[26] Fichte uses this fundamental principle of philosophy and the dialectical reciprocal limiting of non-Ego and Ego as posited by the absolute Ego to derive the Kantian Categories.[27] In this way Fichte manages to explain the possibility of synthetic *a priori* knowledge, and at the same time develop the categories not merely as logical conditions for the possibility of knowledge, but as metaphysical realities. If what the Ego posits is what is real, then the logical conditions for the possibility of knowledge, for being posited by the Ego, are themselves metaphysical realities.

It is worth noting here that Fichte's deriving of the possibility of logical judgment from a consideration of the principle of identity is a procedure that future developments in mathematical logic would render questionable. The principle of identity is not usually one of the postulates of mathematical logic. The parsimonious set of presuppositions that are

23. Fichte, *The Science of Knowledge*, 63–70.

24. Ibid., 72.

25. Kant, *Critique of Pure Reason*, 328–83.

26. Fichte, *The Science of Knowledge*, 70–71.

27. Ibid., 108–89.

necessary in order to do logic in a rigorous way are usually five. It is the interaction of postulates that gives rise to the complex and satisfying structures of mathematics. The postulates must be independent; they cannot be derived from one another. A system derived logically from a single postulate would be rather barren.

Fichte understood his system as a purification and systematization of Kant's critical philosophy. But *The Science of Knowledge* was published while Kant was still alive and working, and Kant rejected the attempt to improve the critical philosophy by eliminating the thing-in-itself.[28] This constituted a refusal to absolutize the subject. In this refusal Kant's commitment to some form of realism, however critical of metaphysics he may have been, can be recognized. Kant's epistemology has an essential modesty to it. Certainly Fichte's metaphysics has its roots in Kant's project and in the difficulties that remained unresolved within that project. But the historical relationship must not be permitted to obscure the underlying incompatibility of the two philosophical systems.

Hegel agreed with Fichte that the deduction of the categories in Kant's philosophy represented the speculative impulse at its best, but that the thing-in-itself represented the hypostasization of the empty form of opposition. Fichte was right in eliminating it from philosophy and seeking to derive everything in philosophy from the self-positing Ego. But Hegel is not satisfied that the dialectic by which Fichte develops his system from its fundamental principle truly resolves all contradictions. Dichotomy or division is the reason that philosophy is needed, and its task is to construct a unified whole. This unified whole is the construction of the absolute for consciousness. The absolute is presumed to be already present, and reason produces it by freeing consciousness from its limits. The problem with Kant's philosophy is that dualisms and oppositions, such as between phenomena and noumena, or between sensibility and understanding, are not reconciled. Fichte rightly sets out to rectify this failing, but fails himself in that the principle of identity does not actually serve the function that Fichte assigns to it, that of being the fundamental principle of the system. For this reason, according to Hegel, the subject-object distinction is not overcome in Fichte.[29]

---

28. Copleston, *Kant*, 223.

29. Hegel, *Difference between Fichte and Schelling*, 79–83, 89–94, 155–56.

For Hegel, the rational is the real, and the real is the rational.[30] This is an assertion that, in reason, objectivity and subjectivity are identical and universal. In the universality of reason the determinations of self-consciousness are as objective for the very being of things as they are for thought.[31] Reality is the necessary process by which the absolute, self-thinking thought, actualizes itself. In Hegel's philosophy dialectic always comes to resolution. His philosophy has a threefold structure even as does his dialectic. The first part is logic, which is also metaphysics, for it is the nature of the absolute in itself. The second part is the philosophy of nature, in which the absolute manifests itself as objective. The third part is the philosophy of spirit, in which the absolute re-identifies itself in conscious knowledge of itself.[32]

The key to Hegel's thought is the metaphysics exhibited in the logic. Within the logic priority belongs to the concept of the absolute. The concept of the absolute, which is prior to everything, is the concept of being. But the logically prior concept of being must be the concept of pure being. The concept of pure being is wholly indeterminate because there is nothing prior to condition it. But a wholly indeterminate, or un-conditioned, being can only be thought as negation, as non-being. But this non-being can only be thought as identical to being. So being and non-being pass into one another in a continual movement. This move-ment is becoming. Therefore being, the absolute, must be conceived as becoming, as a process of self-development.[33]

In this way we can see how far Hegel has come from Kant, and how self-consciously. In this respect, I think that we might regard Hegel's system as one that has no necessary connection with Kant. It does, of course, have an actual historical connection with Kant. Hegel does de-velop his system starting with a consideration of the rethinking of Kant by Fichte and Schelling. But it can easily be imagined that he might have developed his system out of a Platonic or Neo-Platonic background, rather than a background in the critical philosophy of Kant.[34]

30. Hegel, *Hegel's Philosophy of Mind*.

31. Ibid., 58.

32. Ibid., 167–68, 196–97; Copleston, *Fichte to Hegel*, 207–14.

33. Hegel, *The Encyclopedia Logic*, 136–45; Copleston, *Fichte to Hegel*, 231–33.

34. Gadamer, *Hegel's Dialectic* traces Greek roots of Hegel's philosophy. See the reference in Warnke, *Gadamer*. The judgment that Hegel's philosophy has come far enough from Kant that the connection is historical and accidental rather than nec-essary and essential is my own. But the suggestion that Hegel's system could just as

After Hegel's death speculative idealism became a fragmented movement. In the middle of the century materialism was the dynamically growing form of philosophy in Germany. It was in reaction against these two forms of philosophy, the fragmented speculative idealism and the growing scientific materialism, that Neo-Kantianism took its rise.[35] The concern that gave rise to Neo-Kantianism can be seen in the work of G. Fechner who believed Hegelianism to be irreconcilable with the results of modern science, and materialism to be unable to offer a satisfactory account of the human mind.[36] This concern motivated philosophers as well.[37]

A figure that mediates the development of Neo-Kantianism after the period of speculative idealism is Friedrich Adolf Trendelenburg. He was strongly critical of Hegel and all of speculative idealism for attempting to prescribe to the sciences what they must be on account of an analysis of the subject. Trendelenburg's object was to learn from the sciences, rather than to attempt to prescribe to them. He considered Hegel's logic, with so fundamental a role being played by negation, to be nonsense. The logic that Trendelenburg preferred was the more traditional logic first articulated by Aristotle.[38] Kant also considered logic to have been articulated by Aristotle in a form that required no significant revision.[39] In the 1860s Trendelenburg engaged in a long debate with Kuno Fischer over the interpretation of Kant's transcendental aesthetic. Trendelenburg maintained that there was a flaw in Kant's deduction of the forms of sensible intuition because the possibility that these forms were at once subjective and objective had not been considered. It was in the course of this debate, which involved much of the German philosophical community, that Neo-Kantianism first began to articulate itself in a self-conscious way.

---

well have developed from out of a Platonic or Neo-Platonic background derives from Gadamer's interpretation of Hegel.

35. Copleston, *Schopenhauer to Nietzsche*, 134–35. See also Fisher, *Revelatory Positivism*, 7–9. Köhnke, *The Rise of Neo-Kantianism*, 5–6, 201–3, demurs somewhat about this. For him the rise of Neo-Kantianism is much more closely linked with the rise of liberalism in the new German state of the last third of the nineteenth century. Moreover, he identifies a positivist phase in the early Neo-Kantianism of the 1870s, which is commonly ignored in the histories of the movement.

36. Fisher, *Revelatory Positivism*, 18; Copleston, *Schopenhauer to Nietzsche*, 148.

37. Fisher, *Revelatory Positivism*, 13.

38. Köhnke, *The Rise of Neo-Kantianism*, 20–28.

39. Kant, *Critique of Pure Reason*; 17 Kant, *Logic*, 23.

What was general and common to Neo-Kantians was a desire for a new critical philosophy. Both Hegelianism and materialism were considered to have exceeded the critical boundaries on possible theoretical knowledge set by Kant. But none of the Neo-Kantians expected to restore Kant's philosophy in the form in which Kant left it.[40] All of them wished to continue his critique and go beyond it in one way or another.[41] The means for going beyond Kant was to be a continuation or extension of the transcendental method which was able to produce the desired universality and necessity without negating value judgments and without dismissing ethics and culture as proper fields for philosophical endeavor. Neo-Kantian epistemology, in both of its major schools, tended to become more emphatically idealist as it developed, minimizing the role of empirical intuition and emphasizing the constructed character of all knowledge.[42]

The Marburg school of Neo-Kantianism took its most characteristic form in the work of Hermann Cohen. He began his philosophical career as an interpreter of Kant, producing commentaries on each of the three Kantian Critiques as well as a summary of the debate between Trendelenburg and Fischer.[43] Even in his commentaries Cohen is already giving a very strong reading of Kant. He interprets Kant with such a strong emphasis upon the ground of necessary and apodictically certain synthetic *a priori* knowledge that he understands Kant's project as a critique of experience, rather than as a critique of pure reason.[44]

---

40. Fisher, *Revelatory Positivism*, 9.

41. Köhnke, *The Rise of Neo-Kantianism*, 178–80, 262–65, considers that figures like Cohen and Windelband went so far beyond Kant as to no longer be Kantians. Yet these are the key figures for the two most important schools of Neo-Kantianism.

42. Fisher, *Revelatory Positivism*, 9–14. Köhnke, *The Rise of Neo-Kantianism*, offers an analysis of Neo-Kantianism that is complementary to all of this. Köhnke is investigating the relation of the social environment to the rise of Neo-Kantianism. Generally held philosophical positions are not what he considers to bind the Neo-Kantians together into a recognizable movement. Indeed, he sees more variety in the philosophical positions of the Neo-Kantians than either Copleston or Fisher. For Köhnke, the most important binding ingredient in the development and rise of Neo-Kantianism is the relation of academic politics (evaluated in terms of appointments to academic posts and variety of course offerings at the German universities) to the growth of liberalism in Germany in the years in which the country was unified and the Reich founded.

43. Fisher, *Revelatory Positivism*, 20; Köhnke, *The Rise of Neo-Kantianism*, 167–68.

44. Köhnke, *The Rise of Neo-Kantianism*, 180–89.

In its mature form the Marburg system makes an identification between being and being known. Being achieves existence by being thought. Therefore, it understands philosophy to rest upon a transcendental investigation of the necessary, universal, and apodictic structures of cognition. Since being is identified with being known, the necessary structures of thought are the necessary structures of being. Cohen and his followers were consistent idealists.[45] The problem of dealing adequately with what Kant called *Empfindung*, sensible intuition, constantly threatened the Marburg system. Cohen believed that Kant had tackled the task of conducting a transcendental inquiry into epistemological questions imperfectly. He seemed to Cohen to have started well with purely logical considerations, but at times to have abandoned them to develop a psychology of the knowing subject.

Critical philosophy needed to concern itself with the forms of pure thought. In his concern for the purity of thought Cohen attempted "to purify Kantian methodology by formalizing Kant even more and by introducing his new form of transcendental logic based upon the calculus model." Kant had acknowledged two roots of knowledge, the understanding and sensible intuition. "In Cohen's mature system sensible intuition is firmly rejected as a condition of knowledge. Arguing that nothing exists outside thought and that all knowledge has its origin in thought alone, he accounted the presence of sensible intuition in epistemology as absurd and irrational."[46] As such, he rejected the notion of things-in-themselves. Since to be was to be known, there could be no ontological distance between true knowledge and noumenal reality.[47]

Kant had postulated a connecting link between the categories of the understanding and the manifold of sensible impressions. These were the schematized categories, understood and applied in terms of time, one of the two pure forms of sensible intuition.[48] Cohen eliminated the

---

45. Fisher, *Revelatory Positivism*, 22, 31.

46. Ibid., 32–33.

47. This had the interesting consequence that Cohen considered the notion of the thing-in-itself to be a mythical notion. Mythical objects were those that had not been rendered knowable by mathematics and the laws of thought. They were the remnants of pre-scientific understanding and possessed no epistemological significance. This was the understanding of myth that was transmitted to another twentieth-century theologian who was also a student of the Marburg school, Rudolf Bultmann. His relation to the philosophy of the Marburg school is explored in Johnson, *The Origins of Demythologizing*.

48. Kant, *Critique of Pure Reason*, 180–87.

schematism. In this way the Kantian "anticipation of perception" was no longer a principle by which the category was applied to the manifold, but rather a union of intuition and thought in which the anticipation of something to be given in sensible intuition was bound to the category of reality so as to be produced and determined by thought.[49] It is no longer the case that, as with Kant, all knowledge begins with experience, even though it does not all arise out of experience.[50] Rather, it is a problem or a task that calls the mind's cognitive powers into operation. In tackling the problem the mind first posits mathematical-type relations or laws for the problem being addressed. It then investigates these laws to produce a solution to the problem from out of the posited laws. Thought alone is active in this process. No sense data is required for the mind to work upon. Thought generates not only knowledge, but the reality to be known.[51] Since knowledge and being both originate in thought, and both are developed by generative thinking, it follows that there is no such thing as the given, except that which thought gives to itself as task.[52]

Sensible intuition as a root of knowledge, and the notion of the given are eliminated entirely. Instead, "Only thinking itself can generate what validly counts as being," and "*das Denken seinen Stoff sich selbst erzeugen soll*."[53] The material of thinking does not come from *Empfindung*, it is a generated content produced by thought.[54] This notion of the self-sufficiency of thought was considered to be the philosophical expression of the scientific method. The scientific method here was pre-eminently the method of mathematics, which does indeed produce its objects by its choice of axioms, and investigates the lawlike regularities that are to be found among them. But the problem of identifying the actual in the midst of a range of possibilities is impossible to address with pure

---

49. Fisher, *Revelatory Positivism*, 36–37.

50. Kant, *Critique of Pure Reason*, 41.

51. Fisher, *Revelatory Positivism*, 29.

52. Ibid., 43.

53. Hermann Cohen, *Logik der Reinen Erkenntnis*, 81, 59; cited in Fisher, *Revelatory Positivism*, 39.

54. This continues in Cassirer even into the twentieth century. "Thought does not reproduce an outward reality; it is the foundation and the very core of reality . . . There is no being, no objectivity, no 'nature of things' that does not originate in thought. A reality outside the sphere of thought and exempt from its principles and conditions is a meaningless concept." Ernst Cassirer, "Hermann Cohen 1848–1918," *Social Research*, 10 (1943) 226, cited in Fisher, *Revelatory Positivism*, 39.

mathematics alone. Mathematics can be used to describe regularities and symmetries in the relations of the actual, but it cannot, by itself, distinguish the actual from the possible. It can only distinguish the possible from the impossible.

In Kant, the understanding was the faculty of rules. It was more than just the capacity for formulating rules by a comparison of experiences; it was itself the lawgiver to nature.[55] Cohen agreed with Kant's evaluation of the importance of laws for cognition. But for Kant the understanding gives laws to nature in that the categories provide the laws according to which the manifold of sensible intuition is organized into the objects of experience. With the elimination by Cohen of sensible intuition as a feature of cognition laws become the sole feature of known objects. The reality of things is constituted by their being determined by a law of thought.[56] This means that the object is a constructed objectification of laws.

Kant recognized that the logically possible might not be actual, and that the empirical conditions of knowledge might preclude the actuality of the logically possible. For Kant, the actual is that which is bound up with the material conditions of experience, that is, with sensation.[57] In this Kant recognizes the formal character of mathematics and logic. For Cohen, since cognition is independent of empirical intuition, no empirical limits can be set upon actuality.[58] Cohen considered that there was an accent of realism in Kant's epistemology and an agnosticism in his ontology that prescribed limits to his idealism.[59]

The end result of Cohen's system is a metaphysics of precisely the sort that Kant would *not* have countenanced. Cohen was correct. There is an accent of realism in Kant's epistemology, an unwillingness to abandon the notions of things-in-themselves as an expression of the limits of what can be known theoretically, and a bit of agnosticism in his ontology. That which Cohen recognizes in Kant, and criticizes in order to improve upon him, is precisely that which makes it possible to read Kant in a critically realistic mode.

55. Kant, *Critique of Pure Reason*, 147.

56. Fisher, *Revelatory Positivism*, 44.

57. Kant, *Critique of Pure Reason*, 239.

58. Fisher, *Revelatory Positivism*, 49.

59. Ibid., 24.

5.3 BARTH'S READING OF KANT IN PROTESTANT THEOLOGY IN THE NINETEENTH CENTURY

McCormack has established that, as Barth began to do dialectical theology, he was strongly influenced by the particular shape that Marburg Neo-Kantianism took in the hands of his brother Heinrich.[60] In particular, he was indebted to his brother for the manner in which that philosophy could serve as a critical theory which was able to loan concepts to his theological description, in the second edition of *The Epistle to the Romans*, of the crisis in which all human being and knowing stands as a consequence of the divine self revelation.[61] But the God-concept of Heinrich Barth was still thoroughly idealistic, and Karl Barth was already holding idealism in tension with realism in his dialectical theology. In doing so he was following a reading of Kant from a different branch of Neo-Kantianism than that under which he had been educated.[62]

The chasm between realism and idealism, between theoretical knowledge and things as they may be in themselves, is deep. But the concept of the *ding an sich*, the thing-in-itself, emphasized in Kant's explicit refusal to abandon the concept, and his co-ordination of intuition and understanding, in which the categories of the understanding are empty without the material supplied to them by the sensible intuition which is correspondingly blind without the categories to organize its material, and Kant's understanding of his project in the *Critique of Pure Reason* as an explanation of the success of mathematics and Newtonian physics rather than a critique of them, show that he refuses to walk away from the chasm. Kant's idealism is neither absolute nor is the knowledge it describes self-generating. As such, it was more suitable to be coordinated with realism in a form of critical realism. Speculative idealism not only leaves the chasm behind, but denies that there is anything on the other side of it. Barth's embrace of a more classical Kantianism is a product of his need to do dialectical theology in a critically realistic way.

60. McCormack, *Barth's Critically Realistic Dialectical Theology*, 218–26.

61. "And so it was with respect to his use of the category of the *Ursprung*: to speak of God in terms of the category of the *Ursprung* was helpful for pointing to *the* crisis which the being and existence of God means for the whole of reality." Ibid., 225.

62. Ibid., 225–26 As corrected by Lohmann, *Karl Barth und der Neukantianismus*, and Anderson, "The Crisis of Theological Science."

Early in his chapter on Kant in *Protestant Theology in the Nineteenth Century* Barth makes it clear that he is not giving Kant an anti-realistic reading:

> But his own criticism is . . . criticism of knowledge itself and of knowledge as such. This does not mean that it is a complete or partial denial of the possibility, validity and worth of the human method of forming knowledge . . . Those have truly been guilty of misunderstanding him who have taken him to be a kind of super-sceptic, who have looked upon him as the "all annihilating one," as far as the reality of knowledge, the reality of science and morality, art and religion are concerned.[63]

Barth clearly understood Kant's project as an investigation into the limits and limitations of human knowledge. Indeed, he emphasizes that in Kant the Enlightenment commitment to rationality and the unlimited power of untrammeled reason reaches a new height and also takes a new turn. In Kant reason reaches a new maturity, but it is a maturity that expresses itself as an understanding of its limitations rather than a celebration of its powers.[64] But Barth refuses to understand Kant's limitation of the powers of reason as a denial of the possibility of rational knowledge.[65]

Here we have, I think, a crucial pointer to the affinity that Barth felt for Kant. He sees that for Kant the criticism of the human understanding is a product of an examination of the nature and character of the achievement of human knowledge as an event beyond question. Criticism does not dissolve knowledge because knowledge is first of all recognized, acknowledged and affirmed to be real. The reality of human knowledge is the starting point for the criticism that reveals the limitations of that knowledge. Hume had moved Kant to abandon the certainties of dogmatic metaphysics. But against Hume he undertook to explain the truth and certainty of scientific knowledge, concerning which Hume was theoretically skeptical.[66]

---

63. Barth, *Protestant Thought*, 153–54.

64. Ibid., 150.

65. "For him civilization, the achievement of his age, the achievement which is also and in particular the achievement of human knowledge in all those fields, is an event beyond question. It is this event that provides him with the ground upon which he stands. His investigation does not seek to answer the question of whether this achievement has any basis, but the question as to what its basis is." Ibid., 154.

66. Friedman, *Kant and the Exact Sciences*, is, in its entirety, a demonstration of the importance for Kant not only of mathematics, but also of his determination to work

In the short *Foundations of the Metaphysics of Morals* Kant again makes use of that modified form of *modus tollens* that he calls a transcendental deduction. His demonstration of the freedom of the will depends upon the logical meaning of the idea of necessity. First he demonstrates that the freedom of the will is necessary for ethical reflection to be meaningful at all, indeed, in order for there to be any such thing as morals. To say that A is necessary for B means logically that not-A implies not-B. Therefore, if there is no freedom of the will, then there are no morals. But Kant affirms, and expects us to affirm, that there is such a thing as morality. The contrapositive of not-A implies not-B is that B implies A. Therefore, any acknowledgment of the reality of morals implies the reality of the freedom of the will. Again, Kant has not investigated whether there is any such thing as ethics, but rather, if there is, what would be the condition under which alone ethics is possible. Freedom of the will is the necessary presupposition of ethics.[67]

This method of Kant's has correspondences to Barth's method in doing dialectical theology in a critically realistic way. Barth is not inquiring into whether or not there is such an event as revelation, the Word of God.[68] Rather, the reality of the revelation of the Word of God as an event forces him to consider the presuppositions that are necessarily entailed in that event. This is why in part two of volume one of the *Church Dogmatics* the section on the objective *reality* of revelation precedes the section on the objective *possibility* of revelation, and the section on the subjective *reality* of revelation precedes the section on the subjective *possibility* of revelation. Barth explains why the possibility of revelation and the analysis of its necessary conditions and presuppositions derive from a recognition and acknowledgment of the reality of revelation. The opposite procedure, examining the conditions and presuppositions of revelation first and then inquiring whether these conditions and presuppositions are anywhere fulfilled, is in great danger of prescribing to God beforehand what revelation must be and how it must occur.[69] This

---

out an appropriate metaphysics for Newtonian physics. Friedman shows the roots of this enterprise in Kant's precritical writings, but also shows how this concern persisted in the critical period. The work is detailed, precise, and persuasive. See especially ibid., 209–10. It is hard after seeing the extent of Kant's concern for the metaphysical foundations of material nature not to credit him with some realist interest.

67. Kant, *Foundations of the Metaphysics of Morals*, 64–75.

68. Barth, *Church Dogmatics II/1*, 4.

69. Ibid., 5.

presumption upon the freedom and sovereignty of God must not be permitted because the "knowledge" discovered in such a process will not be true and referential knowledge of the actual revelation of God in Jesus Christ.[70]

This order of investigation is a critically realistic feature of Barth's dialectical theology. The actuality of knowledge determines the theoretical conditions and presuppositions that are appropriate to it, just as in the sciences theoretical speculation is dependent upon knowledge obtained in experimentation and observation.[71] Barth sees this feature in the course that Kant takes in doing his philosophy. He calls attention to it at the very head of his chapter on Kant and uses it to dispute the anti-realistic reading of Kant.

Moreover, Barth recognizes in Kant the essential humility of his project. It is aware of its own limitations and eschews metaphysics. But the humility is essential because, guided by it, reason is able to confidently develop positive results that can be built up into a vast architectonic structure.[72] Barth is also engaged in erecting a large and intricate structure in an attitude of essential humility. What is pertinent to the thesis of this chapter is that, in both men, the development of a large body of structured positive knowledge in an attitude of essential humility is a critically realistic mode of operation. It affirms the reality of knowledge while remaining critically aware of its limitations and fallibility.

70. Barth, *Church Dogmatics* I/2, 1–9.

71. Of course, part of the modern dispute over the meaning and character of the sciences has to do with the fact that experimentation and observation are also conditioned by theoretical commitments. But one of the central assertions of critical realism in the sciences is that even though theoretical commitments condition experimentation and observation, they do not finally determine them. Indeed, the history of science is replete with cases where experimentation and observation conducted under one set of theoretical commitments has nonetheless forced upon the scientific community a re-evaluation and revision of its theoretical commitments. See the discussion of the underdetermination of theory by fact in chapter 3.2.3.

72. "And the courage (*Mut*) demanded here from him is not meant to be arrogance (*Hochmut*), let alone faintheartedness (*Schwachmut*) but—lying midway between the two—humility (*Demut*), enabling man to subject himself to a searching critique of his capacities which will show him the right course and which, precisely because it is searching and showing the right course, will clarify and confirm his ability to subject himself to, and, once he has done this, to be guided by the results of this self-criticism. Its pathos is not by any means that of a denial; it is, rather, in the most explicit manner possible, that of an affirmation of reason." Barth, *Protestant Thought*, 154.

In his rehearsal of the basic outlines of Kant's philosophy Barth takes the classic assertion that "thoughts without content are empty, intuitions without concepts are blind"[73] and asserts that the emphasis in it lies in the emptiness of concepts without intuition.[74] His primary purpose in so doing is to emphasize the way the Kantian critique limits or eliminates metaphysics. This can be understood as a product of Barth's intention to combine realism and idealism in the service of dialectical theology, given the history reviewed earlier in this chapter and Barth's own relation to the Marburg philosophy that had departed from Kant at precisely this point. He reads Kant as an idealist whose philosophy is more open to realistic elements than that of Cohen.[75]

Kant is like one who has discovered himself to be standing on ground that is muddy. Spurred by Hume he has recognized dogmatic metaphysics as a mire and taken the critical and brilliant step out of the mud and onto the clear ground of idealism. But he has not lifted his other foot from off the ground of realism. Even if his weight is upon the idealistic foot, the realistic foot is still necessary and Kant's refusal to lift it gives his position a balance and stability that Barth does not find in absolute idealism. The second step into idealism, lifting the foot from realistic ground and attempting to place it upon the absolute, must seem like an attempt to walk upon thin air.

Barth's reading of Kant is strongly colored by his determination to read the first and second critiques as organically joined one to another. This permits him to assert that Kant has not destroyed metaphysics, but rather made it possible as a science.[76]

> Reason . . . will not have come to an understanding of itself so long as it imagines itself merely to be theoretical reason and not active practical reason. In Kant's teaching "practical reason" is not a second form of reason existing beside the theoretical form; it is rather that the one kind of reason, which is also theoretical, is also and, it must be said, primarily practical reason. Surely the union of intuition and concept, whence empirical knowledge derives its reality, is in fact action, practice, having its basis in transcendental apperception. It is in this act as such that man is

73. Kant, *Critique of Pure Reason*, 93.

74. Barth, *Protestant Thought*, 158.

75. Indeed, he says that "Criticism" or "Rationalism" would typify more clearly and comprehensively what Kant wants than the term idealism. See ibid., 157.

76. Ibid., 162.

laid hold of not only by the being of things, i.e., by nature in its reality in time and space, but beyond this and above all by the thing that must be, hidden from us as a "thing in itself," which is, as a thing, undiscoverable; by the world of freedom which limits time and space and resolves them within itself . . . God, freedom, and immortality—these ideas which in their regulative use are indispensable also in empirical knowledge—cannot be perceived *in abstracto*, i.e., by contemplation in isolation, but they can be perceived *in concreto*, i.e. in actual fact. It is in and with the *fact* that their true contemplation is accomplished; it is in practice that the true thing is accomplished. The theory which accompanies provides the basis for and contains within itself all empirical knowledge but now also rises truly and legitimately above it. They have no truth in a theory by itself.[77]

This reading of Kant, which understands the first and second critiques to be related in such a way that both theoretical and practical reason are irreducible features of pure reason, in which practical reason has the priority, and in which knowledge by practical reason is thereby knowledge by pure reason even when it is not knowledge by theoretical reason, is one that some Kant scholars would dispute. But there were interpreters of Kant, primarily Max Wundt, Nicholai Hartmann, and Heinz Heimsoeth, who proposed a reading of Kant very much like this, and at just about the time that Barth was working in Göttingen.[78] There is no clear evidence that Karl Barth was acquainted with their work, but there is good evidence that his brother Heinrich was.[79] It was to his

77. Ibid., 159–60.

78. Scott-Taggart, "Recent Work on the Philosophy of Kant," 2–3. This school of interpretation begins around 1924 and is usually referred to as the ontological interpretation of Kant. The ontological interpretation of Kant also maintains the importance of things-in-themselves. Heimsoeth suggests that the critical limitation of knowledge is determined by the basic metaphysical conviction of the reality of the thing in itself (see ibid., 4–7). This attitude is compatible with both modern scientific realism and the dialectical form of critical realism we find in Barth.

79. Lohmann, *Karl Barth und der Neukantianismus*, 191, says that Heinrich knows both Hartmann and the ontological interpretation. Later, on 387, he says that Karl knows the ontological interpretation and is himself an example of the transformation of Neo-Kantianism in this period. Both Lohmann and Anderson make the point that Barth's adherence to the ontological interpretation of Kant and what I have called its critically realistic character do not constitute a retreat from Neo-Kantianism, but rather the adoption of another form of Neo-Kantianism that was available at this time.

brother that Barth gave credit in the forward to the second edition of *Romans* for helping him to recognize the importance of Kant.[80]

But the issue here is not whether Barth has read Kant correctly, but whether he is reading Kant in a critically realistic manner.

By attributing the status of real knowledge by pure reason to the things which are known by practical reason Barth treats Kant's full system as a sort of pragmatic critical realism in which the first critique serves as a critical theory, calling attention to the limitations and fallibilities of pure reason, but not thereby undermining the reality of human knowledge. We do not have theoretical knowledge of the reality of other persons as centers of will and knowledge, as the *locus* of a freedom that acknowledges universal law. But the practical knowledge that we have of our own freedom is sufficient to make us morally responsible, and the practical knowledge that we have of God is again sufficient for moral responsibility, and most importantly, the practical knowledge that we have of other persons is sufficient to make us responsible for treating them always as ends in themselves as well as means to our own ends. This knowledge of practical reason Barth treats as real knowledge of things in themselves and is what he means by asserting that Kant has made metaphysics possible as a science.[81] Our knowledge of things in themselves does not have the appropriate character to be understood as theoretic knowledge, for then the application of the categories of the understanding would enable us to flesh out this knowledge with empirical detail. But it is real because it is an irreducible and inescapable feature of our moral responsibility as ethical agents. It is real because it refers to things in themselves even as it acknowledges the theoretic limitations upon our knowledge of those things. It is real because the ideals of God, freedom, and immortality "while they do not extend speculative knowledge, they give objective reality to the ideas of speculative reason in general (by means of their relation to the practical sphere) and justify it in holding to concepts even the possibility of which it could not otherwise

---

80. Barth, *Romans*, 4.

81. For a supporting opinion see Silber, "The Metaphysical Importance of the Highest Good," 243: "That Kant should direct metaphysics to the objects of freedom, God, and immortality, only to carry out the inquiry into these objects in terms of the ideas of the soul, the world, and God, clearly shows that Kant presents the inquiry into moral ideas of reason as a genuinely metaphysical and speculative inquiry as well as a moral investigation."

venture to affirm."[82] It is thus from Kant himself that Barth gets the idea that knowledge by practical reason amounts to precisely what theoretic reason cannot even hope to attain, knowledge of things in themselves.[83]

Thus, we can have theoretic knowledge of a person's appearance, and of their activities in the world of appearances. But we cannot have theoretic knowledge of their freedom, since that freedom is precisely freedom from bondage and limitation to the world of appearances, while theoretic knowledge is bound by its nature to the world of appearances, its concepts being empty apart from empirical intuition. But we can nonetheless know their freedom by pure reason in its practical application as an essential attribute of the other person apart from all appearances.[84]

It is also a matter of some importance for Barth's reading of Kant that he understands Kant to be describing the actual knowing of existing individuals. This is neither the self-knowledge of the absolute, only imperfectly realized in finite beings, as is certainly the case in Hegel and probably in Fichte, nor is it the knowledge of an archetypical ideal knower as in Cohen. It is the plain, matter of fact, more limited, and yet also more pragmatic and realistic knowledge of actual existential persons. This is why Barth says that abstract man is not real man and that we are not real human beings because of our capacity to have empirical knowledge of things in the transcendental unity of apperception. What makes us real human beings is our freedom to perceive by reason the necessity and lawfulness of things. But this is a metaphysical feature of our being, our true noumenal being. Though it touches the abstract, though it is precisely the ability to recognize the abstract, it is itself not abstract but concrete.[85]

Though Barth reads Kant in a critically realistic way, he does not make the mistake of treating him as a critical realist outright. For one thing, Barth still takes for granted the validity of the Kantian epistemology as it applies to our knowledge of empirical reality, and our lack of theo-

---

82. Kant, *Critique of Practical Reason*, 137.

83. "By pure rational knowledge Kant means that necessary knowledge which refers not to what is, but to an object that transcends all experience, to what must be and only in this sense 'is.'" Barth, *Protestant Thought*, 157. In saying this Barth is understanding Kant to regard pure rational knowledge which is ideal in character as knowledge of "an object that transcends all experience." Such an object is, of course, the kind of thing usually addressed in metaphysics.

84. Rescher, *Kant and the Reach of Reason*, 29, suggests that for Kant things in themselves are to phenomena as the rational will is to its free acts.

85. Barth, *Protestant Thought*, 160.

retical knowledge of the noumenal reality behind phenomenal appearances. Barth is not a critical realist about human knowledge in general but about the knowledge of God. Moreover, he is well aware that Kant is idealistic about the knowledge of God.[86] But he sees in Kant's system a suitable dialogue partner over against which to develop the critically realistic knowledge of God as a dialectical consequence of God's own act of self-revelation.[87] This will be addressed in detail at the beginning of the next section. Barth is well aware that he is using Kant in a manner that Kant himself would not have accepted. But when he suggests that there might be an insight in Kant's treatment of the problem of religion which was unable to bear fruit in the framework of Kant's own undertaking, but which might bear fruit in theological reflection, he clarifies for us his own relationship to Kant.[88] He is granting Kant credit for attempting to speak of and refer to the same reality of which Barth himself claims to speak, so that even where he departs from Kant's system and disputes Kant's conclusions, he also accepts that Kant may be right in some ways and give essential insight to the inquiry into our knowledge of God. This kind of generous attitude toward another position is critically realistic in character, and tends to give a critically realistic reading to the materials that it interprets.

5.4 BARTH'S USE OF KANT (AND OF PHILOSOPHY IN GENERAL)

Barth understands Kant as a "critical rationalist" whose system is best understood as a form of idealism. Barth did not have available to him the concept of critical realism by that name and in the form it takes in the twentieth century. Nonetheless, Barth's reading of Kant is critically realistic on three counts.

First, Barth returns to a careful consideration of Kant after the excesses of speculative idealism and in particular the form of Neo-Kantianism to which he was exposed at Marburg.[89] He needs for his

86. Ibid., 188.

87. Ibid., 191–92.

88. Ibid., 195–96.

89. He calls it "the heaven storming Idealism of the first half of the century," and asks, "Is it with impunity that we can train man to titanism, as the Idealists with their faith in God finally did?" Not only was the idealism that followed Kant wrong in itself, but so

theological purposes a form of idealism which does not reject the notion of the thing in itself and which does not try to eliminate the function of empirical intuition in the field of knowledge. This need is produced by the experience of the Word of God in the church as something that asserts itself over against all human speculation about the nature and character of God. The strongly idealistic theology produced by Barth's predecessors in the nineteenth century, despite its affection for transcendental method, seemed to Barth to be inadequate to a God who was truly transcendent. Barth needs and desires for his theological purposes a theory of human understanding in which we can have real, true, referential knowledge of actualities that are other than and more than our knowledge of them. Knowledge does not have to be absolute, final, and theoretically certain in order to be real knowledge. Moreover, for Barth's purpose, which is to explicate the self-revelation of the transcendent God, the self-critique of reason in an absolute idealism is inadequate. Only the actuality of God is an adequate critique of reason.

Second, Barth lays emphasis upon the importance in Kant of empirical intuition. Instead of looking for ways to minimize or eliminate empirical intuition Barth takes it to be an essential part of Kant's system. As so many of Kant's successors pointed to empirical intuition as a realistic remnant in Kant's system, Barth's emphasis upon it must be recognized as a realistic element in his reading of Kant. Barth is not doing philosophy, and he does not take advantage of the importance of empirical intuition in order to develop a critically realistic understanding of our knowledge of the world and all that is in it. But he needs the idea of intuition in order to address the problem of how God remains the subject even in the self-objectification of revelation. The grounds upon which he understands our knowledge of God in a critically realistic way are not such that they can be employed to treat our knowledge of the rest of reality in the same way.[90]

Third, Barth refuses to accept an anti-realistic reading of Kant. As was said above, the net effect of these realistic elements in Barth's reading of Kant is to treat him as a pragmatic critical realist.[91] This binding to-

---

excessive that its collapse was still debilitating for theology and philosophy leaving "nothing but a positivistic historicism and psychologism." Barth, *Church Dogmatics II/1*, 73.

90. "Barth presupposed the validity of that [Kant's] epistemology insofar as it touches upon our knowledge of empirical reality in order to transcend its limitations in describing our knowledge of God." McCormack, *Orthodox and Modern*, 144.

91. Rescher, *Kant and the Reach of Reason*, 1, interprets Kant as a protopragmatist.

gether of the pragmatic reality of our knowledge and the idealist critique of our knowledge is a feature of Barth's commitment to doing theology dialectically.[92] By taking notice of and giving emphasis to the realistic elements in Kant, Barth gives him a critically realistic reading.

Many of the features that make Barth's reading of Kant critically realistic are formal and structural in character. Barth is addressing the problem of the knowledge of God. Kant is addressing the problem of human scientific and ethical knowledge. Barth is not ascribing to Kant a form of critical realism about scientific and ethical knowledge. Rather, he is describing an *unrealized possibility* in Kant's philosophy that can be used to describe the meaning of a critically realistic knowledge of God. This makes it difficult, at times, to distinguish Barth's own theological work from his reading of Kant. But Barth was aware of the distance that lay between them, even if he attempted to reduce that distance by bridging it from the theological side.

> It is only necessary to take what Kant said half in mockery, in order to hear something very significant, even though we reserve in every respect our right to object to his formulations. Or is it not the case that the philosopher of pure reason has said something very significant to the theologian in telling him in all succinctness that *"the Biblical theologian proves that God exists by means of the fact that he has spoken in the Bible"*?[93]

Karl Barth was, and remained, a theologian and not a philosopher. He was not unaware of philosophy and its questions and problems, but he did not undertake to resolve them. Even the philosophies that he takes the most seriously, Kantian Idealism and Existentialism, he treats

---

92. Contrast Bradshaw, *Trinity and Ontology*, 4, who finds a different root for Barth's dialectics: "The important concept in this exploration resembles the Hegelian idea of the *relation of opposites*. This concept, with its development into the relationship between freedom and conditionedness, helps us to understand Barth's interpretation of the Trinity *ad extra* and *in se*, and from there his view of man and reconciliation. Barth's theology is, accordingly, found to be dialectical in character." Though Bradshaw does not anywhere reference the term "critical realism" I believe that his arguments can be understood as supporting the critically realistic interpretation of Barth. Certainly he is correct about the background of Barth's use of Hegelian concepts, for Barth knew Hegel and his effect upon theology well. Bradshaw argues that Barth's use of Hegelian concepts is a product of his need for them in his doctrine of the trinity. This need is not *a priori* but an *a posteriori* consequence of material decisions in theology. This is a pattern that I am arguing to be critically realistic.

93. Barth, *Protestant Thought*, 196.

as tools with which to explicate his theology. His use of existentialism is clearly seen in works like *Romans* and *Die christliche Dogmatik im Entwurf.* That it was nonetheless a tool of explication and not a central commitment can be seen in the way that Barth moved to explain himself differently in *Die kirchliche Dogmatik*, with special concern for correcting readings of *Die christliche Dogmatik* that seemed to take his use of existentialist motifs more seriously than he himself did.[94] His use of Kant, despite the seriousness with which he took Kant's philosophy, to describe a theological possibility, the knowledge of God, of which Kant would have denied the theoretical possibility, is key evidence for this.[95]

For Kant, the knowledge of God is solely ideal. The concept of God has no substantial content.[96] It functions as a regulative ideal and Kant regards any attempt to fill this regulative ideal with content as a misuse of the categories of the understanding which can only lead to irresolvable antinomies. Yet Barth is determined to discuss a knowledge of God that has substantial content as well as functioning as a regulative ideal. In doing so he both uses Kant, and also exceeds the limits which Kant had set.[97]

It was not the case that Barth considered the Kantian philosophy to be a correct description of our knowledge of empirical reality, while we have some other structure of mind which we use for knowing God. The structure of the mind that we use for knowing God is the same one that we use for empirical reality.[98] When we have knowledge of empirical reality we do not yet have knowledge of God, because God is not identical with any of its elements, not even the set of the whole. Some additional specification is necessary to identify God. For dialectical theology, as Barth conceives it, that additional specification is revelation. But revelation does not make that specification by using some other, perhaps higher, intellectual faculty than that which we use in seeking, gaining, having, and using the knowledge of empirical reality. Revelation uses the ordinary mental faculties with which we are endowed but gives their

94. See McCormack, *Barth's Critically Realistic Dialectical Theology*, 421, 443–44.

95. "All of his [Barth's] efforts in theology may be considered, from one point of view, as an attempt to overcome Kant by means of Kant, not retreating behind him and attempting to go around him, but going through him." Ibid., 465–66.

96. As Barth reads him. See Barth, *Church Dogmatics II/1*, 183.

97. McCormack, *Orthodox and Modern*, 125–26.

98. Barth, *Church Dogmatics II/1*, 21.

products a new reference and a new meaning.[99] God does this from a direction at right angles to all the ordinary four-dimensional events and actions and causes of empirical reality as we experience them. This is what Barth means by the language in Romans about revelation touching reality as a tangent does a circle at a single point, or the plane of eternity intersecting the plane of time in a line.[100] That line has no extension in the plane of ordinary reality. This is the way Barth speaks when emphasizing that revelation comes from outside and is not bound by time. But he also says that Jesus Christ is that intersection, and Jesus obviously does have extension in time. Indeed, he is how the unintuitable becomes intuitable.[101] Because this is God's own action it comes from outside the four-dimensional space-time of this empirical reality, and cannot be our action. Any action we could exert, being exerted by four-dimensional creatures in a four-dimensional world, could not have any component in a fifth-dimensional direction.[102] It must be God's doing.[103]

99. "It is God himself who opens our eyes and ears for himself. And in doing so he tells us that we could not do it for ourselves, that of ourselves we are blind and deaf. To receive the Holy Spirit means an exposure of our spiritual helplessness, a recognition that we do not possess the Holy Spirit. For that reason the subjective reality of revelation has the distinctive character of a miracle." Barth, *Church Dogmatics* I/2, 244. Note that in citing this passage in support of this argument I am taking the eyes and ears that God opens to be a synecdoche for the entire cognitive machinery by which one knows empirical reality. The language I introduce about four and five dimensions is also but a metaphor, as is Barth's language about eyes, ears, blindness, and deafness. It is a transformation of Barth's metaphor into the idiom of the philosophy of science. See also Barth, *Church Dogmatics* II/1, 94.

100. Barth, *Romans*, 29–30, 40, 60. This way of using n-dimensional geometry to conceive of what Barth means is also useful in explaining what he means when he says: "The fact that God's Word is God's act means first its contingent contemporaneity." Barth, *Church Dogmatics* I/1, 145. Since God's act comes from beyond the four dimensional world of empirical reality it intersects time, rather than being trapped in time. As such it intersects time in three different ways, in Jesus Christ in the early first century, in the witness of the prophets and apostles in the times both before and after, and in the hearing of the church even today. But all of these times are one contemporaneous act of God that cuts across empirical time at three different places.

101. The apparent contradiction is to be resolved in 6.1 on the dialectic of veiling and unveiling.

102. This is simple vector analysis. See, for instance, Kolman, *Elementary Linear Algebra*, 89–99, chapter 2, "Real Vector Spaces," section 2, "Linear Independence."

103. The idea that the action of God comes from a further direction beyond or behind the usual four of space-time is to be used to recognize what Barth is asserting in his repeated insistence that the Word of God, that revelation itself, is always a miracle, something that is not a possibility of this world. "If we have understood that the knowability

All of this is merely an understanding in mathematically modeled terms of the traditional Reformed (and, indeed, Roman Catholic, considering that the Reformed viewpoint is so strongly descended from Augustine) theological understanding of the prevenience of grace in salvation and in revelation. But mathematical modelings with strict logical consequences were exactly what Barth's Kantian commitments would lead him to expect of high-level theological judgments. Barth accepts plainly the idea that we think within the Kantian limitations even when we do theology. But when revelation occurs an actor from outside the Kantian limitations intersects with empirical reality and acts within it, as well as acting from without.

We do not say that when revelation occurs an actor from outside *must* intersect, not even if the logic of the only way we can think of to frame the question implies the intersection, and thus justifies the addition of the word "must." We only report that in the case to which we give witness as Christian theologians this intersection *did* occur. Indeed, the reality that we meet in revelation claims that, "I will be who I will be." This means, at least, that it claims not to be who it must. God intersects with empirical reality by choice, not by necessity. This is but the doctrine of election, as Barth conceives it, and as applied to the doctrine of revelation. Moreover, that revelation is by choice, by grace, rather than by necessity, emphasizes the reason that it must be conceived as acting from a direction outside the four dimensional space-time of empirical reality. If it were by necessity, then it would be conceivable that the necessity was coded or structured into empirical reality, so that no further dimensions need be conceived in order to understand God's word. When the word of God, by a free choice, intersects with empirical reality it makes itself present to empirical experience. The presuppositions of that experience

---

of God's Word is really an inalienable affirmation of faith, but that precisely as such it denotes the miracle of faith, the miracle that we can only recollect and hope for." Barth, *Church Dogmatics I/1*, 247. "To say 'the Word of God' is to say the miracle of God." Barth, *Church Dogmatics I/2*, 528. "'God reveals himself'—if the statement is made in respect of the revelation attested in Holy Scripture, it is made in view of the actually *miraculous event*, the special new direct act of God in the breaking in of new time in the midst of the old. In the Bible miracle is not some event that is hard to conceive, nor yet one that is simply inconceivable, but conceivable only as the exponent of the special new act of God in time and in history. In the form in which it acquires temporal historical actuality, biblically attested revelation is always a miracle, and therefore the witness to it, whether direct or indirect in its course, is a narrative of miracles that happened. Miracle is thus an attribute of revelation." Ibid., 63–64.

are made necessary by the actuality of the event of the Word of God, rather than by the logic of human experience or pure reason.[104] It is the contingent actuality (that is, actuality by choice, rather than by necessity) of the word of God that makes it intuitable as an empirical reality, even though it is more than the empirical reality in which it is intuited.

> With Kant, Barth believes that human knowledge is limited to the intuitable, phenomenal realm. And that means that if God (who is unintuitable) is nevertheless to be intuited (and therefore, *known* in the strict theoretical sense), God must make himself to be phenomenal, that is, God must assume creaturely form. But at this point a further problem arises. In making himself phenomenal, God has entered into the subject-object relation in which the constructive role played by the Kantian categories of the understanding make the human knower the "master" in any and every knowledge-relation. So the problem is: how can God remain God (i.e. the subject of the knowledge of God) even *as* God takes on phenomenal form? The answer has everything to do with the fact that God does not make himself directly identical with a phenomenal magnitude, but only indirectly so. What occurs in revelation is that the divine Subject lays hold of or grasps the human knowing apparatus through the phenomena from the other side. In this way, the limitations placed on human knowing by the Kantian subject-object split are overcome by a transcendent, divine act.[105]

The difficulty here referred to is at the heart of Barth's commitment to dialectic in theology. The very language of "if God is to be intuited, he must make himself to be phenomenal" has itself already "entered into the subject-object relation in which the constructive role played by the Kantian categories of the understanding make the human knower the 'master' in any and every knowledge-relation." The mastery in question is shown by the use of the language of logical necessity. Yet Barth clearly intends for us to understand the incarnation to be a free choice on God's part. One of the purposes of dialectic is to remind us that the necessity here referred to is a necessity imposed upon *us*, imposed upon our cognitive machinery, by God's free act.[106] In this, dialectic is partly reflecting a Kantian theme, that the perceived necessity of theoretical knowledge

---

104. Barth, *Church Dogmatics I/*1, 246; Barth, *Church Dogmatics II/*1, 30.

105. McCormack, *Orthodox and Modern*, 111.

106. Barth, *Church Dogmatics II/*1, 21.

is a product of the structure of *our* minds, and that freedom lies with the things themselves, whatever they may be, that stimulate and engender our knowledge.

This means that when "the divine subject lays hold of or grasps the human knowing apparatus through the phenomena from the other side" and "the limitations placed on human knowing by the Kantian subject-object split are overcome by a transcendent, divine act," it remains *un*-contained by the Kantian limitations. I have modeled this with the language of n-dimensional geometry. But when I suggest that the action of God in revelation comes from a direction beyond the four (or fourteen or eighteen, depending on your flavor of string theory) that we use in our knowledge of empirical reality, it might still be possible to say that the Kantian transcendental unity of apperception—which acts to combine the categories of the understanding and the manifold of sensible intuition into the objects of empirical knowledge—is also in a fifth dimension beyond the four of empirical space and time (metaphorically, just as the use of this language for God's action is metaphorical). Then it might be possible to see and understand God as being beyond empirical reality, but still within the plane of transcendental thought as Kant conceived it. But Barth is going beyond Kant as well as using him and taking him for granted within his own sphere of thought. Barth would simply say that the action of God in revelation comes not merely from beyond the four dimensions of empirical space and time but also from beyond whatever additional dimensions are necessary to hold transcendental philosophy's understanding of the nature of reason and the character of empirical knowledge.[107]

In revelation God neither uses some native capacity for n-dimensional understanding that we have but do not commonly use for empirical judgments, nor does he endow us with some new capacity. Rather, he gives us a new interpretation of cognitive events within the limits of the human imagination. We can, by way of illustration, draw a two-dimensional figure in the plane that consists of three contiguous parallelograms. Viewed as a two-dimensional figure and subjected to the operations of plane geometry it will never become otherwise. But when

---

107. This lies behind the difference between Karl Barth and his brother Heinrich on the subject of the *Ursprung*. Karl made use of it in the form given to it by Heinrich, but the difference prompted him to say, "Have we come to the point with the philosophical police when we must hear their warning without obeying it?" McCormack, *Barth's Critically Realistic Dialectical Theology*, 218–26. The quote is on p. 223.

we add to the drawing the interpretation that it is a sketch in two dimensions of an ordinary four-dimensional object, a child's toy block sitting still for the length of time necessary to recognize and draw it, it then becomes something more. The interpretation does not make the sketch to be more than two-dimensional, rather the interpretation makes the sketch into a two-dimensional *projection* of a four-dimensional object. In the same way revelation is a projection by God into the world of space and time and empirical knowledge, with all its dimensional and cognitive limitations, of an object that is not limited to space and time and the structures of empirical knowledge. Just as in geometrical projection, where a higher dimensional object is represented by its projection into a space of fewer dimensions, so also in revelation an act of God is projected into the world of empirical reality. Again, this is an attempt to model, not to justify, what Barth means in asserting that in revelation God makes himself to be phenomenal and more than that, to be known, and known in and with the same cognitive structures and processes by which we know empirical reality, without thereby becoming subject to the limitations of empirical knowledge.

Barth's use of philosophy is conditioned at every point by theological requirements and theological purposes. It is because his theological purpose has a realistic intention as well as a critical one that Barth gives Kant a reading that emphasizes those elements in the Kantian philosophy that are open to realistic concerns. But note well that Kant's critical philosophy is not sufficiently realistic to be used immediately and directly for Barth's theological purpose. Theology must stand on its own and philosophy is used, where it can be, to explain where theology stands. The incarnation is not a response to the problems of the Kantian epistemology. Rather, the Kantian philosophy is used to explicate the meaning and character of the knowledge that we have of God in the incarnation. Philosophical considerations do not determine material theological issues. Rather, material theological decisions determine what philosophy will be useful in explicating those decisions and condition how that philosophy is used making those explanations.[108]

108. "Now all that I have said to this point might seem to suggest that Barth was working with an a priori *Erkenntnistheorie* and tailoring his Christology to it. But, in fact, just the opposite is the case. Talk of what God "must" do if He is to reveal himself rests upon *a posteriori* reflection upon what "must" be the case if God has done what God is said to have done in Jesus Christ by the New Testament witness. Thus, I would argue, Barth's anhypostatic-enhypostatic Christology ultimately controlled his use of

Anyone speaking of an axiom of *theology* and even specifying that it is the *first commandment* . . . must understand from the outset that this concept is being given a content and a meaning which it can have only in theology. In no way must it be assumed that the choice of this concept has provided a common platform, a "point of contact" for the dialogue with logicians, mathematicians and physicists . . . Indeed, the concept "axiom" will not be chosen to describe that instance because it is believed that the first commandment can be subsumed under this concept. Nor will the concept be chosen because one can discern an intrinsic similarity or an immanent analogy to the first commandment— and thus provide the ability to understand it. The concept will not be chosen, therefore, because of its suitability. We assert that it is not *through* the concept axiom, but only *by means* of it (to be precise, *in spite* of it, only by trespassing on its customary usage, even reversing it, only by a misuse of this concept) can we designate the presupposition for theology and its significance for theological statements.[109]

Here Barth makes utterly clear the relation of his theology to the mathematical and philosophical concepts that it uses. The content of revelation controls the formal concepts used to express that content. The first commandment itself, "I am the Lord, your God, you shall have no other gods before me," announces that it may not be subsumed under any concept. For Barth, theological use of mathematical and philosophical language is, and must be, metaphorical. But despite the refusal to submit to the standards of philosophy and the sciences, Barth's understanding of the relation of the object of his discourse to the discourse itself is critically realistic. The object controls the meaning of sentences about it. The interpretation of those sentences in a model of the object is tested always by continuing interaction with the object onto which the model is being mapped. The physical sciences have learned to hold theory secondary to fact, and to change theories whenever anomalies in the mapping of models of theories onto the actual behavior of the world become numerous and recalcitrant. Theology has had to learn this lesson at its very beginning from God, who announces that he will be who he will be and that we shall have no other gods before him.

Kantian categories. Kantian epistemology is brought into play in order to explicate the *erkenntnistheoretischen* implications of his Christology." McCormack, "Beyond Nonfoundational and Postmodern Readings of Barth," 83.

109. Barth, "The First Commandment as an Axiom of Theology," 63–64.

Moreover, a recognition of the metaphorical character of language wherever it is applied to any other than purely formal realities is an integral part of critical realism. The model as a model of knowledge, and the understanding of the bidirectional meaning and use of the model (that the model of the theory is used as a model of the object) imply that language is metaphorical. The theory may well be abstract and direct, but the model is a metaphor. It can be difficult, and sometimes very difficult, to use and understand the sentences of a theory directly, without a model, unless the theory is about a purely formal object such as logic or mathematics.

Barth was not consciously a critical realist. He did not first have a critically realistic understanding of the nature and character of human knowledge and then apply it to the problem of rescuing our God talk from the difficulties into which liberal theology had led it. In this respect the thesis of this book is anachronistic. Nonetheless, when compared to the work of others among the dialectical theologians, and even more, when compared to the work of the liberal theologians who preceded him, it can be seen that there is a critically realistic character to Barth's theology.

Kees van Kooten Niekerk, describing the range of positions that can legitimately be called critical realism, says that "In German philosophy, it [critical realism] designates those positions which take account of Kant's critical epistemology but deny that the subjectivity of our experience makes it impossible to acquire knowledge of the external world as it is in itself."[110] By this definition, Barth's use of Kant, coupled with his understanding of how God reveals by taking control of the human knowing apparatus from the noumenal side, amounts to critical realism in theology. The critical limits of human knowledge are neither violated nor ignored, so Barth's position remains critical in the Kantian sense. But God gives to our limited knowledge what it cannot have by its own act, true correspondence to God's own act of revelation. This correspondence is not a product of the transcendental unity of apperception. The correspondence is an actualistic product of God's revelatory act, so that without our experience becoming any less subjective thereby, we are nonetheless gifted with real knowledge of an external reality: God in self-revelation. It can, of course, be contested whether this is, in fact, how God reveals. But by making such a realistic claim for our knowledge of God in the context of and with all due respect to the Kantian critical

110. Van Kooten Niekerk, "Critical Realist Perspective," 51.

epistemology, Barth is clearly making a critically realistic claim about our knowledge of God.

It is important to note here that the way that Barth uses Kant makes Barth a postfoundationalist in theology even though he is a thoroughgoing modern and a foundationalist in philosophy. The object of his discourse, God in self-revelation, is one that cannot be captured in human thought built upon human foundations. The object of his discourse forces him to sit loose to his foundations. He might not have adopted the postmodern attitude that "anything goes," but he also steadily refused to let philosophical foundations dictate theological conclusions. This attitude towards the foundations that he is using makes Barth post-foundational.[111]

Neither nonfoundationalism nor postfoundationalism suggest that all structure in human thought, and all primacy in that structure, is improper. They rather criticize the notion that some of the primary items in that structure are "noninferential principles whose certainty and stability ground other epistemic claims."[112] For Barth it is God's own action that grounds our epistemic claims about him, and God's own faithfulness that gives our epistemic claims about him certainty, and not any principles of thought. Barth's dialectical insight—that in revelation God gives us true referential knowledge of himself even though human thought is, in and of itself, incapable of grounding, framing, or judging the knowledge of God—means that he would not have accepted the *anti-realistic* element in postmodern thought, but would have been sympathetic to the *nonfoundationalism* of postmodern thought. This sympathy combined with some form of realism we have been calling *post*foundationalism.

---

111. McCormack, "Beyond Nonfoundational and Postmodern Readings of Barth," 83–84, coins the term transfoundationalist to describe Barth's practice of having a foundation but holding it loosely.

112. Thiel, *Nonfoundationalism*, 1.

6

Karl Barth's Dialectical Critical Realism

When I speak in this chapter of Barth's dialectical critical realism I am not describing a philosophical position that Barth articulated. Rather, I am describing a philosophical position that can be constructed from the implications and presuppositions of Barth's theology. This philosophical position is useful in understanding Barth's own theology.

The contention of this chapter is that Barth's critical realism is not just an historical accident resulting from his theological determination to speak realistically of God despite his philosophical commitment to a Kantian epistemology. It is rather a function of his dialectical theology. The critically realistic elements in his understanding of the knowledge of God are a product of his dialectical conception of the problem of the knowledge of God. Indeed, dialectical theology itself is the *product of,* rather than a presupposition of, the reality of our knowledge of God in the revelation of Jesus Christ.

6.1 THE CRITICALLY REALISTIC CHARACTER OF THE DIALECTIC OF THE DIVINE VEILING AND UNVEILING IN REVELATION

It is important to note that I speak of the critically realistic *character* of the dialectic of the divine veiling and unveiling in revelation, not of its critically realistic *nature*. The latter locution would imply that critical realism, as the underlying form of all human knowledge, was the rock bottom upon which all understanding of the knowledge of God everywhere and at all times must be erected. For Barth, the only possible rock bottom is the reality of God as *God*. The reality of God as *God*, that is, as sovereign, prevents any epistemological consideration from having determinative character.[1] The source and nature of our knowledge of God in self-revelation is God's own decision to reveal. Critical realism is descriptive rather than prescriptive of what we have in our knowledge of God.

The particular character of Barth's doctrine of revelation is of crucial importance for understanding his whole theology. In what follows I will be taking for granted that there is substantial continuity in Barth's work from the first edition of *Romans* all the way through the *Church Dogmatics*. There is development, but it is continuous. There are changes, but they are primarily in the mode of explication. If this were not to hold, then my argument here would be flawed. But more than a few scholars now agree on this substantial continuity.

Some basic features of Barth's doctrine of revelation follow:

6.1.1 Revelation Does Occur

This means that there *is* a God to be known and we *do* have real knowledge of God in revelation. None of the questions to be addressed in theology can even be raised as questions about God apart from the reality of revelation. Barth is not beginning with an inquiry into whether there is any such thing as revelation, and what revelation must be if we encounter it. Rather, he takes it for granted that we have been encountered by God in revelation and that all theology is a *post hoc* investigation of what we encountered in revelation and who we must be because we have encountered it.[2] This does not mean that Barth denies the question as to whether or not revelation does occur. As we will see later, Barth recognizes that *all* theology is done in the face of this question, and cannot wish it otherwise. But theology, and in particular church dogmatics, does not even begin until we have given, at least provisionally and hypothetically, a positive answer to this question.

---

1. Barth, *Church Dogmatics* II/1, 5.
2. Barth, *Church Dogmatics* II/1, 4–5. See also Barth, *Church Dogmatics* I/1, 12.

The order is critical here. We do not first investigate who we are in order to determine what revelation must be if it is to be possible for us to encounter it. It is, rather, revelation that determines who we are when we encounter it. As revelation is an integral act of the one who created us, who made us to be who and what we are, this is the correct logical order in which to put these things, regardless of what order they may have in the history of our encounter with revelation.[3]

This underlying attitude is also common to most forms of critical realism. The subject matter of our knowledge is assumed to exist, as well as the reality of our knowledge of it. (The quality or veracity of our knowledge is always in question.) This assumption cannot be guaranteed in advance. If the knowledge we gain turns out to be self-contradictory or incoherent, we may abandon the assumption. If not we may retain it, but it still rests upon the assumption of the reality of that which we investigate in our learning and knowing. The possibility of real knowledge depends upon the reality of that which is the case, and the power of that reality to assert itself in the knowing relation. Scientific Realism sees this witnessed in the history of science as the realities encountered in observation and experimentation have forced scientists to rethink their theories. Barth sees it in the history of the church's interpretation of Scripture. "As the orthodox Protestants were fond of saying, Holy Scripture was the *facultas semetipsam interpretandi* which at any rate means the power sooner or later to throw off every foreign sense attributed to it, to mark and to expose its perversity, and in contrast to assert itself in its own characteristic meaning."[4]

It might be thought that a critically realistic attitude would mean, first of all, being critical about whether or not there is any such thing as revelation. But this would be a critically realistic question for the philosophy of religion, or for each human being in the existential reality of their life, but *not for theology*, or, at least, not Christian theology as Barth has defined it. In parallel fashion, the question of metaphysical realism is a question for the philosophy of science, not for the science of

3. Again, this logical order is structurally reflected in the *Church Dogmatics* when the objective and subjective *reality* of revelation is treated prior to and as the condition of the objective and subjective *possibility* of revelation. See Barth, *Church Dogmatics* I/2, 1–7 for the explanation of the necessity of this ordering.

4. Barth, *Church Dogmatics* I/2, 681–82. On page 684 Barth explicitly cites the Reformation recovery of the theme of salvation by grace alone after centuries of other interpretations as evidence of the power of Scripture to assert itself in the knowing relation.

physics. This does not mean that Barth's doctrine of revelation is to be held immune from criticism, nor even that faith can avoid the question, but rather that theology need not confine itself to prolegomena and may proceed to develop a positive teaching on the assumption of the reality of that revelation.[5] It is in times of crisis, when a position develops anomalies that resist resolution despite continuing efforts, that we begin to question first principles.

The reality of revelation and the justification of the assumption of revelation as a starting point for theological reflection depend upon the power of revelation to assert itself in the knowing relation. For Barth that power is the simple sovereignty of God, exercised in grace.[6] In the earliest form of critical realism that power was the ability of objects to communicate the pattern of their essence to the knower in perception and conception. In scientific realism that power is the ability of the world to confound even the most carefully erected theoretical structures by not conforming to theoretical expectation in experiment and observation. In all three cases knowledge is dependent upon the reality of that which it knows. If the reality in question does not force itself upon us in some way, then there is no knowledge of external reality, but only a knowledge of our own structure of thought. In the sciences we design our inquiries, our experiments, to put the question to nature in such a way that we are ready to accept the answer that is given even when it forces us to change our theoretical structures and their questions. For Barth it is God in self-revelation who puts the question to us.

The reality of revelation fulfills my characteristic I-a of a critical realism, the reality of the object. Revelation is the revelation of *God*. Barth's theology practices ontological realism. It also practices epistemological realism and theoretical realism, for revelation is the *revelation of God*. There is a knowledge of God and human beings can have it, although it is subordinate to God's self-knowledge.[7] This fulfills part of my characteristic I-b, the reality of knowledge of the object.

---

5. "If in faith we have moved on the *circulus veritatis Dei* we must openly and honestly let ourselves be asked whether and how far this really took place in faith." Barth, *Church Dogmatics II/1*, 246.

6. Barth, *Church Dogmatics II/1*, 69.

7. Ibid., 128, 150.

6.1.2 God Remains God

God remains the subject in all revelation.[8] This is not something that we know about God prior to revelation. It is, itself, revealed. Barth extends himself in several places to explain the meaning of Exodus 3.[9] First, God's announcement of his name to Moses in the form "I am Who I am," means that God is the one who cannot be named by another, cannot be contained in a name, cannot be controlled by a name. It is God's self-revealing announcement that even in revelation God is still the subject and not the object. Barth's insistence upon the irreducible subjecthood of God is a product of his realization that any doctrine of the knowledge of God that treats God as subject to a theory of knowledge amounts to a violation of the first commandment.[10]

This is a confession that the other which is known is truly other. It is not subject to us and to the structure of our knowing. It is what it is, whether we know and understand it or not. This means that in its reality it is constantly challenging our knowledge of it. For Barth, this is the sovereignty of God expressed as irreducible subjecthood in revelation. God is other than the creation, indeed, *wholly other* than the creation.[11] But God reveals and makes himself known in relation to the creation. This making known in revelation does not compromise the otherness of God precisely because one of the most basic things communicated in revelation is God's sovereignty and irreducible subjecthood. "In his revelation in which he distinguishes himself from all gods and idols, God is and exists only as subject. His revelation consists precisely in his refusal to be a He or an It, an object."[12]

We must understand this in the context of Barth's Kantian and Neo-Kantian background. To be an object here is to be a construction of the mind in the transcendental unity of apperception. This would not be a reality other than the knower. But it is basic to critical realism that the reality known is other than the knower. (Even introspection is a re-cursive process in which the self that is known is in a different iteration

---

8. Ibid., 10.

9. Barth, *The Göttingen Dogmatics*, 327–28; Barth, *Church Dogmatics* I/1, 316–24; Barth, *Church Dogmatics* I/2, 53; Barth, *Church Dogmatics* II/1, 60–61.

10. Barth, "The First Commandment as an Axiom of Theology," 75–77. See also Barth, *Church Dogmatics* II/1, 22.

11. Barth, *Church Dogmatics* II/1, 76–77.

12. Barth, *The Göttingen Dogmatics*, 327.

than the self that knows.) For scientific realism this is expressed in the attitude that the world is what it is, not what we wish it to be, nor even what we think we know it to be. Whenever reality does not match our theoretical understanding of it, then it is theory that must change to accommodate reality. This is why critical realism in general and scientific realism in particular regard even true and real knowledge as nonetheless incomplete and fallible. In their different fields, but for similar historical and philosophical reasons, Barth and the philosophy of science found it necessary to put behind them Neo-Kantian forms of idealist thought. If the other to be known is truly other, then there can be no guarantee that it must conform to the structure of human thought, even if that structure should turn out to be logically necessary.

It is the reality of that which is known that is at the heart of a critical understanding of the limitations of our knowledge. For Barth, the reality of God in revelation actively criticizes all our knowledge. This is expressed in its first clarity in the central theme of *Romans* in its second edition. The revelation of God is the *krisis* of all human knowledge of God. It criticizes, judges, and rejects all our presumption that we know God. All our positive knowledge of God has this negative moment at its heart and only in the act of revelation is our rejected knowledge of God reconstituted on a higher plane.[13]

Barth objects to natural theology because its triumph in the church (when this takes place) domesticates revelation and hides it.[14] Natural theology attempts to build up some kind of knowledge of God (admittedly less than that which is had in revelation) from a consideration of the nature of this world and an understanding of our nature as experiencers of the knowledge of God. The essence of Barth's complaint is that this is an attempt to achieve the knowledge of God apart from an encounter with the reality of God in action.[15] The *analogia entis* suffers this failing as well. If God can be known by analogy from the nature of being itself, which we as human beings share, then God can be known apart from his acts. But if so, then God can be known apart from our interaction with him, the object of our knowledge. Unless, of course,

13. "The dialectic of 'veiling and unveiling' in revelation . . . was taken up into his doctrine of analogy and preserved in it as its first moment." McCormack, *Barth's Critically Realistic Dialectical Theology*, 18.

14. Barth, *Church Dogmatics* II/1, 141.

15. Ibid., 85–90.

being is understood as action, in which case the *analogia entis* would be subordinated to a knowledge of God's being in action, and then we would have the knowledge of God only in interaction with him.[16] The reality of God in revelation rejects and criticizes any attempt to build up knowledge of God from below. It is not possible to prescribe in advance what we may or may not find when we encounter God in revelation, nor even how we may know God in that encounter.

The attempt to know God apart from God's acts seems to Barth as misguided as the attempt to impose Aristotelian metaphysics upon the science of physics seemed to the scientists of the seventeenth and eighteenth centuries. God remains hidden even when God reveals God's self, because revelation is the revelation of the God who veils himself when he unveils himself.[17] We know God only in the moment of gracious interaction with us (in the sense of moment of action, as in physics, rather than moment of time). This attitude Barth shares with critical realism, especially in the sciences, where history has proven that, although metaphysical commitments may be an element of any theory that can possibly be formed, they cannot be permitted to bind in advance what we may discover the world to be.

The curious outcome of these points is that Barth is critically realistic about the knowledge of God, which only exists in an encounter with the wholly other God, because human beings are not the master of the knowing relation, as demonstrated in revelation. But Barth would, in strictly Kantian terms, be willing to grant human beings the mastery, the right to impose theoretical structures, in their knowledge of the world because they share being with the world and their theoretical structures are the objectification of their epistemological subjectivity.[18] The philosophy of science is critically realistic about the knowledge of science because the world is truly other and human beings are not the master of the knowing relation, as demonstrated in the history of science. But many philosophers of science would be willing to grant human beings the mastery, the right to choose and impose theological structures upon the knowledge of God. They judge that human beings share being with God as God is primarily the objectification of their subjectivity in faith. This converse relation between Barthian theology and the philosophy of

16. Ibid., 79–84.

17. Ibid., 40–41, 55.

18. Ibid., 22, 188–89.

science is an indicator that it is time that each side in this conversation ceased to misunderstand the other.

Barth insists that the revelation of God is not and never does become the revealedness of God.

> If, therefore, we are serious about the fact that this miracle is an event, we cannot regard the presence of God's Word in the Bible as an attribute inhering once and for all in this book as such . . . We recollect, in and with the Church, that the Word of God has been heard in this book and in all parts of it . . . Yet the presence of the Word of God itself, the real and present speaking and hearing of it, is not identical with the existence of the book as such. But in this presence something takes place in and with the book, for which the book as such does give the possibility, but the reality of which cannot be anticipated or replaced by the existence of this book.[19]

It is the Holy Spirit who is the revealedness of God, not the doctrine of Holy Scripture, nor the doctrine of the Holy Spirit, nor even the Scripture itself.[20]

In volume II of the *Church Dogmatics, The Doctrine of God*, Barth says that the revelation of God as Lord, creator, reconciler, and redeemer, criticizes all our human ideas of lordship, creation, reconciliation, and redemption. Therefore, no human analogy of these can give us direct access to God's being.[21] God remains God, even in revelation. The event of revelation, the act of God in revelation, is the brute fact to which Christian theology gives witness and about which it theorizes. The relation of its doctrines to this event is analogous to the relation between matter-energy events in space-time and scientific theorizing. But this analogy only holds where Christian doctrine remains dialectical and scientific theory remains critical. The analogy would hold inside out if theology became self-righteous and identified its doctrines with revelation and science became strongly positivist and identified its theories with the nature of the world itself. The analogy fails when only one of the two is critical and self-critical.[22]

19. Barth, *Church Dogmatics* I/2, 530.

20. Thompson, *The Holy Spirit in the Theology of Karl Barth*, 20–21.

21. Barth, *Church Dogmatics* II/1, 75–79.

22. In 7.1.4 I will argue that this is what happens in T. F. Torrance's work, where the analogy is made, but the dialectical element in theology is so attenuated that it does not hold.

Barth's refusal to confound the object of knowledge, God in revelation, with the human response to that event is also present in the section of volume I of the *Church Dogmatics* entitled "The Revelation of God as the Abolition of Religion."[23] The church is only the *locus* of true religion.[24] Revelation is the reality to which religion refers. Religion is the theoretical and practical response to that reality. But the reality retains priority and always criticizes the theoretical structures which are used to describe it. Barth accepts this radically. Christianity is a religion, with all the limitations and faults common to such, and is not to be identified directly with the revelation to which it is a response. This amounts to a critically realistic interpretation of the *semper reformanda*: the church that has been reformed must nevertheless always be reformed according to the Word of God. Working scientists take the same attitude towards their theories. Scientific knowledge, which has been revised in the face of observation and experiment, must nevertheless always be revised in response to further observation and experiment. The necessity of further revision or reformation is not taken as evidence of impropriety in the knowledge that we have in hand, but only as evidence of the character of the relationship between knowledge and that to which it refers.

Scientific realism also considers that the reality of the world criticizes all our knowledge of it, but in a slightly different manner. For Barth, God in self-revelation is a person actively engaged in criticizing the human response even in making himself known.[25] Scientific realism certainly considers the world to be active in its interaction with us. But it is not active as a person, with will and intent. (Or if so, we haven't discovered it and have, as yet, no reason to hypothesize it. The religious supposition that we should hypothesize it is bad theology for all the reasons given in Barth's critique of natural theology.) Our theoretical structures are criticized by other theoretical structures at the point in a scientific discussion where it is seriously debated whether one theory should supplant another. The

23. Abolition translates *Aufhebung*, which, for Barth, is "affirmed, negated, and then reconstituted on a higher plane." Hunsinger, *How to Read Karl Barth*, 98; see similar locutions on pp. 193 and 223. Abolition is correct as far as it goes, but it only goes part way. It is also "dissolved" as a partnership or a marriage, "annulled" or "invalidated" as a contract, "rescinded" or "repealed" as a law. But it is also, in other meanings, to lift or to raise up, to keep or to save, or even to "put up" as jam or preserves.

24. Barth, *Church Dogmatics* I/2, 298.

25. "The knowledge of God is unlike all other knowledge in that its object is the living Lord of the knowing man." Barth, *Church Dogmatics* II/1, 21.

event that is the world is the ground upon which the debate takes place and the reference for testing truth claims in both theories. The history of science makes it clear that the cogency and applicability of the criticisms of one theory against another are a product of the world first behaving in such a way as to produce anomalies in our theoretical description of the world. The mere fact of another theory that criticizes some scientific theory is not sufficient to force that scientific theory to revise itself. But the actual behavior of the world to produce an anomaly in our theoretical description of it is sufficient reason to consider a revision of theory. The persistence of anomalies despite efforts to resolve them is sufficient reason to try to develop either a revised theory or a replacement theory.

That God remains God even in revelation, and that the church's doctrines do not possess the authority of revelation, but stand under it and under its judgment, is at the heart of the critical element in Barth. Dialectic in theology, and in particular in the doctrine of revelation, is the theorized form of this critical element and constitutes Barth's critical theory, my characteristic II-b of critical realism. In the critically realistic philosophy of science the history of science and fallible epistemology constitute the critical element. Again, the difference lies in the object of knowledge. In theology the critical element is a person and the critical theory is a response to God. In the philosophy of science the critical element is a human act, but it is a response to the actions of the world recorded in the history of science.

Be it noted here that Barth's critique of natural theology also works as a respectful recognition of the freedom of the sciences in their own spheres, since it invalidates any attempt by theology to co-opt the sciences to do its own work. I hope that it will be clearly understood that I am using mathematics and science in this work as analogies to explain the meaning and intent of Barth's work. They in no way prove that it is right or demonstrate its validity. But the existence and the validity of the analogies (if the reader agrees that they are valid) do argue that theology done in the school with Barth is a legitimate participant in the current dialogue between science and theology.

6.1.3 Indirect Identity in Revelation

The God who remains subject in all revelation nonetheless also makes himself objective for us in revelation so that we may truly know him.[26]

26. "He is really object, in the same way as this may be said of other objects of man's

God makes himself objective without becoming a *mere* object by becoming indirectly identical with a creaturely medium of revelation.[27] This identity is and remains indirect because God is still sovereign and also still other than the creaturely medium in which revelation takes place.[28] But it is identity because God chooses to become one with it, to identify with it.[29] In this identity our knowledge of God is made to correspond to God's own self-knowledge. The creaturely medium becomes transparent in revelation because God makes it to correspond to himself.[30] Thus God unveils himself. But the creaturely medium remains a veil in that it *corresponds* to God and is not the immediate and direct presence of God.[31] The recognition of this indirectness is a criterion by which to recognize the knowledge of God. "At bottom, knowledge of God in faith is always this indirect knowledge of God, knowledge of God in His works, and in these particular works—in the determining and using of certain creaturely realities to bear witness to the divine objectivity. What distinguishes faith from unbelief, erroneous faith, and superstition is that it is content with this indirect knowledge of God."[32]

Barth's language of veiling and unveiling is particularly dialectical. He frequently uses paradoxical locutions such as, "the unveiling of God in his veiling or the veiling of God in his unveiling."[33] The dialectical point can be maintained, yet the paradoxical language mitigated, in the following way. God is both infinite and complex in a way that makes God inaccessible to our cognitive machinery. God arranges a correspondence

---

cognition: as the opposite of another, which man can distinguish from himself and from which man can distinguish himself, which he can therefore perceive and contemplate and of which he can speak. For if this is not the case he does not know God." Barth, *Church Dogmatics II/1*, 205.

27. Barth, *Church Dogmatics II/1*, 199, 201.

28. Ibid., 52.

29. This locution in theology must not be misunderstood as a reference to the philosophical and logical principle of identity. In that technical sense, God is *not* identical with any of the creaturely media. But that is the point of recognizing revelation as a miracle. God's *act* of identifying with the creaturely medium, and making himself known faithfully thereby, is the identity in question, which is only analogous to logical identity.

30. McCormack, *Barth's Critically Realistic Dialectical Theology*, 17, 159; Chia, *Revelation and Theology*, 105.

31. See Barth, *Church Dogmatics I/1*, 162–76 for an extended discussion of veiling and unveiling.

32. Barth, *Church Dogmatics II/1*, 17.

33. Barth, *Church Dogmatics I/1*, 175.

between some feature of the world that is accessible to us and himself. That correspondence is itself the veil, whether it be expressed as the flesh of Jesus, the history of Israel, the preaching of the prophets, or the proclamation of the gospel. The correspondence veils God because it is a correspondence, a finite, or, at best, denumerably infinite, *model* of who God is and what God is doing. God's self remains beyond our grasp and the correspondence, precisely because it is the correspondence that we grasp, hides whatever may be beyond our grasp.[34] But the correspondence is also what unveils God, for, in this context, to have a correspondence is to have knowledge. The correspondence is to God's own knowledge of himself in revelation and thus qualifies as true referential knowledge. The veil in the veiling and unveiling is analogous to the duality of a model in the model theory of knowledge. But this knowledge comes to us in such a way that we are forced to admit that one of the things this knowledge knows is that there is more there than this knowledge knows.[35]

The idea of the veiling and unveiling of God in revelation has this critically realistic feature: it treats the knowledge that we have in theology as co-determined by the reality which is the object of our discourse and the cultural background and philosophical presuppositions which we bring to that discourse. We cannot know God pure and simple apart from any cultural background or without presuppositions. These things are part of the fabric that constitutes the veil. This is why Barth says that God never unveils without veiling. But God uses the veil and gives it meanings which correspond to his own self-knowledge and which it does not have in itself. This is why Barth says that God unveils *by* veiling. Our knowledge of God is co-determined and God is rightly counted as one of the determinants of that knowledge.

It might easily be presumed that Barth would deny this co-determination because God is the Lord, and entirely determines the knowledge of God in revelation. It is certainly true that he argues that the Lord God entirely determines this knowledge, for the readiness of God to be

34. "To receive the Word of God does not mean on either side to be able to see and know and state the relation between the two sides, to be able to say why and how far the veiled Word now means unveiling or the unveiled Word means veiling . . . The speech of God is and remains a mystery to the extent that its totality as such, and hence with all the weight and seriousness of God's Word, is always manifest to us only on one side and always remains hidden on the other." Barth, *Church Dogmatics* I/1, 174.

35. "Knowing God we necessarily know His hiddenness." Barth, *Church Dogmatics* II/1, 184.

known includes the readiness of human beings to know God, and the human readiness is entirely *subject* to God's readiness to be known. But precisely because the readiness of God to be known *includes* the human, it also *establishes* the human, for in grace God's readiness to be known is readiness to be known *by* human beings.[36] God's adoption and adaptation of our human knowing apparatus is God's acceptance and establishment of the co-determination of our knowledge of God.

> God is known only by God. We do not know Him, then, in virtue of the views and concepts with which in faith we attempt to respond to His revelation. But we also do not know him without making use of his permission and obeying his command to undertake this attempt. The success of this undertaking, and therefore the veracity of our human knowledge of God, consists in the fact that our viewing and conceiving is adopted and determined to participation in the truth of God by God himself in grace.[37]

The correspondence present in the veiling and unveiling of revelation is both realistic and critical. As God's act of self-revelation it is a complete correspondence because God reveals not this and that, but self, self alone, the whole self.[38] But the correspondence of our thought to God in theology is analogy, partial correspondence and agreement, similarity. "In Himself He is quite different from what He is in our work. Therefore the relationship between what He is in Himself and what He is in our work is only a relationship of similarity." Nonetheless, "on the basis of this similarity there is true human knowledge of God." What is said about God is truth in Him, in revelation, but in us it is contingent, improper, and in error.[39] We are forced to use the concept of analogy, of similarity, by the truth of both the veiling and the unveiling of God in revelation.[40] We are given the knowledge of God in the same faculties for knowledge and understanding that we use for all other knowledge.[41] By God's grace the knowledge corresponds to God's being. But because God's grace is knowledge of God given to *human beings* the correspondence is partial and can only be called analogy.

36. Ibid., 126, 128.

37. Ibid., 179.

38. Barth, *The Göttingen Dogmatics*, 88–94.

39. Barth, *Church Dogmatics II/1*, 225–29. The quotation is on 227.

40. Ibid., 234, 236.

41. Ibid., 15, 21, 181–82.

Antirealistic positions usually deny correspondence. Naively realistic positions take correspondence so much for granted that it becomes direct identity.[42] Both the original form of critical realism and scientific realism work with the idea of correspondence truth. But both of them also find the correspondence in a medium, even as Barth does. In the early form of critical realism that medium is psychical existences, units and structures of thought in our own minds. In scientific realism that medium is the theoretical entities and structures we create in our minds in order to understand the world and its behavior.

Antirealists deny the meaningfulness of the notion of correspondence by pointing out that: "To single out a correspondence between two domains one needs some independent access to both domains."[43] But independent access to the noumenal realm is precisely what we do not have. Our access is only through our knowledge. But the correspondence in question is the correspondence of our knowledge to noumenal reality, so that the access we have is not independent. With Barth it is also the case that we have no independent access to God's self. Our only access to God is in the knowledge of God given in revelation. But it is precisely this knowledge whose correspondence is in question.

Barth's doctrine of revelation accepts these limits. Barth does not assert that we have independent access to God. On the plane of human knowledge we have no right to claim correspondence between our knowledge of God and God himself. This is part of the reason that Barth is so firmly set against natural theology. But the correspondence of which Barth speaks is not one that we create in our minds by our powers through our independent access to both domains. The correspondence of the creaturely medium to God in the veiling and unveiling of revelation is one that is created by God in the act of revelation.[44] God does have independent access to both domains. God knows God fully and apart from any creaturely medium. God knows his own creatures. God knows any and every creaturely medium that he may take to himself in an act of revelation. Moreover, all of these things are in God's power. God's own

---

42. This is the substance of the criticism of the "new realism" by the American authors in Drake, et al., *Essays in Critical Realism*, 5–10.

43. Putnam, *Reason, Truth and History*, 74.

44. McCormack, *Barth's Critically Realistic Dialectical Theology*, 14–20, points this out in great detail. The key point is that the analogy of faith is not a theological method, nor an inherent structure of human thought, but an *event* in God's act of revelation.

being is self-determined, as Barth describes it. The creature is determined by God in creation. The creaturely medium is determined by God in providence.[45] The independent access necessary for correspondence is real and present, but it is present on God's side of the division. This is why Barth speaks of our being grasped by revelation from the other side.

Knowledge whose correspondence depends upon our being grasped from the other side is not knowledge that is guaranteed by the nature and structure of our thought. In Kantian terms, knowledge that is guaranteed by the nature and structure of our thought is theoretical knowledge, which is, in the end, only knowledge *of* the nature and structure of our thought, and not of things as they may be in themselves. At best, it is knowledge of the way that things may appear in the structure of our knowledge. In terms of scientific realism, knowledge that is guaranteed by the nature and structure of our thought is axiomatic mathematical knowledge, which is formal in nature and empty of content. When those formal structures are applied to empirical reality, then we have knowledge of the world, but that knowledge is thereby fallible, being dependent upon both the nature and structure of our thought and the nature and structure of the world that interacts with us in the field and in the laboratory. Critical realism understands that the real knowledge that we have of another is, from our side, always fallible knowledge whose truth and trustworthiness are dependent upon that other that we are making knowledge claims about.

This is the answer now to the inherent problem of critical realism, to explain how knowledge that is admitted to be both mediated and fallible can be claimed to be true.[46] All our knowledge is a construction with which we attempt to model some reality. Being a construction makes knowledge mediated. If the construction corresponds to the reality, then it will be true. If some of the realities which we model are truly other than ourselves, then when we judge them to be other than ourselves, we are judging that in any difference between our model and the actual behavior of the reality when we encounter it, the model is to be adjusted to maintain its correspondence to the reality being modeled. This means that we adopt fallibility as a critically realistic criteria for true knowledge of a truly other.[47] Infallible knowledge, if there be any such, can only

45. Barth, *Church Dogmatics II/1*, 59.

46. Posed in 2.1.

47. Which Barth does as well. See 6.2.4.

be knowledge of the inner structure of our knowledge. The problem is inherent because of how critical realism understands the idea of truth.

The Word of God is necessary for knowledge of God, for if God does not reveal, then nothing that we take as knowledge of God can be trusted not to be merely the knowledge of a power greater than ourselves.[48] Between our finite selves and the transcendent God there is room for an infinity of infinities. The phrase infinity of infinities is not poetic rhetoric, but mathematical exactitude. In modern set theory, based upon the work of Georg Cantor, infinities of different sizes, each greater than all those preceding, can be built upon one another forever.[49] In this world and this life we are finite beings. Even in the resurrection, if we take seriously the notion of the resurrection of the body, though we shall become infinite we shall only be denumerably infinite.[50] This is the smallest infinite cardinal number, that of the counting numbers. But if God is transcendent, then God must be infinite at least on the order of a regular inaccessible cardinal number. A regular inaccessible cardinal number is an infinite number that cannot be reached by any operation of set theory starting from any smaller set or number. It cannot even be reached as the limit of any series unless the cardinal number of the series is equal to that of the regular inaccessible cardinal number that we are trying to reach. The existence of a regular inaccessible cardinal number cannot be proven in set theory,[51] as indeed the existence of God cannot be proven in this finite world,[52] but some of the characteristics that a

48. "The possibility of knowledge of God's word lies in God's word and nowhere else." Barth, *Church Dogmatics* I/1, 22.

49. Boyer and Merzbach, *A History of Mathematics*, 563–69; Boyer, *History of the Calculus*, 296–300.

50. This is because human thought, occurring in and mediated through a human brain, can be described mathematically in the field of discrete mathematics, which is confined to the realm of the denumerably infinite.

51. These assertions about set theory, and the ones that follow are not speculations, but standard features of set theory as it is taught at the upper division or graduate level. See Boulos and Jeffrey, *Computability and Logic* and Hrbacek and Jech, *Introduction to Set Theory*. My application of these mathematical themes to Barth's theology is, of course, my own.

52. Barth, *Anselm*, 171, where he says at the end of his discussion: "That Anselm's Proof of the Existence of God has repeatedly been called the 'Ontological' proof of God, that commentators have refused to see that it is in a different book altogether from the well known teaching of Descartes and Leibnitz, that anyone could seriously think that it is even remotely affected by what Kant put forward against these doctrines—all that is so much nonsense on which no more words ought to be wasted."

regular inaccessible cardinal number must have if it does exist can be proven. Similarly, even though God's existence cannot be proven, some of the properties God must have if given in self-revelation can be proven on the basis of the content of that revelation.[53]

One of the properties of a regular inaccessible cardinal number is that there must be an infinity of infinite numbers bigger than the denumerable infinity of the counting numbers and smaller than the regular inaccessible cardinal number. Another of the things that must be true of it is that any characteristic or property that such a number can have that can be described by a finite or even a denumerably infinite mind must also be a characteristic or property of some infinite number less than the regular inaccessible cardinal number itself. This means that any characteristic that we can ascribe to God may be a characteristic that can also be found in some infinite being that is nonetheless less than God. Thus no knowledge that we can have of God can be trusted simply because of its own character as knowledge not to be knowledge of something that is less than God, even though it may be knowledge of something greater than ourselves.[54] Unless God reveals we cannot have any way of knowing that what we know is God and not some other. Even if God does reveal, the knowledge that we have in revelation is still, as human knowledge, only denumerably infinite at best and it remains the case that the only way that we have of knowing that knowledge as knowledge of God is by faith, by trust in the one who makes, gives, and renews such knowledge. Any such knowledge cannot be justified as knowledge by the form of its content or by the method of thought by which we obtain and hold it. It must be justified by its object fulfilling the conditions for the truth of its statements.[55]

---

53. Barth, *Anselm*, 171: "God gave himself as the object of his [Anselm's] knowledge and God illumined him that he might know him as object. Apart from this event there is no proof of the existence, that is of the reality of God. But in the power of this event there is a proof which is worthy of gratitude."

54. Barth, *Church Dogmatics* I/1, 164: "For according to all that we can know of the how of the Word of God, one thing is ruled out. It cannot be an entity which we can demarcate from other entities and thereby objectify . . . All our delimitations can only seek to be signals or alarms to draw attention to the fact that God's Word is and remains God's, not bound and not to be attached to this thesis or that antithesis."

55. I think that it might be possible to make an argument that the existence of a transcendent God *cannot* be proven modeled on the proof that set theory cannot, within its own bounds, prove the existence of a regular inaccessible cardinal number. In natural language such an argument would show that if we could prove the existence

This is a mathematical model of why Barth insists so strongly all through *Romans* that every knowledge that we have of God that is built up from ourselves, or from this world, or even from the presuppositions of reason as a possible form of human thought, is still only knowledge of the No-god of this world. It is also thereby a model of one of the reasons for Barth's uncompromising resistance to natural theology. It also models why Barth insists in the *Church Dogmatics* that even the knowledge we have of God in revelation, if we take it to be a permanent possession, at our disposal to do with as we wish, is still only knowledge of the No-god of this world. The knowledge of God can only be justified by faith. But justification by faith is the content of the knowledge of God. Therefore, in the knowledge of God, the content, action, and justification of the knowledge of God are one.[56] The knowledge of God is thereby analogous to the Trinity. This is no surprise, as Barth has insisted from the time of the *Göttingen Dogmatics* that "the content of revelation is God."[57] In the *Church Dogmatics* Barth argues in depth that revelation itself is the root of the doctrine of the trinity because revelation is the act of the triune God.[58] Again, these mathematical ideas are only a model, and not the justification, of what Barth is saying about the knowledge of God that we have in revelation.[59] The source and justification of Barth's doctrine of revelation, if it is justified at all, is the actual content of the revelation to which Barth refers.

---

of a transcendent God within the bounds of human reasoning, then we would also have proved that such a God is not transcendent. Since this would make the proof self-contradictory, the proof of the existence would be rendered invalid. If God is transcendent then the only possible knowledge of God as *God* is by revelation. All other forms of knowledge of God are incompetent to establish that it is God that they know, and not some other. They may, perhaps, be taken up and used by revelation as a medium, but even such use does not give them the power to reveal.

56. "*God* reveals himself. He reveals himself *through himself*. He reveals *himself*. If we really want to understand revelation in terms of its subject, i.e., God, then the first thing that we have to realize is that this subject, God, the revealer, is identical with his act in revelation and also identical with its effect." Barth, *Church Dogmatics I/1*, 296.

57. Barth, *The Göttingen Dogmatics*, 88.

58. Barth, *Church Dogmatics I/1*, 121.

59. "We must not, therefore, base the hiddenness of God on the inapprehensibility of the infinite, the absolute, . . . etc. For all this . . . is the product of human reason, in spite of and in its supposed inapprehensibility. It is not, therefore, identical with God." Barth, *Church Dogmatics II/1*, 188.

Moreover, the use of this model illustrates, in both its content and its application, how and why Barth's doctrine of revelation is critically realistic. It is not so from the beginning, as a method for obtaining knowledge, for the knowledge to which it refers cannot be obtained from below by any means, whether it be mathematical proof or philosophical critical realism. Rather, it is critically realistic about the character of the knowledge that we have in revelation, the knowledge that takes possession of us, and it is the nature and character of that knowledge that forces us to be critical, not realism that enables us to obtain the knowledge. This, too, parallels the situation in the sciences and the philosophy of science. Scientific realism is a thesis about the nature and character of the knowledge that we have in the sciences, not a prescriptive method for obtaining that knowledge. Scientific knowledge is obtained by any method that comes to hand because it is an investigation into an unknown object. It cannot be obtained without method, but neither can it be limited to any given method.[60] This necessity that reality imposes upon us, to sit loose to our method, is a feature of scientific knowledge, even as it is of the knowledge that we have in theological reflection upon the Word of God.

For this reason Barth acknowledges plainly that everyone who approaches the Scripture to interpret it does so with some sort of philosophy, either more or less explicit, not excepting even the most biblicist of interpreters. The received view of science envisioned theories as things that were only constructed after the facts had been gathered and inductive generalizations about them made. Scientific realism understands that scientists are indoctrinated into the theoretical structures of their specialties, and that facts are theory-laden.

That the Word of God reveals itself precisely to such theory-laden interpreters, for there are no others, means that every manner of thought that we bring with ourselves in reflecting upon Scripture can only have the character of an essay or an hypothesis. Scientific realism considers hypothetical method to be characteristic of the sciences. It is the appropriate way to approach an unknown reality or one only partly known. Hypothetical method coupled with the unknown character, or inexhaustible complexity, of the object under investigation is the reason that "anything goes."

---

60. This is the respect in which even Feyerabend can be treated as a sort of critical realist. See Feyerabend, *Against Method*, 249.

If they are not already so, the philosophies with which we approach Scripture will be forced to become, not merely critical, but also self-critical. For in being used to approach and interpret Scripture such philosophies are subjected to criticism by Scripture. Danger arises when such philosophies are not treated as hypotheses, but are posited absolutely. This holds in scientific practice and in critical realism as well. No matter how necessary they may seem, the history of science has demonstrated many times the danger of positing theories absolutely.

But when not posited absolutely the philosophies with which we approach Scripture are hypotheses. The supposition that the necessity of holding our philosophies as hypotheses means that it would be even better to withhold our hypotheses and try to approach Scripture as blank slates is nonsense. In the first place, we cannot do it. In the second, it would not be good even if we could. It is necessary to venture such hypotheses in order to practice obedience in the task of interpreting Scripture.[61] We must put ourselves at risk of being changed in order to learn from and interpret Scripture. Even so, it is necessary in science and philosophy as well, once we have learned not to hold our theories absolutely, to venture our hypotheses boldly. It is our tenacity in holding theories and our boldness in advancing hypotheses that expose the accumulation of anomalies and sharpens the crisis that leads to new theories, and more importantly, new knowledge of the world.

In theology these attempts and their risks are justified by grace.

> I shall have to remember that grace is implied if my attempt and therefore my mode of thought can become useful to this end. After each attempt I shall also have to be willing and ready to proceed to new attempts. And I cannot exclude the possibility that the same attempt can and must be ventured with the application of quite other philosophies than mine. Therefore I shall not radically deny to other philosophies than my own the character of useful hypotheses in the service of the same end.[62]

Barth takes this very seriously and understands it as applying even to his own theological project. He shows that in sitting loose to his own Kantian foundations he is also aware that other structures of thought are possible. He admits that, "there is no essential reason for preferring

---

61. For the preceding three paragraphs see Barth, *Church Dogmatics* I/2, 728–32.

62. Barth, *Church Dogmatics* I/2, 731 This theme is also repeated throughout chapter V: The Knowledge of God in Barth, *Church Dogmatics* II/1.

one of these schemes to another."[63] This is a product of his conviction that the truly active party to the knowing relation here envisioned is God. Since one of the functions of the Word of God is to convert sinners, it must be supposed that even if one were to come to the scripture with a philosophy that other interpreters or even the same interpreter at a later time might regard as largely erroneous, the effect of Scripture upon that philosophy in the course of the work of interpretation will modify the philosophy so that it becomes more suitable to its material.[64] But even good theology, which has been subjected to the criticism of Scripture and modified thereby, is still only an essay or an hypothesis in the continuing work of interpreting Scripture.[65] Critical realism is not a philosophical method for producing theories that are beyond criticism, but an understanding of the critically fallible character of all theories, no matter how advanced they may become.

Because the end result of Barth's work is vast, detailed, architectonic, and systematic it is easy to suppose that it is a system; that it has a fixed and final philosophical core from which the whole system derives by exposition and development. But Barth denies that his work constitutes a system, even if he admits as one of its canons the duty to be systematic.[66] Barth intends quite consciously the humility that is implied in doing theology in a critically realistic way. But he considers that such

63. Barth, *Church Dogmatics* I/2, 733. An example of this is given in Barth, *Church Dogmatics* IV/1, 274–83, where, after developing a portion of the doctrine of reconciliation in great detail in the form of forensic justification he sketches two other forms that the doctrine might take without loss.

64. Barth, *Church Dogmatics* I/2, 734: "We can say, therefore, that the use of a human scheme of thought in the service of scriptural exegesis is legitimate and fruitful when it is a critical use, implying that the object of criticism is not Scripture, but our own scheme of thought, and that Scripture is naturally the subject of this criticism."

65. Barth, *Church Dogmatics* I/2, 734: "Theology itself, which in itself and apart from its subject can only be the fulfillment of a human way of thought, and therefore a kind of philosophy, should not forget its hypothetical, relative, and incidental character in the exposition of Scripture." See also ibid., 733: "The necessity which is there is particular: in a specific situation this or that particular mode of thought can be particularly useful in scriptural exegesis, and it can then become a command to avail oneself of it in this particular instance. But it has always proved fatal when this particular necessity is elevated at once into a general one, when this or that mode of thought is enjoined upon all, when, by means of this particular mode of thought it is hoped to apprehend and interpret all the words of Scripture, or even one such word fully, and when it is treated as normative for all situations and times."

66. Barth, *Church Dogmatics* I/2, 181, 280; Barth, *Church Dogmatics* I/1, 73.

humility no more bars him from producing an extended, detailed, and architectonic work than it does in the physical sciences.

Barth's humble attitude towards the theoretical structures used to understand and interpret Scripture is not merely critical, or self-critical, for that might easily lead to a kind of theology that is endlessly trapped in the work of prolegomena. It is critical and self-critical as a response to its own actual history of encounter with its object, an object that has proved itself to be a subject that is able to exert itself in the knowing relation. It is the reality of the object as a subject that communicates itself that forces theology to be self-critical, not a general philosophical rule about the nature of human knowing. The rule may be assumed to be general, as it usually is in the sciences, but it arises from a specific history, and not from abstract speculation. Such humility is essential for any knower who wishes to know something that is truly other, as do the physical sciences, or wholly other, as does theology. The fallibility of human knowledge is a product of that which also gives it any possibility of being true, its dependence upon the other that it knows.

Indirect identity in revelation, the *Realdialektik* of the veiling and unveiling of God, falls under my critically realistic characteristic II-a, mediated knowledge. It corresponds to Niiniluoto's R4 thesis, fallible realism. Indirect *identity* in revelation is semantic realism, Niiniluoto's R1 thesis and thus falls under my I-b, real knowledge. Dialectical theology, a human response to the *Realdialektik* of the veiling and unveiling of God, is the heart of Barth's critical realism and corresponds to Niiniluoto's R5 thesis, falling under my II-b, critical theory.

6.2 THE CRITICALLY REALISTIC SHAPE OF BARTH'S UNDERSTANDING OF THE TASK OF THEOLOGY

In 1929 Barth gave a series of lectures in Dortmund later published under the title "Schicksal und Idee in der Theologie." In these lectures Barth pulls together in the most self-conscious fashion the themes that give us reason to call him a critical realist: realism, critical idealism, and dialectical theology. In his 1986 introduction to the English translation of these lectures by George Hunsinger, S. W. Sykes very clearly calls Barth a critical realist.[67]

67. Thomas F. Torrance was probably the first person to understand Barth as a critical realist. His writings about Barth throughout the sixties and the seventies continually

> Barth presents himself, in philosophical terms, as a critical real-
> ist, that is to say one who primarily is concerned with actuality
> and occurrence, but who acknowledges the necessity of attend-
> ing to the conditions and limitations of human knowing. Even
> when it is faithful to its own business theology cannot escape the
> problem of philosophy . . .
>
>   At root this is the position of the critical realist who asserts
> the irreplaceability and cognitive content of metaphorical lan-
> guage in both science and theology and decries the possibility
> of adequate "translation" into non-metaphorical speculative ab-
> stractions of philosophical origin.[68]

A close look at these lectures is therefore in order.

First of all, Barth has chosen the terms "fate" and "idea" as indicating the more directly experienced and lived version of what could also
be called "'reality and truth,' or 'nature and spirit,' or 'the objective and
the non-objective,' or . . . 'experience and reason,' . . . or 'realism and
nominalism,' or 'romanticism and idealism.'"[69] This catalogue of terms,
offering an attempt at an extensive definition of those things of which
Barth wants to speak in this article, amounts to "realism" and "critical
idealism" in the terms that I have been using. In the course of the lectures Barth both affirms and denies the propriety of each of these terms
for a theology that attempts to speak of God's self-revelation. But the
need to speak of both he regards as inherent in any serious reflection
upon human experience.[70]

Barth binds these two—realism and critical idealism—together in
a dialectical relationship. If he had been doing philosophy, rather than
theology, it might have been conceivable that he would have integrated
the two into a synthesis, which he might have called "critical realism."

---

suggest that Barth's procedure in theology was, in the best sense, scientific. See several of his articles collected from the sixties and seventies in Torrance, *Karl Barth*, 14,
52–60, 62–63, 68. See especially p. 58, where, in an introduction to another work first
published in 1962, Torrance calls Barth's position "Critical Realism in Theology." But
see my critique of Torrance's understanding of Barth's critical realism in chapter 7.1.4.

68. Sykes, "Introduction," 12, 18–19.

69. Barth, "Fate and Idea," 25.

70. "Whenever it probes more or less deeply into human existence, philosophy
eventually strikes upon what these and similar concepts indicate, namely, the two
boundaries of human thought. It strikes, in other words, upon the problem of how
these two boundaries are related to one another, upon the question of their priority
(because one might take precedence over the other), and upon the problem of their
higher unity." Ibid., 25.

Certainly the two work to criticize one another and each necessarily attempts to bring the other under its own concepts.[71] But because Barth is concerned with realism and critical idealism in *theology*, because the object of discourse is not the world and the knowledge which human beings have of the world in which they dwell, but rather, God's self-revelation, Barth regards any attempt at synthesis as illegitimate with respect to this object, and this is why he binds the two together dialectically rather than synthetically.

This does not mean that Barth does not appreciate any possibility of synthesis at all. He regards the possibility of a synthesis as a legitimate philosophical possibility with respect to our knowledge of the world. Indeed, it is a possibility that he considers to be almost necessary in philosophical discourse. He says that "the relationship between fate and idea is not symmetrical . . . Knowledge is first and foremost a knowledge of experience or of existing reality. When it proceeds to clarify itself critically, by advancing into knowledge of truth, then that is simply a second step which presupposes the first."[72] But he also acknowledges that from the point of view of idealism the asymmetry may well be on the other side. When idealism "discovers itself as a criterion that must at least be taken into account" then "whether openly or secretly, it discovers itself as original and superior to mere being."[73]

For Barth it is not merely an historical accident that in realism a critical corrective and in idealism a realistic corrective tend to arise. "The material itself apparently requires each to deal with the other's concern."[74] The context of this sentence, a discussion of the ways in which the mutual interaction of realism and idealism in theology is parallel and has connections to that same mutual interaction in philosophy, makes it clear that the "material itself" of which he speaks here is our lived experience, whether of the world or of the Word of God. Moreover, good philosophy, of either kind, tends to include its opposite dialectically.[75]

71. Ibid., 52: "We have also observed how with equal strength a corrective tends to arise in each case. The material itself apparently requires each to deal with the other's concern. Each side seems impelled to bring the other's opposing thesis somehow under its own denominator."

72. Ibid., 32–33.

73. Ibid., 43.

74. Ibid., 52.

75. "In philosophy such an inclusion always means proposing and promoting, or at least attempting, a synthesis—that is, some third postulate superior to the two opposites.

The way that Barth describes the relation between realism and idealism here makes it clear that the synthesis towards which he expects philosophy to work is what we have come to call critical realism. He regards pure realism as too naïve[76] and pure idealism as too formal and empty to be good philosophy.[77] If Barth had known of critical realism as we have described it, he would probably have recognized it as the philosophical synthesis of which he is speaking here. But he was probably unaware of the early critical realism of the American pragmatists, even though it was already in print at the time Barth was doing this work. If he had been aware of it, the inadequate understanding of Kant that so strongly colors that work would very likely have made it difficult for Barth to recognize it as a form of the philosophical synthesis of which he was speaking. The critical realism that arose in the philosophy of science in the 60s and after came too late for Barth to be aware of it. Barth shows clearly that he was unaware of critical realism as a philosophical movement when he expresses doubt that philosophy ever has produced any synthesis between realism and idealism.[78]

But even if critical realism, as we understand it now, had been available to Barth, he would have regarded it as a philosophical synthesis that had no necessary claim upon theology. "Theology may be oriented toward realism or idealism, but as theology it has neither the *primum* nor the *secundum* as an overarching *tertium*. It has no *tertium* at all—neither to propose and promote, nor to suggest, nor even to approximate. The art of theology cannot be the art of synthesis."[79] This serves to remind us once again that *Barth* is not using critical realism to do theology. We are attributing a critically realistic character to his theology, but that theology is originally, and remains throughout his work, dialectical theology.[80]

To that extent the realist makes a crucial concession to the idealist, and vice versa. For each would claim—what philosophy has not?—that from its own standpoint the dualism of the two boundaries can be surveyed, criticized, and ultimately overcome." Ibid., 52.

76. "As already hinted, even realist theology cannot be good theology without drawing heavily on idealism." Ibid., 43.

77. "Anyone who wanted to reject this position [realism] *in globo* would not be a particularly good theologian, not even a particularly good Protestant theologian. Instead he would show himself to be an idealist, and not a particularly sophisticated one at that." Ibid., 37.

78. Ibid., 55.

79. Ibid., 53.

80. McCormack, *Barth's Critically Realistic Dialectical Theology*, 464.

In order to see clearly why it is legitimate to call this dialectical theology critically realistic we need to examine (1) why it is realistic and how Barth is dialectical about its realism, (2) why it is critical and how Barth is dialectical about its critical character, and (3) why it is dialectical and how Barth is dialectical about its dialectical character. Then we will be able to see why being dialectical makes Barth critically realistic.

6.2.1 Dialectical Realism in Theology

Dialectical theology means, in the first instance, that having encountered and experienced the Word of God, theology is bound thereby to give witness to that Word despite the fact that what is proclaimed in that Word is the God who is beyond the power of our speech.[81] God proves that he is a God of such transcendence by coming to us in speech that in and of itself, not merely before but also during and after God's use of it to come to us, is an inadequate vehicle by means of which to go to God. This dialectical dilemma is the heart of dialectical theology, and the method of statement and counter statement so commonly associated with the early days of dialectical theology is a mere methodological reflection of the dilemma.[82] This dialectical dilemma controls Barth's understanding of revelation and his understanding of the nature and character of the knowledge that we have in revelation. But it also produces the critically realistic features that Barth's theology exhibits so clearly in "Fate and Idea."

Barth says that "theology has God as its object only to the extent that it strives to have absolutely no other origin than the communication which God actually gives of himself."[83] Though this is, in brief, only a statement of the necessity for and character of dialectical theology, it has a realistic implication. God acts, and theology is a response to God's action. But the action of God as a determining factor in theology is a causal reason in justification of theology's right to refer to God realistically. As we saw in chapter 4, even in the sciences, the power of the objects we

---

81. This characterization is, of course, an interpretation of Barth famous words from "The Word of God and the Task of Ministry," in Barth, *The Word of God and the Word of Man*: "As ministers we ought to speak of God. We are human, however, and so cannot speak of God. We ought therefore to recognize both our obligation and our inability and by that very recognition give God the glory." This dialectical dilemma persists even in the positive and highly structured *Church Dogmatics*.

82. McCormack, *Barth's Critically Realistic Dialectical Theology*, 18–19.

83. Barth, "Fate and Idea," 27.

study to be rightfully listed among the various causes of our knowledge is a justification for referring to those objects realistically.

Making this claim, that God acts and that theology is entitled to speak of God's act, involves a difficulty, even though it is a realistic claim. The difficulty is that we are making a claim that is not based upon the regular and ordinary course of events, but rather upon a miracle.[84]

The miracle in question here is that the theologian speaks of God by virtue of God's self-revealing act. If God does not so act then the speaking of the theologian is subject to Feuerbach's criticism that it is but speech about humanity writ large. It is realistic to make a claim that suffers this difficulty because the difficulty, the miracle, is intrinsic to the object being spoken of. The truth of the claim is dependent upon the actuality of the event of which the theologian speaks. Realistic speech is speech that depends upon that to which it refers. But note that even though Barth speaks here of "the presupposition of divine miracle" he is not taking this miracle for granted. If Barth were taking the miracle for granted he would not speak of the miracle as a *limit* to the theologian's speaking of God; he would not call attention to the doom of failure that threatens the theologian's speaking of God. Barth does not treat the pre-supposition of miracle with the casual hubris of a fundamentalist, but applies the presupposition of miracle dialectically so that it both justifies and *criticizes* our speech about God.

Nonetheless, Barth is uncompromising about the need to be realistic in our speech about God.

> If we are going to talk about God as the *object* of theology, then we will already be advancing a typical realist position . . . The proposition that "God is" is a realist utterance, not easily dispensed with if theology is not to fall into mystical silence the first time it ventures to speak. The situation does not get any easier, but even more exacting when we recall that by the term God we do not mean some sort of "God as such," but rather, according to our agreement about the nature of theology, the God of the Christian Church, the God revealed in his word.[85]

---

84. "If we want to disregard this great limit to the theologian's activity, or the great fulfillment which alone can make it meaningful, then it needs to be said that considered by itself, this undertaking is completely exposed and dangerous. Only one thing keeps it from being doomed to failure: the presupposition of divine miracle." Ibid., 29.

85. Ibid., 35.

Note that Barth is not merely being realistic, but being specifically and concretely realistic. Indeed, speech that claimed to be realistic but failed to become specific, concrete, and detailed about its object would come under suspicion of not being realistic at all. Barth is concrete, specific, and detailed about the object of theology, God's self-revelation, because he has a concrete, specific, and detailed field of inquiry in which to seek that object: the Word of God attested in Scripture and proclaimed in the church. But the dialectical reservation upon such seeking is that it has no hope in its own power to find that which it seeks. Indeed, when it finds that which it seeks the first thing such realistic theology is forced to confess is that the seeking was upon the other side, and that it was the theologian who was found and thus enabled to speak of God. But this again is only to claim realistically that the causal justification of our ability to speak of this object is upon the side of the object.

Barth makes it clear that realism is not merely a different possibility to one side of a dialectical theology of the Word of God (with critical idealism on the other side) but a necessary moment *in* a dialectical theology of the Word of God. "God's being revealed" means that "God becomes an object of our experience." Revelation makes God accessible to experience. Experience means the "process of perceiving ourselves, our world, and the two in indissoluble correlation."[86]

> At least at first we judge the things, that is the possibilities that we meet, according to the standard of reality . . . Do I experience them? Do I experience them in the unity and totality of inner and outer experience? Are they *real* for me? Are they real for *me*? . . . It should not be surprising that instinctively we even measure God by this standard, at least as a first step in our reflecting about God. How could God be anything other than real, real at least in the same sense that I experience myself and the world in which I live—real as act, being and fate? Don't we have to pose this question simply by virtue of the concept of revelation?[87]

Barth's answer to these questions is neither a simple affirmation, rendering them merely rhetorical, nor a simple rejection. Their legitimacy, even for dialectical theology, is acknowledged. A complete rejection would "mean tossing the baby out with the bath water. No theology can afford not to share completely the intentions evident here." "A theology

---

86. Ibid., 36.
87. Ibid., 36.

not open to the aspirations of realism would be neither Protestant nor Christian."[88] Barth intends and claims to be speaking realistically about God. But that realism stands under a reservation.[89] The reservation is not simply the necessity to be critical as well as realistic. Even being critical stands under the same reservation. The reservation is a dialectical product of the actuality of the object of our knowledge, the *Realdialektik* of the divine veiling and unveiling in revelation.

The reservation that is necessary here is primarily a product of the theologically necessary proposition that it is by grace that we know God. It is by grace that our speaking of God can refer to God realistically. It is not a product of our ability. It is not realism that is capable of describing God, but God that is capable of using realism for self-description. If realism were in and of itself capable of knowing God and appropriate to the knowledge of God, this would imply that there is an inherent human capacity for the knowledge of God. But this is precisely what Barth denies, not because of the difficulties inherent in the knowledge of a higher being by a lower being, but rather on the grounds of the doctrine of grace. Grace is grace to sinners, and it is the doctrine of sin (a part of the doctrine of grace, not a separate doctrine) that forces us to acknowledge that we have no natural capacity for the knowledge of God.[90] Barth is here taking the doctrine of grace in the Reformed manner, not supposing that grace completes and enhances nature, but that grace confounds nature, making actual what is not even a possibility in nature.[91]

> For grace is the event in which God comes to us in his Word, an event over which God has sole control, and which is strictly momentary. Otherwise God could not be distinguished from a hidden feature of reality as such . . . God distinguishes himself from fate by the fact that He is not so much there, as rather that he comes. Confidence in God's self-giving is therefore rather different than realism's confidence in God's givenness . . . We can think

88. Ibid., 37, 38.

89. "It is by no means obvious that the guidance realism offers can be simply equated with the final and authentic guidance to be received from God's Word." Ibid., 38.

90. "The reason is not merely because we have a weak, creaturely will, made even weaker through sin. It is rather because our will is perverse, fundamentally incapable of knowing God and of acting obediently toward him." Ibid., 41. This theme is repeated and taken into the doctrine of God in chapter V in Barth, *Church Dogmatics II/1*. See especially 213.

91. Barth, "Fate and Idea," 39. This is an extended discussion and the footnote applies to all the preceding five sentences.

and speak realistically only by presupposing the act-character of God's reality . . . We can think and speak realistically only by pre-supposing that the very thing realism posits—the possibility and necessity of finding God in experience—is such that it must be taken up, negated and transformed. Such a possibility and neces-sity, in other words, is a matter of God's free will, not our will.[92]

This is the characteristic dialectical attitude toward realism: that the grace of God both limits and criticizes the realism of our knowledge of God because it reminds us forcefully and repeatedly that it is not by our abilities, not by the accuracy of our judgment, not by the correctness of our philosophy, not even by the nature of reason and knowledge itself that we know God. Yet, at the same time, it is grace that establishes our knowledge of God in revelation and gives it a realistic character. This is not precisely critical realism as we have encountered it in the philosophy of science, in which realistic intention is combined with critical reflec-tion to enable us to make critically realistic judgments. But it is similar and parallel in that we are, by grace, forced to be both realistic and also self-critical. The judgment that we have heard and must give witness to the Word of God has this character even if its source is to be found in grace rather than in second order epistemological reflection.

6.2.2 Dialectical Idealism in Theology

Idealism, for Barth, means first and foremost, the critical rationalism of Kant. Idealism serves as a critical check upon realist thinking. But beyond that it deals with what is not given as over against the immanent reality given in realist thinking. It deals with what is pre-supposed rather than given.[93] In theology, idealism's orientation to the non-given also serves to give witness to the Word of God.[94]

This witness that idealism gives to the transcendence of God is also an essential element in any theology that seeks to give witness to the

92. Ibid., 40.

93. Ibid., 43: "Idealist thinking is critically chastened. It worries about the realist's naive confidence. It poses a fundamental question about what the realist simply takes for granted—about how self-evident the way really is from object to subject, and from subject to object. In other words, it asks about where the givenness of this correla-tion comes from, and about the limits to knowledge within it. Idealist thinking is also critically strengthened, however, for by posing this question it discovers something not given over against the given subject and object."

94. Ibid., 44.

Word of God. It can be expressed radically, despite the fact that Barth has already given affirmation (under the dialectical reservation, of course) to realism's assertion of God's being.[95] Barth understands the relationship between idealism and realism as both dialectical and necessary. Reality is such that both of them are required, and they each strengthen and correct the other. This is all the more the case in theology, where the particular object of theology makes this dialectical relationship between realism and idealism even more necessary.[96]

In this understanding of how idealism interacts with realism Barth shows a grasp of the interaction between positive and negative knowledge in the act of knowing. In scientific realism the need to be aware always of the negative limits to all positively expressed knowledge on the grounds of its historically demonstrated fallibility and in the face of the legitimate philosophical questions that can be raised about its justification was coupled with an awareness of the positive achievement of knowledge that was gained in every negative discovery that previous theories were inadequate or wrong. Of course, simple realism can always insist that we are merely at a long distance from a complete and accurate theory of everything that will not be subject to such faults. Antirealism can always insist that such faults are pervasive and inherent, so that all positive knowledge must be regarded as finally false. Critical realism attempts to hold both these insights together in an understanding of the nature and character of our knowledge. Barth's reason for holding the two together is different in that he has a different object of knowledge, but similar in that it is the action of the object upon us that forces us to hold both positions together if we are to be at all faithful to the object of our discourse. The structural relationship between realism and idealism (or critical theory) is also analogous.

95. "Doesn't it have to be said that all theology must be just as necessarily idealist as realist? Isn't all theology necessarily idealist to the extent that thinking about God's given reality always involves referring to its non-given truth? Doesn't all theology understand the given in the light of the immanent reality not given to it?" Ibid., 45.

96. "In its own way genuine idealism does not exclude but includes the given. That is what makes Christian theological idealism possible: a critical understanding of revelation's givenness . . . Crisis does not mean negation. It means chastening the knowledge of the given for the sake of its strengthening—chastening it by rejecting the self-evident status it has for realism; strengthening it by restoring its true connection . . . It [idealism] aspires to do justice to God's hiddenness even in the midst of his revelation, to the divine hiddenness that points to the divine disclosure." Ibid., 46.

Idealism in theology also performs the important function of reminding us constantly of the difference between the object of discourse in theology and the object of discourse in science and philosophy. But despite the witness it gives to God's transcendence "the Christianity of idealist theology is not beyond jeopardy." Even as with realist theology, Barth retains a dialectical reservation, a reservation in harmony with his rejection of natural theology. "We will need to make certain that this critical view of reality as the context where truth is found has nothing to do with a general way to God open and accessible at all times to everyone."[97] This is to say again that it is always and only by God that God is made known and not even in the idealist witness to the non-givenness of God in revelation is a way made open to God. It remains but a witness that the way that has been opened has been opened *from* God.[98] The truth of our knowledge of God is "substantiated by God's action—not by God's action along with ours, but by God's action alone."[99]

6.2.3 Dialectical Critical Realism in Theology

Barth has now described how both idealistic theology and realistic theology have valid things to say about God in his self-revelation. He has observed how a dialectical reservation must be held against each, and moreover how each serves to criticize and compliment the other. He notes how realism attempts to do justice to the receptivity of human knowledge and how idealism attempts to do justice to the spontaneity of human knowledge. He holds them together in a critically realistic fashion, and yet is still aware that there is a distinction between the knowledge of God and all other human knowledge.[100]

The knowledge of God is both like and unlike other knowledge. It is like theoretical knowledge in that it makes assumptions or takes

97. Ibid., 47.

98. Ibid., 54: "Theology must therefore set out from the point at which philosophy thinks it can arrive or at least would like to arrive. Moreover, theology claims that this very point can only be given in advance, that reflection on God can only proceed in the form of a thinking from, rather than a thinking toward. It must reject the claim that we might arrive at this point by reflecting on the truth and reality of human existence—if by 'this point' we mean an ultimate word, a naming of God worthy of the name."

99. Ibid., 49.

100. "No, reason's normal activity is not interrupted; but it is directed, guided and ordered by something superior to itself, something that has no part in this antithesis . . . That is the oddity about knowledge of God as compared with other knowledge." Ibid., 50.

presuppositions as postulates as they seem to impose themselves upon us by their necessity. From these presuppositions we may derive a large body of implied knowledge by the familiar process of proof, explication, implication, and further development of the consequences of our assumptions. It is like empirical knowledge in that it seems to be bound to an external reality to which it must respond and by which it must measure all of its knowledge, and even its underlying assumptions. But it is unlike all other knowledge in that our fundamental faith is here not to be found in ourselves, and the powers of our intellect, and the intelligibility of the world of which we have knowledge, but in God and God's action in our behalf.

Confidence in the necessity and self-evidence of our postulates, given their object, is like faith in that it is trust of what cannot be proved and demonstrated, as it is itself the form and structure of all demonstration and proof. But it is unlike faith in that the choice of postulates is our own, by our will, chosen because of a seemingly necessary relationship to reason and the object of our discourse. But faith is trust in another, rather than ourselves.

Conformance of our theoretical structures to the object known in critically realistic scientific understanding is like faith because it is conformance to another in which all our theoretical commitments are made by reference to their value in knowing this other. But it is unlike faith in that our faith in the power of the world to confound our expectations and force us to change our theoretical commitments is really a product of our own deep commitment to the process of further investigation and questioning.[101] But Christian faith is trust that the other, an active living being that exerts their own will upon us, will force us to re-examine and adjust our theoretical commitments even when we are sinfully determined not to. It is faith in grace that is given to sinners and not faith in the inherent capacities of human beings.

"As we now remind ourselves for the third time, it is the concept of sin, of fallen humanity, which we have had to bring to bear against realism and idealism."[102] Even if we had philosophical and scientific reason

101. Barth clearly understands that our knowledge of the world is, in part, a product of our own creative efforts. But the knowledge of God is different in that it does not depend upon our creativity, but God's. "Since faith is knowledge of the creator, not knowledge of some existing object in the antithesis previously mentioned, it follows that faith is not the kind of knowledge in which we can see ourselves as creative." Ibid., 51.

102. Ibid., 54.

to believe that human knowing and human reason were perfectly suited to knowledge of the reality and truth of the creation in which we have our being, under the doctrine of sin we would still have to be critical, devastatingly critical, of any possibility that we might have knowledge of God.[103] Even if we had philosophical and scientific reason to believe that all human thinking was vain imagining with no knowledge of anything in this creation, not even itself, under the doctrine of grace we would still have to be critical of our own incapacity for knowledge and acknowledge that we have in revelation real and referential knowledge of God.[104] This is the deep meaning of the dialectical reservation that Barth holds with respect to both theological realism and theological idealism. It is critically realistic in form and also in substance, for it is material doctrines derived from the raw material of theology, the Word of God attested in Scripture, that force this character upon theology, and not general philosophical considerations about the nature of knowledge. Theology is not critically realistic because it is in the nature of human knowledge to be critically realistic, but because the material content of our knowledge of God is knowledge of the grace that forgives sinners.

> Anything said about this God can only be said as a matter of obedience, never mind its being set forth in the form of objective human knowledge, in the same framework as philosophical discourse, under the constraint of the same dialectical movement. It can only rest on God's having spoken, not on our having said something to ourselves . . . It is strictly a matter of the command in which we know our obedience to be grounded. We have not proved that such a command exists. We will take care to refrain from doing so. We can only establish that on the basis of this command theology speaks of God.[105]

In the context of Barth's discussion of realism and idealism, and the dialectical reservation that must be held against them in theology, this passage cannot be interpreted as revelational positivism, as a simple assertion that what we have is the Word of God written and from that we may proceed freely to develop whatever positive knowledge flows from

103. See Roland Chia for further discussion of the relation of Barth's theological anthropology to his theological epistemology. Chia, *Revelation and Theology*, 116.

104. Barth, *Church Dogmatics* II/1, 212.

105. Barth, "Fate and Idea," 51. See also p. 27: "That is, theology has God as its object only to the extent that it strives to have absolutely no other origin than the communication which God actually gives of himself."

it. The obedience spoken of here is just as much submission to judgment as it is giving positive witness. It must be understood as an assertion that the reality of our knowledge of God is dependent not upon the structure and character of our own knowledge but upon the actuality of the object to which it refers. That object imposes itself upon us in such a way that even as we are bound to make positive assertions about it, we are also forced into a critical awareness of the limitations and dependence of our knowledge. The knowledge of faith is a form of obedience. But that obedience is obedience to grace rendered unto sinners, and thus takes the characteristic form of a turn around, of repentance. It is a positive knowledge in obedience springing immediately out of and inseparable from the negative knowledge of repentance, the realization that we have not known God rightly. It is analogous to a paradigm shift in the natural sciences, for negative and positive knowledge are here bound together inseparably.[106]

6.2.4 Dialectic in Theology

Finally, and most importantly, the dialectical reservation that Barth maintains against realism and idealism in theology, he also maintains against dialectics in theology. Dialectical theology is not a method for doing theology that releases it from bondage to the nature and limits of human knowledge. Dialectical theology, just as realistic and idealistic theology, is still only a human endeavor and its work and its products are still human work and human products. "So is theology very much the human undertaking of a technical or academic discipline. Its tools are nothing more than ordinary human thought and speech with their own definite laws, possibilities, and limitations."[107] This means that the indirect character of all theological knowledge is expressly acknowledged and accepted. Dialectical theology is not a method for obtaining unambiguous direct knowledge of God.

"Despite the divine origin and object of its knowledge, theology has no divinely unambiguous categories at its disposal, none which might

106. Ibid., 46, where he clearly shows an understanding that the negative and positive aspects of theological knowledge are bound together. "It [idealism] aspires to do justice to God's hiddenness even in the midst of his revelation, to the divine hiddenness that points to the divine disclosure." See also chapter V, paragraph 27, section 1 "The Hiddenness of God" in Barth, *Church Dogmatics II*/1.

107. Barth, "Fate and Idea," 27.

not be countered or canceled by categories from elsewhere. It has no categories by which it might be able to differentiate its knowledge, the knowledge of God's word, from the knowledge of the philosophers."[108] In this admission Barth points out not only the indirect character of our knowledge of God, but also its fallibility and its vulnerability to criticism by other standpoints and other philosophies. Only strictly mathematical, logical, or totally *a priori* knowledge, which is by its nature empty of all content except its own formal structure, is, by that very emptiness, infallible and invulnerable. All knowledge with content, all knowledge of an other, whether it be scientific knowledge or theological knowledge, is understood to be vulnerable and fallible. The Word of God may be infallible, but our own theological formulations of what we have in the Word of God are only too fallible. But fallible knowledge is better than absolute knowledge.[109]

Barth makes it clear that dialectic is necessary in theology because it is the only way that theology has to give witness to the dialectical dilemma. The apparent contradiction contained in the dialectical dilemma is not one that is founded in the nature of human thought as such (though Barth acknowledges that there may be some contradiction there also), but in the revelatory act of God. It is because of how God acts in revelation that theology finds itself forced to be dialectical.[110]

The same dialectical reservation that was held against realistic and idealistic thinking in theology holds for dialectical thinking as well, and therefore dialectical theology has an essential modesty.

> Not because my dialectics are so great, but because God condescends to make use of me and this my doubtful tool . . . Not because I can demonstrate how fate is really idea, or idea really fate, or how my synthesis of them is really God; but rather because it has pleased God, as the one superior to the contradiction of my existence and my thought, to step in for me as Revealer and Reconciler so that I should confess him; and therefore because it has pleased God to confess himself to me . . . We thus cannot boast to others about our hearing the Word. In hearing the Word we either stand by obedience or we do not stand at all. For not only the Word's being spoken but also our reception of it is always a matter of God's grace. It is not therefore a matter in

108. Ibid., 28.

109. See 4.3.2.

110. Barth, "Fate and Idea," 54.

which one might adopt a so-called standpoint by which to exalt oneself over others . . . God's Word is not bound nor ever will be bound. Theological dialectic can be genuine only as it is open to this conception, that is, as it serves the freedom of God's Word.[111]

We saw this modesty before, when Barth admitted that any number of other philosophies than the one he was using might properly be used to essay the task of interpreting the Scripture. We now see it again as Barth makes the same judgment about his own characteristic style of theology, dialectic, that he makes about all other forms of theology: when it works it does so by God's grace and not by any intrinsic suitability it may have for knowing God nor by any accomplished superiority it may have over any other human way of knowing. The dialectical reservation does not mean that we do not have real knowledge, but only that that knowledge must be held in a critical fashion that does not mistake its correspondence to the Word of God for direct possession of the Word of God.

It is with this essential modesty in mind, this dialectical view of the status of dialectical theology, that Barth formulates fallibility as a criterion of true knowledge of God. "To determine whether a particular theology has as its object merely a deified concept or the living God, the first criterion might be whether that theology is conscious of its own relativity."[112] Relativity here is not a reference to relativism. Barth means the relativity of theology to its object. But he means that relativity to be understood as the fallibility of theology relative to its object. If God is transcendent, then God transcends even the knowledge that is given in revelation, even though God is also immanent in it. Fallibility is here being offered as a criterion of the truth in theology, for to succeed in referring to the living God rather than to some deified concept is to have corresponding referential truth. Infallible knowledge of God is knowledge of an idol rather than knowledge of the transcendent God.

6.3 CONCLUSION—DIALECTICAL CRITICAL REALISM

Karl Barth's dialectical theology is properly to be characterized as a form of critical realism. Dialectical theology understands its own place as a form of human thought as well as its primary object, God's self-revealing address to humanity, in a critically realistic manner. Dialectical theology

111. Ibid., 58–59.
112. Ibid., 58.

in Barth exhibits, in the ways pointed to throughout section 6.2 of this chapter, analogies to the following features of scientific realism elucidated in section 3.2:

(1) It presumes the reality of the object of its discourse. This is why theology and science are both *post hoc* investigations into what is the case, rather than what must be the case. (2) It is postfoundational. (3) It is both critical and self-critical. Moreover, it acknowledges that it is the reality of the object of knowledge that forces us to be critical. (4) It finds that positive and negative knowledge are bound together in the act of knowledge.[113] (5) It considers that knowledge is co-determined by the structure of our minds, our cultural antecedents, and the external reality to which we refer in our discourse. (6) The referential power of our discourse is founded upon the power of the reality to which we refer to be a cause of our knowledge. (7) It uses a referential, correspondence idea of truth. (8) It recognizes that our knowledge is always indirect and mediated. (9) It accepts that all our knowledge is fallible and dares to propound fallibility as a criterion of truth. (10) It uses hypothetical method for an investigation into an unknown object.

Dialectical theology and the dialectical critical realism that may be developed from it differ from other forms of critical realism in their object and their understanding of the relationship in which we stand to that object such that we have knowledge of it. For dialectical theology the object of discourse is God, not the world. The possible confusion of the two arises from the fact that all our discourse about God consists of metaphors, analogies, and models drawn from our knowledge of the world. Our relationship to God is fundamentally different than our relationship to the world. It is by our own efforts in research and investigation, and by our own modesty and good judgment in holding our theories in a postfoundational way, that we obtain critically realistic knowledge of the world. But the active agent in our knowledge of God is God himself. Barth does not consider that God has put his revelation out there in the world so that, by using critically realistic dialectical thinking, we can find it and understand it. Even our reception of the Word of

---

113. In "The Ideal and the Real in the Theology of Karl Barth" in Roberts, *A Theology on Its Way?*, 59–79, Roberts accepts the Neo-Orthodox misinterpretation of Barth's mature theology as "supremely positive" (ibid., 60). He interprets the relation between ideal and real without any reference to "Fate and Idea," and so criticizes Barth for concluding in an uncompromising and improperly founded realism.

God is part of the miracle of revelation, so that without the witness of the Holy Spirit even the best theology that can be imagined cannot hope to find or understand the Word of God. God's act of self-revelation is out there, in the sense that it is empirical, that it is incarnation. But recognizing it as revelation, interpreting it as revelation, and understanding it as revelation are acts that require God's continued action, and not acts of which the human knowing apparatus is capable by itself.

This difference of object, and of relationship to object, is why Barth is not a critically realistic philosopher. But it is precisely this object, and the relation that theology has to it, that force Barth's dialectical theology to assume a critically realistic character. Nonetheless the difference must be held clearly in mind. Critical realism in the philosophy of science is second order epistemological reflection on the nature and character of our knowledge of the world. Critical realism in theology is an epistemological consequence of the doctrine of grace.[114]

---

114. I made this judgment and wrote this line in my dissertation. While revising it for publication I found this statement: "In this sense, dialectical thinking is a correlate of justification by grace alone, in its epistemological reference." Torrance, *Karl Barth*, 88.

7

Some Critics of Barth

Here I examine several classic criticisms of Barth's theology. They were developed before the generation of work that led to the critically realistic interpretation of Barth's dialectical theology.[1] In some ways this interpretation answers those criticisms by claiming they involve a misunderstanding of the character of Barth's doctrine of revelation. In other ways the answers given here will depend upon the reading of Barth as postfoundationalist. Answering criticisms only clears away misunderstandings and leaves open the possibility that these criticisms could be reformulated.

The three questions to be examined are: whether Barth's theology constitutes a sort of revelational positivism, as posed by Wentzel van Huyssteen; whether it is radically irrational, as posed by W. W. Bartley; and whether it is incurably subjective, as posed by Wolfhart Pannenberg.

7.1 REVELATIONAL POSITIVISM

Dietrich Bonhoeffer in several places in the *Letters and Papers from Prison* refers to Karl Barth's "positivism of revelation." Bonhoeffer approves of Barth's critique of religion and his identification of Christianity as a religion against which the same dialectical reservation must be held as against all religion. But his doctrine of revelation seems to Bonhoeffer to depart from that critique.

---

1. McCormack, *Barth's Critically Realistic Dialectical Theology*, 5–14, 24–28.

Barth was the first theologian to begin the criticism of religion, and that remains his really great merit; but he put in its place a positivist doctrine of revelation which says, in effect, "Like it or lump it": virgin birth, Trinity, or anything else; each is an equally significant and necessary part of the whole, which must simply be swallowed as a whole or not at all . . . The positivism of revelation makes it too easy for itself, by setting up, as it does in the last analysis, a law of faith, and so mutilates what is—by Christ's incarnation—a gift for us. In the place of religion there now stands the church—that is in itself biblical—but the world is in some degree made to depend on itself and left to its own devices, and that is the mistake[2] . . . It was not in ethics, as is often said, that he subsequently failed; . . . it was that in the non-religious interpretation of theological concepts he gave no concrete guidance, either in dogmatics or in ethics. There lies his limitation, and because of it his theology of revelation has become positivist, a "positivism of revelation," as I put it.[3]

It is not fully clear what Bonhoeffer meant by "a positivism of revelation," but it is certain that he was not dealing with the problem of the model of rationality in Barth's theology, and he was not in conversation with concepts from the philosophy of science that have arisen in the dialogue between science and theology.[4] The idea of a positivism of revelation seems to have been closely connected with his desire for a "religionless" interpretation of Christian faith.[5] In this context the meaning of positivism of revelation is "that proclamation of God's revelation which presents its truths for mere acceptance without being able

2. Bonhoeffer, *Letters and Papers from Prison*, 144–45. See also the brief comment on 140.

3. Ibid., 170–71.

4. It was not fully clear to Barth, either. Barth, "Letter of Karl Barth, 21 December 1952."

5. Nineteenth-century German liberalism often made use of the idea that there was an element of human being and nature that was "religious." This made and preserved a safe place in the life of human beings and human culture for religion, and thus for Christianity. Both Bonhoeffer and Barth refuse this notion and regard the revelation of God as something that stands over against human nature and culture, and Bonhoeffer gives Barth credit for seeing this first. But Bonhoeffer believes that the need is for a theology that brings the world face to face with its creator, to interpret the revelation in such a way that the world cannot hide from it, that is, in non-religious language. This is what he misses in Barth. See Prenter, "Dietrich Bonhoeffer and Karl Barth's Positivism of Revelation," 96–100.

to show clearly how they are related to the life of a world come of age."[6] This is the point at which Bonhoeffer's complaint has been picked up and amplified by others.

There seem to be three meaningful complaints against Barth here and in the criticisms that adopt this language. The first is that his doctrine of revelation is positivistically foundationalist. It treats its own structure of thought about revelation as a *necessary* structure whose presuppositions, definitions, and methods tend to be considered necessary as well. The second is that it is phenomenalistic about revelation. The third is that it cuts off dialogue with other positions by setting up a rigid and unjustified standard for what constitutes meaningful theological discourse, which parallels the logical positivist adoption of the principle of verification as a standard of meaningful scientific discourse.

Wentzel van Huyssteen develops this charge of revelational positivism more thoroughly than Bonhoeffer's fragments. In the second chapter of his book, *Theology and the Justification of Faith*, he characterizes Barth's theology as a reaction to the positivist model of science, which, by reaction, becomes positivist itself.

The positivist conception of the character of science is marked by the following characteristics: (1) axiomatic method; (2) the development of the consequences of axioms by means of a strict two valued logic which is considered to be universally valid; (3) induction from empirical observation to generate possible new axioms; (4) the supposition that scientific theories are based upon direct factual observation free from theories and ideologies; (5) the testing of possible new axioms by empirical verification of their logically developed consequences; and (6) the demarcation of meaningful from meaningless discourse on the basis of empirical verifiability. The rationality inherent in this characterization of science is the classical model. All scientific statements, whether axioms, empirical observations, hypotheses, or deductions must be either true or false. It may be at issue which is the case, but bivalence is presumed and contradiction is sufficient evidence of falsehood.[7]

6. Ibid., 105.

7. See van Huyssteen, *Theology and the Justification of Faith*, where he characterizes positivism primarily in terms of characteristics 1, 2, 4, and 5. Kolakowski, *The Alienation of Reason*, 1–11, characterizes positivism as phenomenalist (corresponding to characteristics 3 and 4), nominalist, demarcationist about statements with cognitive value (corresponding to characteristics 5 and 6), and dedicated to the unity of scientific method (corresponding to characteristics 1 and 2).

Even though logical positivism was probably the beginning of the modern practice of the philosophy of science, several of its features caused it to be abandoned when work in the history of science began to impact the field.[8] It was strongly foundationalist. Contemporary critical realism is postfoundationalist, while most postmodern theories in the philosophy of science are nonfoundational. Logical positivism is phenomenalist. A modern understanding of the theory-laden character of observation and the underdetermination of theory by fact has displaced phenomenalism. And logical positivism was strongly demarcationist. But the abandonment of both foundationalism and phenomenalism in the philosophy of science have undermined the idea of any clear demarcation between meaningful and non-meaningful speech. This has given rise to opportunities for dialogue between the natural sciences and other fields.

With this understanding of the nature and character of logical positivism in mind, and fully aware of its inadequacies, van Huyssteen formulates his criticism of Barth. "I shall argue that the rationality model of logical positivism might bear down so heavily on theology that the theologian would react almost automatically by devising his own esoteric and peculiar conceptual model for theology. But by its nature and structure such a theological model of thought, even if seen as a theology of revelation or of Scripture, lapses both epistemologically and methodologically into a model of rationality analogous to the standard positivistic concept from which it sought to escape."[9] This says that the demarcation criteria of logical positivism—a criteria by which logical positivism dismissed not only religious statements but also all metaphysics as empirically meaningless and cognitively empty—would so impact the practice of theology that in self defense theology would create its own foundationalist approach to its subject matter and its own demarcation criteria which would render it independent of the criticisms of logical positivism.[10] In Barth's theology this would mean that the assumption that all theology begins with a given revelation which theologians must interpret faithfully and obediently is necessary to its foundation. The rule of theology that says that every doctrine must be understood in the light of the particular event of the self-revelation of God in Jesus Christ functions as a demarcation criteria whose primary

8. Kolakowski, *The Alienation of Reason*, 3–4.

9. van Huyssteen, *Theology and the Justification of Faith*, 11.

10. Ibid., 22–23.

purpose is to render criticisms from philosophy irrelevant. In this way theology would have duplicated in mirror image the rationality model of logical positivism. But because one of the key flaws in logical positivism lay in its model of rationality, theology would inherit the same flaw even though it was arguing against logical positivism. "But the assumed axiomatic datum of God and His revelation offers no escape from this dispute, because the positive quality thus given to revelation can offer no alternative to subjectivism in theology. A positivistic theology of revelation that adopts a highly esoteric method makes it extremely difficult to convince others that the basic tenets of theology—God, revelation, Holy Scripture, inspiration, etc.—are not the constructs of subjective whim, whether personal or directed by an influential tradition."[11]

The substance of van Huyssteen's critique of Barth's procedure is that the status that Barth thinks he is giving to God in his revelation alone, he is actually giving to his own particular and peculiar conception of God and his revelation. In this way the most basic methodological and epistemological assumptions of Barth's work are both concealed and granted immunity from critical examination. At the same time the model of rationality in use in his work is uncritically assumed to be the only possible form of rationality appropriate to the object of theology. Were all this to be the case, then in the very act of announcing that all human endeavor lies under the judgment of God, Barth would nonetheless be denying the possibility of any critique of his theology. If this is so, then the model of rationality in Barth is certainly analogous to the positivistic concept and shares similar faults.

The answer to these criticisms lies in reading Barth as a *critical realist*.[12] The rationality model that Barth uses is not positivistic; it is postfoundational, uses three-valued logic instead of two, and is not phenomenalistic about revelation. It does not need to be demarcationist, but in practical application it sometimes is, and that will remain a concern.[13] Let us take these matters in turn.

---

11. Ibid., 22.

12. Van Huyssteen, *Postfoundational Theology*, 141, calls Barth's doctrine of holy Scripture a "naive realist position."

13. This is dealt with most fully in 7.2.4.

7.1.1 Barth's Postfoundationalism

In section 6.3 I characterized Barth's doctrine of revelation as post-foundational, so it is a matter of some concern that many criticisms of Barth consider him still to be using a classical foundationalist model of rationality. The reason for this, I believe, is that Barth is just barely postfoundational, and only in theology, with just a few degrees of freedom, whereas we have become used to a postmodernism that is either nonfoundational or postfoundational about everything, and with many degrees of freedom.

Postfoundational thinking is not, of course, structureless, nor is nonfoundationalism. Even as anarchistic a thinker as Feyerabend makes it clear that rule oriented classical thinking is a necessary part of all good thinking.[14] But having rules and structure is not sufficient to make a position foundationalist. It becomes foundationalist only when some inner subset of those rules is taken to be a set of "non-inferential principles whose certainty and stability ground epistemic claims."[15] If the most basic rules of a structure of thought, its foundations, are understood to be fallible and revisable, then the structure is not foundationalist even though it may be large and highly structured. Modern science is a huge and highly structured object that is nevertheless postfoundational because even its deepest rules are understood to be fallible and revisable. Not only are the high level structures, theories, and paradigms revisable, but even the core of logic and mathematics is understood to be revisable.[16] Where the core rules are not regarded as absolute foundations, then the knowledge that the structure of thought contains, even when it is asserted as true and considered to be in no

14. Feyerabend, *Against Method*, 249.

15. Thiel, *Nonfoundationalism*, 1.

16. Feyerabend, *Against Method*, 204: "It is the dogma that all subjects, however assembled, quite automatically obey the laws of logic, or ought to obey the laws of logic . . . This dogmatic assertion is neither clear nor is it (in one of its main interpretations) true . . . Then the assertion is not *clear* as there is not a single subject—LOGIC—that underlies all these domains. There is Hegel, there is Brouwer, there are the many logical systems considered by modern constructivists." See also Boyer, *History of the Calculus*, 308: "Materialistic and idealistic philosophies have both failed to appreciate the nature of mathematics, as accepted at the present time. Mathematics is neither a description of nature nor an explanation of its operation; it is not concerned with physical motion or with the metaphysical generation of qualities. It is merely the symbolic logic of possible relations, and as such concerned with neither approximate nor absolute truth, but only with hypothetical truth."

need of revision at present, is held with a reservation. It is hypothetical truth, and not final and absolute truth.

Barth's theology is highly structured and well equipped with basic motifs and recurring patterns that articulate that structure. As previously pointed out, he is a foundationalist in philosophy, and the foundation that he uses is Kant. But in theology he uses the Kantian philosophy in a postfoundational way. He does not assume that the foundation is suitable to the object of his discourse, God's self-revelation. He maintains a dialectical reservation against it, and that reservation leads him to regard all theological work as fallible and revisable. The dialectical reservation also requires him to regard even the products of his own work as only hypothetically true.[17] Most importantly, he holds the dialectical reservation against even his own theology in its analogical-dialectical form.[18] This means that he does not regard dialectical theology as a device for pointing out the relativity and hypothetical nature of all *other* thought.

Barth is a late modern. He uses a large, modern, foundational structure, but because he does not regard its foundations as absolute for the object of his discourse, he uses it with at least one degree of freedom. He is able to step back from his own structure of thought and look at it from a new angle and then come back to it with new insights. He is able to do this because he regards God's self-revelation as not being captured by any structure of human thought at all, not even by the necessities of logic. But I refer to this practice as postfoundational with *only a few* degrees of freedom because Barth does not follow the postmodern practice of using several different structures and letting the collisions between them produce interesting dialogue which may manage to touch some previously unrecognized feature of reality. A few degrees of freedom are sufficient to make a position postfoundational, but are not always sufficient for being *recognized* as postfoundational.

Ernest Sosa has proposed a metaphor for this issue.[19] Foundationalism regards knowledge as being like a pyramid, built with rigid structure upon timeless and unshifting sands. Nonfoundationalism regards

---

17. See 6.1.3.

18. See McCormack, *Barth's Critically Realistic Dialectical Theology*, 19: "It should be noted that no privileged claim is being made here for Barth's doctrine of analogy [which McCormack has identified as inherently dialectical]. It was a *doctrine* like any other. It did not fall down from heaven; it was constructed by a human being."

19. Sosa, "The Raft and the Pyramid," 3–6.

knowledge as a raft, whose structure is less ponderous and rigid, which floats upon a sea of time and culture. In most cases, postmodernism acts like a fleet of rafts. There may be design similarities to the rafts, but they are also built with an enormous amount of variation and act in a varied manner. This strategy allows the fleet to survive in changing conditions. In the terms of this metaphor, Barth's theology is like a huge cruise ship. Because of its size and intricate structure it often seems to the passengers, or those floating on the rafts it sometimes passes, something like a pyramid, a huge floating medieval cathedral.[20] But no one knows better than the architect and captain that it too is a boat afloat on an endless sea. Like Barth, postfoundationalism is willing to build larger structures than rafts, but still clearly understands them to float on a sea of interpreted experience, rather than considering them to be like pyramids built on unshifting sands.

This metaphor for representing how Barth's postfoundational theology is easily mistaken for a foundationalist one is useful because of the common perception of Barth as a foundationalist. The rationality model of Barth's thinking argued here is much more like that proposed by Harold Brown.[21] The essential element of rationality is the judgment by means of which one is able to step back from the rules and structures one is using in order to make a decision about changing the rules or how to apply them. Rationality inheres in the rational agent who is able to exercise such judgment, not in the propositions, principles, or rules that such an agent formulates.

Further support for this postfoundational reading of Barth is to be found in his insistence that theology could never become a system, which is what a foundationalist structure of thought is normally expected to become. There are two reasons for this. First, the motif of particularism in Barth's theology, the defining of every concept used in theology on the basis of the particular event called Jesus Christ, means that revelation cannot be understood as other than mysterious. Secondly, the motif of actualism, which always regards being as an event or an act and never as an unchanging substance, means that revelation cannot be understood as other than miraculous.[22] Theology can and must be systematic, in the

---

20. I am indebted to George Hunsinger for the image of Barth's theology as being like a cathedral. See Hunsinger, *How to Read Karl Barth*, 27–28.

21. See 4.2.

22. Hunsinger, *How to Read Karl Barth*, 4.

sense that it attempts to understand and explicate all the implications of what it is given in its object and apply them to the full range of human experience. But theology can never be a system, that is: "a general conceptual scheme capable of encompassing the totality of relevant terms and explaining more or less exhaustively their underlying formal unity . . . But (if anything) only concepts and principles, not persons and histories, could be systematized in this way, to say nothing of a mysterious person available to us only by way of a miraculous history, as Jesus Christ is affirmed to be by faith."[23] Because, for Barth, theology as rational is bound not to self consistency, but rather to consistency with its object, Jesus Christ as witnessed in the Scripture, and because this revelation is mysterious and miraculous, no consistent system can be developed.[24]

7.1.2 Multi-Valued Logic

Barth's theology can be interpreted as using a sort of three-valued logic, not in conformity with the two-valued logic that is intrinsic to the classical model of rationality, and thereby to logical positivism. Barth was probably not aware of this as different logics were only fully developed in modern mathematics after Gödel's incompleteness theorem suggested that logic itself might also be a formal and axiomatizable field of inquiry in which different axioms might be developed into self-consistent but independent structures of thought.[25] Barth was probably aware of using ordinary logic as far as it would take him, knowing that the attempt to remain faithful to his object was going to drive ordinary logic to its limits in dialectical statements that sounded paradoxical. The dialectical and paradoxical statements produced thereby constitute a witness to the inability of any human frame of reference to capture the knowledge of God. This implies a need to shift frames of reference, not in order to resolve the paradox and capture the knowledge of God, but rather, in order to continue the inquiry into what God says and does when human knowledge is both affirmed and denied in revelation. Barth does not use a three-valued logic out of a conscious methodological decision made in advance. Indeed, he was probably not particularly conscious of it at

23. Ibid., 53.

24. See also McCormack, "A Scholastic of a Higher Order," 10, an unpublished dissertation that was revised to become his *Karl Barth's Critically Realistic Dialectical Theology.*

25. That is, after 1931. See 4.3.1.

all. His use of three-valued logic is an expedient forced upon him by the object of his inquiry.

The implicit third value in his logic is a product of using a foundationalist system postfoundationally. The mere fact that further inquiry always necessitates a revision of our structures of thought, even at the level of their most basic rules, does not necessarily imply a third value in logic. Two additional points imply the third value in Barth's logic. First, the object of discourse in theology is God, who is always other than the structures of thought in which we know him, even when those structures have been revised in light of further encounter with revelation. No amount of ongoing revision will ever be such as to capture God in our knowledge of revelation because God is other than and more than our knowledge in a direction at right angles to that in which we are revising and correcting it. Second, even this dialectical awareness of the difference between God and our knowledge of God does not give us direct access to God but only a qualification of our knowledge of God. If shifting to a new frame of reference were to be understood as shifting to a better or the correct frame of reference, then the shift would not imply a third value in logic. But where the need to shift is understood as meaning that every frame of reference is inadequate to the knowledge of this object, even the new one we shift to, so that the need to shift frames of reference is not merely expedient but necessary as a witness to both the inadequacy of any frame of reference and the grace by which God unveils himself in inadequate frames of reference, then it represents a third value in logic.

The three values in Barth's logic might be formally specified as "true," "false," and "shift."[26] My suggestion that there is a third logical value present in Barth's theology is derived from my reading of George Hunsinger's valuable book *How to Read Karl Barth*, and is to be associated with the term "*Aufhebung*."

Hegel's logic is classically understood in terms of a three-valued logic. The thesis, antithesis, and synthesis all take place in an ongoing

26. The value "shift" corresponds roughly to Robert Pirsig's explanation of the logical value *Mu* from Japanese Zen philosophy. See Pirsig, *Zen and the Art of Motorcycle Maintenance*, 313–16: "Because we are unaccustomed to it, we don't usually see that there's a third possible logical term equal to yes and no which is capable of expanding our understanding in an unrecognized direction. We don't even have a term for it, so I'll have to use the Japanese *Mu. Mu* means 'no thing' . . . It points outside the process of dualistic discrimination. *Mu* simply says 'No class; not one, not zero, not yes, not no.' It states that the context of the question is such that a yes or no answer is in error and should not be given. 'Unask the question' is what it says."

process. The synthesis is an advance over the thesis and the antithesis which does not change their truth values but does have a logical value in which the thesis and the antithesis are no longer statements that exclude one another's truth. Hegel uses the term *Aufhebung* for this process and Barth adopts it for his own use.[27] In Hegel the synthesis is itself to be transcended by an iterative continuation of the process. For Barth even a synthesis is subject to the dialectical reservation. The transcendence lies in God's continuing act of self-revelation, rather than iterative process. *Aufhebung* is God's act, not ours. Theology accepts, follows, and appropriates God's *Aufhebung* of its propositions, not initiates it as a part of theological method.

I am using the mathematical fact that several different varieties of multivalent logics can be developed as evidence that if we decide that the way we want to think about a particular object requires something more or different than traditional two-valued logic it is, at least, not formally impossible to develop some sort of rigorous logical description of such ways of thinking.[28] One of the approaches to quantum theory attempted this.

In the prologue to *How to Read Karl Barth* George Hunsinger examines several attempts to identify a general methodology in Barth's work and agrees that there is none to be found.[29] He then goes on to explain that instead there are six different thought motifs, each of which has a methodological character, which are used by Barth to do his work. These motifs are not used successively or alternatively, but in, with, and against one another in dialectical inclusion to develop the full statement of the positive content of Barth's theology.[30]

---

27. Hunsinger, *How to Read Karl Barth*, 85–86.

28. Kolakowski, *The Alienation of Reason*, refers to Jan Lukasiewicz as the creator of multivalent logics and a common member of the Louw-Warsaw school in which Alfred Tarski did much of his work. See also references to different basic approaches to mathematical logic and the multivalent logics of Lukasiewicz and Tarski in the brilliant but idiosyncratic Korzybski, *Science and Sanity*, 93, 210, 310, 748.

29. Hunsinger, *How to Read Karl Barth*, 5–23. See also van Huyssteen, *Theology and the Justification of Faith*, 16, where he refers to a suggestion by Erasmus van Niekerk that no general methodology has been recognized in Barth's work.

30. Hunsinger, *How to Read Karl Barth*, 4–5. The motifs are introduced here. In chapters one and two they are surveyed in detail. In chapters 3 through 6 they are examined again in greater detail as they are used to explicate the notion of truth as it appears in Barth's work.

The six motifs cannot be reduced to one another nor can they be regarded as a sheaf of axioms in a two-valued logic. Such a sheaf of axioms would have to be logically consistent. The six motifs sometimes work in inconsistent opposition to one another, underlining the need for *Aufhebung*. Hunsinger identifies two patterns in how the motifs are applied. These are dialectical inclusion, a pattern related to the doctrine of the Trinity, and the Chalcedonian pattern, related to the problem of Christology.[31] Now the six motifs and the two patterns in which they are sometimes applied do serve the function in Barth's theology of rules of inference. They are a way of producing new statements from old statements that preserves an epistemic value. In a chapter on the problem of double agency Hunsinger shows carefully how the six motifs work together to explicate the problem of the relationship between the freedom of God in bestowing grace and human freedom in responding in faith.[32] The Chalcedonian pattern is dominant. But the end result is an understanding which is not self consistent, at least not from the viewpoint of two-valued logic, but is rather consistent with Scripture, the inconsistencies being accepted as pointing to the mystery to which Scripture witnesses.

In a sequence of four chapters Hunsinger uses the six motifs to examine the notion of truth in Barth's work. What emerges from the dialectical application of the motifs is a recognition that Barth is not working with a two-valued logic, but rather a three-valued logic. The third value associated with the term *Aufhebung* is best described by the phrase "affirmed, negated, and then reconstituted on a higher plane."[33] Dialectic is not merely an *alternation* between affirmation and negation. In the analogy of faith the *simultaneous* affirmation and negation of a concept under the judgment of God reconstitutes it so that it is able to function positively on a higher plane. This positive value that emerges only from affirmation and negation together is the third value in Barth's logic.

In mathematics Gödel's theorem demonstrated that any sufficiently rich system must have statements that can be neither proved nor disproved. This did not imply a third value in logic, but only demonstrated

31. Ibid., 58–59 for the definition of dialectical inclusion, which is then used throughout the book; and 185–88 for the definition of how the Chalcedonian pattern is used by Barth, and then throughout the remainder of the book.

32. Ibid., 185 ff.

33. Ibid., 98, 193, 200. Hunsinger clearly identifies *Aufhebung* as an important feature of Barth's thought. The characterization of *Aufhebung* as pointing to the third value in a three-valued logic is my own.

the limits of two-valued logic. The statement that could be neither proved nor disproved could be chosen as an additional axiom, giving rise to a new and richer theory. But if a statement was both affirmed and negated, proved and disproved, then it was an indicator that the theory was inconsistent in two-valued logic. In most forms of three-valued logic, and other multivalued logics, the third value is in some way intermediate between true and false.[34] This is especially true in the infinite-valued logic of Jan Lukasiewicz where the values a statement can take are a probability function rendering its truthlikeness.[35] In Barth's three-valued logic the simultaneous affirmation and negation of a statement is not used as a contradiction by means of which anything whatsoever can be proved. It is used as indicator of the third value which is not intermediate, an indicator that here God has acted and transformed the meaning of regular human statements.

Three- (and more) valued logic is often useful where the principle of bivalence, the semantic assertion that every statement of a theory must be either true or false, does not hold. The related law of the excluded middle, the syntactic assertion that either a statement or its negation is true, and which permits proof by contradiction, also does not hold in every formulation of mathematics.[36] They both hold in the classical model of rationality and in purely formal fields, such as the sentential logic.[37] But once statement variables are replaced with actual statements

34. Emil Post developed a three-valued logic in which the values were distinct, rather than the third being in some way intermediate between true and false. Zinov'ev, *Philosophical Problems of Many Valued Logic*, 16–18. See also ibid., 23–41, where Zinov'ev explains a variety of many valued logics, some of which are equivalent to one another, some not, due to Jas'kowski, Boc(v)var, Kleene, Reichenbach, and S(u)estakov. Some of these were designed to meet various needs that two-valued logic did not seem to be meeting, such as quantum mechanics in the case of Reichenbach.

35. Ibid., 10–16.

36. Ibid., 4–7. See also 19: "An important role in the development of many valued logic was played by the ideas of Brouwer. The following statement of Brouwer served as a starting point: 'The general validity of the law of the excluded middle is limited to that part of mathematics (and this means to that part of natural science) which is developed within a determinate, finite mathematical system (i.e., onto which a determinate, finite mathematical system can be projected).'"

37. However, even in the sentential logic, the proof of the independence of the axioms (a proof about the sentential logic, rather than in it) can be done conveniently in a multivalued logic, one that has as many values as there are axioms whose independence from one another is to be demonstrated. See Lukasiewicz, *Elements of Mathematical Logic*, 67–81.

about entities that are not abstract, problems can arise. According to the principle of bivalence any apparent statement that cannot be clearly affirmed as true or false is actually not a statement at all. But once we are talking about reality there are many things that we want to say which appear to us to be statements, to make assertions about things, but which cannot be clearly affirmed as true or false. Even in mathematics, a more formal field, Brouwer questioned whether the process of proof by contradiction, which depends upon the law of the excluded middle, was proper.[38] He was especially concerned about its legitimacy when applied to infinite quantities, where it seemed to produce many counter-intuitive results.

This doubt about the propriety of two-valued logic is thus especially appropriate in theology where the object of our discourse is at least infinite. The chief reason for preferring three-valued logic to two-valued logic is that we don't have statements that are precise enough for two-valued logic. The weakness of two-valued logic is that it only works for statements that are perfectly and entirely true or perfectly and entirely false. Three-valued, and other multi-valued logics, are often useful for those situations in which our statements may not manage to be disjunctively true or false. But this is an element of the dialectical dilemma which is so important to Barth's doctrine of revelation. If ever a field of discourse were ripe for three- or multi-valued logic, it is *theology*.

Natural language is not burdened by the strictness and specificity of mathematical and philosophical languages whose domains and rules of inference are rigorously defined. This has both advantages and disadvantages. On the one hand, no demonstration in natural language can truly be a rigorous proof, but only an argument. But, on the other hand, natural language is the only effective instrument for addressing the unknown, and it is often the most effective instrument for discovery. Even in mathematics and logic, discoveries are often made in natural language that are then tested and proved in formal language. Natural language tolerates ambiguity, fuzziness, and even contradiction without losing meaning, which again suits it to the address of the unknown and objects of discourse which, even though known, have aspects or characteristics which are still unknown or beyond the grasp of linear rational

---

38. Barrow, *Pi in the Sky*, 185–87. See especially p. 187: "The application of mathematics to the physical world has to *assume* a particular logic applies to its working. At present there is no reason to believe that it has to be the standard two-valued logic."

thought. One of the advantages of three and more valued logic is that they sometimes approximate the freedom of natural language while retaining some of the rigor of two-valued discourse. If natural language (and multi-valued logic) is valuable even in the sciences and mathematics, then it is no surprise that it is an appropriate vehicle in theology. But the conscious use of natural language and the implied use of three-valued logic then constitute a step away from the positivism that embraces two-valued logic, the principle of bivalence, and the law of the excluded middle. The argument that Barth's theology thus distances itself from positivism is dependent upon the argument that it remains dialectical and that the analogy of faith is a witness to the miraculous act of God in revelation and not a Neo-Orthodox technique for extracting truth from the interpretation of Scripture.

But this is precisely McCormack's argument, that the analogy of faith is not a method or a technique for doing theology. "The analogy of faith refers to a divine act over which human beings have no control."[39] The simultaneous affirmation and negation of a concept under the judgment of God is a self-revealing act of God, not an act performed by a human theologian. It is the act of God that forces the shift. Pitting statement against counter-statement in dialectical method and using a three valued logic to develop a discourse that regularly shifts its frames of reference are human acts, human methods. But the use of those methods does not guarantee the truth of our talk about God. We use such methods in a critically realistic fashion, as the best method we have been able to work out for giving an account of the reality of God's self-revelation. It is not simply the case that God is beyond the grasp of straightforward unambiguous two-valued discourse, and must therefore be grasped in a paradoxical and dialectical manner. God is also beyond the grasp of paradoxical and dialectical speech. Dialectical theology is no closer to God than any other theology. But it may be better than non-dialectical theology in that it is able to give witness to the otherness of God while also being able to generate positive assertions about who God is and what God is doing in revelation.

---

39. McCormack, *Barth's Critically Realistic Dialectical Theology*, 19.

7.1.3 Phenomenalism

Barth's Doctrine of revelation is not a form of phenomenalism.[40] In positivism this is the supposition that scientific theories are based upon direct factual observation free from theories and ideologies and that statements about realities can be reduced to statements about their phenomenal appearances. Phenomenalism in the doctrine of revelation would be the supposition that theological theories are based upon direct factual observation of the content of the Scripture free from theories and ideologies and that all the truth about God could be put into statements that are verifiable in the Scripture. I specify the Scripture here because the Scripture is the written phenomenal appearance of the self-revealing act of God in Jesus Christ.

Barth's doctrine of revelation is not phenomenalistic because it is critically realistic and dialectical, as explained in section 6.7.2. There is no *direct* factual observation of revelation because revelation is indirect and mediated. In the dialectic of veiling and unveiling, even when God unveils he does so by veiling. What we *observe* is not the revelation, but the veil. Moreover, the revelation is actualistic. It is not always there, at our disposal whenever we want to examine it.[41] There is no direct *factual* observation because there is no neutral observation language in which to report God's revelation. All the language we have for observing and reporting revelation is ordinary fallible human language. Barth even understands the written text of the Scripture to be composed of fallible human language.[42] There is no direct factual observation of revelation *free from theories and ideologies*. We come to the Scripture with whatever philosophy we have in hand, and there are no observers who come free of all prejudice.[43] Speaking of the act of interpreting Scripture, Barth says, "Even in the act of observing and representing, no interpreter is merely an observer and exponent. No one is in a position, objectively

---

40. The phenomenalism at issue in any discussion of Barth and the critique of his theology as positivist must be recognized as epistemological phenomenalism, not the more radical ontological phenomenalism. The being of objects behind the phenomena is not being denied; it is rather asserted that knowledge is confined to phenomena. Whether there are objects behind the phenomena or they are mental or logical constructions is not a subject of our knowledge.

41. Hunsinger, *How to Read Karl Barth*, 30–32.

42. Barth, *Church Dogmatics* I/2, 462–64, 532–34.

43. See La Montagne, "Gadamer's and Barth's Hermeneutics," 67–74 for a more extended discussion of hermeneutical issues in Barth's doctrine of revelation.

and abstractly, merely to observe and present what is there. For how can he do so without at the same time reflecting upon and interpreting what is there?"[44]

Barth's doctrine of revelation does frequently function as though all the truth about God could be put into statements that are verifiable in the Scripture. But critical realism in the modern philosophy of science also frequently speaks as though all meaningful statements about realities could be put into correspondence with statements about phenomena. Logical positivism is an early form of critical realism in the philosophy of science and its phenomenalism is corrected, not negated, in later critical realism. By abandoning belief in theory-free observation language and accepting that statements about realities cannot be *reduced* to statements about their phenomenal appearances, but only put in *correspondence* with them, both modern critical realism and Barth's doctrine of revelation escape positivistic phenomenalism, even if they remain committed to speaking of those realities in correspondence with their phenomenal appearances.

Barth's actualism does not only mean that revelation is not subject to the human knowing apparatus, it also means that revelation is actual and does utilize that knowing apparatus. Because it does occur it also has a phenomenal appearance, to wit: Jesus Christ, not as a concept, but as a person walking around on earth for thirty-some years; the Scripture, the written witness to Jesus Christ; and the preaching and hearing of the church in the present day. All statements about revelation are put into correspondence with these phenomena, but Barth's actualism and his doctrine of analogy (as a divine act of revelation, not a human act of understanding) prevent these statements from being reduced to statements about the phenomena. Phenomenalism in the doctrine of revelation is thereby avoided.[45]

Van Huyssteen says, "The critical question that must, however, be asked about the rationality model of Barthian thought is . . . the question whether Barth did succeed in finding the basis of a true theology in God and His revelation, or whether he found it in a subjective conception of God and His revelation."[46]

---

44. Barth, *Church Dogmatics* I/2, 727.

45. See the long footnote in Rumscheidt, *Revelation and Theology*, 209–12.

46. Van Huyssteen, *Theology and the Justification of Faith*, 16.

However, it is not the rationality model of Barth's theology that raises the question whether he has found a true basis of theology in God and his revelation or in a subjective conception of God and his revelation. The rationality model implicit in Barth's thought is critically realistic, not positivistic. The question is raised because his dialectical and actualistic doctrine of revelation makes the basis of his theology entirely dependent upon God and his revelation.[47] This is a material decision about the content of theology, not a methodological one. Wherever God is not revealed theology must appear to outsiders as a subjective conception. Because God is God, revelation can only be miracle and there is no rationality model or theological basis that can make it appear other than a subjective conception to those who have not recognized and acknowledged that revelation.

The dependence upon revelation is not an immunization strategy by which Christian theology may proceed no matter what may be the case in the world. It is a material conclusion about who and what is revealed, and far from immunizing theology it exposes it to the threat of emptiness should no revelation manifest itself. But it is Barth's understanding that the duty of theology is to conform itself to revelation, not interpret revelation in the world's terms. It is for God to use or not use theology as a veil in which to unveil. But it is to be noted that, far from advocating that theology simply put the content of revelation out there to be accepted or not, Barth spoke against the repristination of older theological language, affirmed not only the right but the propriety of using philosophies other than his own to approach and to interpret revelation, addressed theological ethics directly to the most worldly of issues, and engaged in some radical reconceptualizing of the traditional orthodox concepts that he was affirming.

So, if Barth's doctrine of revelation is not foundationalist, not phenomenalistic, and exhibits a complex logical structure not strictly reducible to two-valued logic, then we should conclude that it is not positivistic in its rationality model. But the legitimacy of these claims is dependent upon giving his dialectical doctrine of revelation a critically realistic reading.

---

47. Prenter also identifies the actualism of Barth's doctrine of revelation as the root of the appearance of positivism in Barth's Theology. Prenter, "Dietrich Bonhoeffer and Karl Barth's Positivism of Revelation," 106–12.

7.1.4 Critical Realism in Van Huyssteen and Barth

It should now be a matter of some interest to understand how van Huyssteen could come to characterize Barth as a positivist by reaction. What makes this question particularly telling is, first, that van Huyssteen is himself a critical realist in theology, though of a different sort than Barth. Secondly, the term "postfoundational"—which I have found apt for describing Barth's dialectical use of foundations, not only philosophical but also theological—is borrowed from van Huyssteen. He says many things that sound very much like what Barth is saying when interpreted in the critically realistic manner developed by McCormack. He calls theology "a purely human activity."[48] Barth agrees with this explicitly in many places, among them the essay on "Fate and Idea," examined in section 6.3. Revelation is a divine activity, but theology is a human. Van Huyssteen notes that, "systematic theology has no justifiable claims to any methodological prerogatives in its search for truth."[49] Barth would agree with this on the dialectical ground that no theological method, not even critically realistic dialectical method, can rightly claim to be the only appropriate method for giving witness to revelation. The only advantage that critically realistic dialectical theology has is a built in awareness of its own dependent character and its own need to regard its products as fallible hypotheses.

Van Huyssteen expresses his own critically realistic understanding of the realism of the biblical text when he says: "Calling the biblical text a reality could therefore never mean a "closed" reality, with a meaning that the historical writer has put there *once and for all*. Reading and interpreting the biblical text in an interactionist and relational way is therefore a creative and imaginative experience in which the text will permit several readings, but definitely also resist others because it has its own inner patterns and limits."[50]

Barth agrees that the biblical text is not a closed reality when he calls attention to the fact that the biblical text does not become the permanent revealedness of God, not even as a result of being used by God to reveal God.[51] Barth's insistence that we must come to the task of

---

48. Van Huyssteen, *Postfoundational Theology*, 107.

49. Ibid., 108.

50. Ibid., 149.

51. Barth, *Church Dogmatics* I/2, 530.

biblical interpretation with our presuppositions open to being addressed by the text and modified in encounter with it is a form of reading and interpreting the text in an interactionist and relational way. Barth's oft repeated themes of the sovereignty of God in revelation, the irreducible subjecthood of God in revelation, and of the power of the Scripture to throw off false readings, treat the biblical text as one that "will permit several readings, but definitely also resist others because it has its own inner patterns and limits."[52]

Van Huyssteen says in another place of his own critically realistic position:

> By seeking theoretical and theological clarity concerning its own premises, critical theology does not denigrate the revelation any more than was the case in other or earlier situations. What it does mean is an insistence on theological and theoretical clarity and a warning against an uncritical approach to philosophical presuppositions when divine revelation is adopted as a premise in opposition to contemporary thinking. In any event, the theologian must bear in mind that the "positiveness" of the revelation, that is, divine revelation as the (supposedly) unmediated premise of a theological model, offers no alternative to theological subjectivism.[53]

Barth's relationship to Kant, the way he uses Kant's epistemology, not uncritically, but with a dialectical reservation that renders it postfoundational, shows that he does not have an uncritical approach to philosophical presuppositions. The discussion of the important essay "Fate and Idea in Theology," where Barth examines carefully the philosophical presuppositions of both realism and idealism and determines to hold them with a dialectical reservation also shows that Barth's approach to philosophical presuppositions is not uncritical. Because Barth does, in fact, adopt divine revelation as a premise it is particularly important to remember that he also holds the dialectical reservation against even his own work. In this way Barth remains critical even when his premise permits him to do "positive" work in theology. The premise Barth adopts contains as one of its tenets the assertion that revelation itself is always

52. See ibid., 681–85 for evidence that he interprets Scripture in the manner suggested by this quote from van Huyssteen. See also 6.1 of this book for argumentation about how these materials from Barth apply to this question.

53. Van Huyssteen, *Postfoundational Theology*, 108–9.

mediated. If revelation itself is mediated, then the premise of revelation must also be understood as mediated. Barth does not consider his premise to be, in and of itself, a protection against theological subjectivism. Relative to the object of theological discourse, God's self-revelation, all theological and philosophical presuppositions must seem subjectivistic. It is revelation itself—God's sovereign self-revealing address to humanity in Jesus Christ—that breaks into our presuppositions and forces them to adapt themselves to the content of that revelation. This, and not dialectical method, is the ultimate protection against theological subjectivism. It forces us to hold every presupposition, even the presupposition of divine revelation, in a critically realistic manner.

Notice that van Huyssteen does not say that divine revelation cannot or should not be adopted as a premise by critical theology. "Critical theology does not denigrate the revelation any more than was the case in other or earlier situations." His critical warning is that *when* it is adopted as a premise it must not thereby treat itself as excused from theological and theoretical clarity nor permit its own philosophical presuppositions to remain unexamined. I have argued at length that Barth's critically realistic dialectical theology does not make these mistakes.

But if Barth's doctrine of revelation were to be stripped of its dialectical character, if the essential dialectical heart of the analogy of faith were to be ignored, if the *Realdialektik* of veiling and unveiling were to be understood undialectically as a simple explanation of how we have in the text of the Scripture a positive revelation, then all of van Huyssteen's criticisms would be both appropriate and devastating.

But this is precisely what happened to the interpretation of Barth in the English-speaking world between World War II and 1995.[54] McCormack's thesis about how to understand and interpret Barth (as a critically realistic dialectical theologian) is intended to address errors

---

54. Before World War II, before 1951 when the interpretation of the development of Barth's theology as a turn from dialectic to analogy offered by von Balthasar was largely adopted as part of the Neo-Orthodox reading of Barth, there were interpreters whose approach to Barth did not suffer the faults of Neo-Orthodoxy. See, for instance, Momsa, *Karl Barth's Idea of Revelation*. He correctly understood the limits to Barth's use of Kierkegaard in *Romans* (ibid., 56); did not over-interpret the relation of the theology of crisis to the crisis of the postwar years (ibid., 66); understood there to be an essential continuity between *Romans*, in both editions, and all subsequent work (ibid., 90); and considered the first volume of the *Church Dogmatics* to be a continuous revision of the 1927 *Die christliche Dogmatik im Entwurf* (ibid., 95–96). See also McCormack, *Barth's Critically Realistic Dialectical Theology*, 209–15, 235–40.

on the right, as well as on the left. One of the primary purposes of his work is to address and correct the undialectical reading of Barth that was standard in Neo-Orthodoxy.

> Karl Barth remained—even in the *Church Dogmatics*—a *dialectical theologian*. Where this has not been recognized, the temptation to view Barth's mature theology in an all-too positive light (as, e.g., a "Neo-Orthodox" theology) has rarely been avoided[55] . . . Thus, the Barth who was received in the Anglo-American world was to a large extent a Barth stripped of his dialectical origins. The Barth who belonged to the sources of "Neo-Orthodoxy" in the Anglo-American world was himself a product of a "Neo-Orthodox" reading. This "Neo-Orthodox" reading was simply reinforced in the 1950s by the assimilation of von Balthasar's thesis of a second "conversion" in Barth's development [the famous turn from dialectic to analogy]. To this day [1995] the Neo-Orthodox reading of Barth remains the predominant one in the English-speaking world.[56]

This finds specific support in Hunsinger's characterization of Thomas F. Torrance's *Karl Barth: An Introduction to His Early Theology, 1910–1931.* He says that the motif in Barth that was of the greatest interest to Torrance was revelational objectivism, and that it "so dominates Torrance's reading of Barth that the other motifs have difficulty emerging in their own right."[57]

> From Torrance, however, one cannot help but feel that one is somehow getting revolutionary theology without the revolution, and the theology of crisis without the crisis. The energy, dynamism, and sense of collision which enter Barth's theology by way of the actualistic and particularistic motifs never quite come through in Torrance's account. Instead of actualism and particularism enlivening the objectivism, the objectivism is allowed to

55. Ibid., 18. See also the very first paragraph of the preface, vii, where the first thing that McCormack says about his own work is that it is "intended to challenge the view which has dominated the historiography of twentieth-century theology in the English speaking world: namely, that Karl Barth was the leading representative of the 'Neo-Orthodoxy' which was dominant in the period 1930–60 . . . The central goal here will be to demonstrate that the turn to a 'Neo-Orthodox' form of theology which is usually thought to have taken place with the *Church Dogmatics* in 1931–32 is a chimera. There was no such turn."

56. Ibid., 24–25. McCormack draws his historiography here from Richard Roberts, "The Reception of the Theology of Karl Barth".

57. Hunsinger, *How to Read Karl Barth*, 9–12. The quote is from page 10.

mute and soften the actualism and particularism . . . Revelational objectivism in Barth's later theology is more powerfully informed by an audacious "exceptionalism," if you will, actualistically and particularistically rooted, than Torrance's analogy seems to allow.[58]

Barth's revelational objectivism is rooted in the *Realdialektik* of veiling and unveiling in revelation. Using this motif to mute the actualism and particularism of Barth's theology is precisely to mute objectivism's own dialectical roots. Barth himself says of the "obligation" and "obedience" which mark "the knowledge of God in faith": "We do not say all that so as to commend some sort of realism or objectivism."[59] Barth does not mean here to reject realism and objective knowledge in theology, but rather that we are given them in faith as a consequence of the Word of God, not as a presupposition by virtue of which to claim that we have the word of God in hand in our theology or interpretation of Scripture.

Certainly there are many passages in the *Church Dogmatics* that supply Torrance with reasons to give revelational objectivism the priority. "Not the veiling, however, but the unveiling is the purpose of His revelation . . . But He does unveil Himself: it is for this reason and to this end that He veils Himself and to this extent that His unveiling is the goal of his way and ours."[60] But the end of the way spoken of here is God's way in revelation and our way in the faith that is established in revelation. The end of the way is not that theology may speak of God in undialectical realism and objectivity. Many other passages maintain the need for dialectic in theology and make it impossible to read positive passages as a graduation from dialectic into objectivity. Our objectivity is prompted by and established in revelation but the positiveness is limited because we still speak of God only by analogy. The analogy of faith is God's act and does not suffer limitation. But the analogy of theology does, and, as was seen in 6.1.3, it is only similarity and truthlikeness. The dialectical limit of analogy cannot be exceeded.

> We then saw that this ability becomes reality—i.e., our words receive analogy to God's being—as God disposes concerning them in His revelation, giving Himself to them as object and thus giving them veracity . . . The relationship between the knower and the known on the basis of revelation is to be understood as

58. Ibid., 11–12.

59. Barth, *Church Dogmatics* II/1, 13.

60. Ibid., 215.

a positive one. But we must now be clear that this positivity is definitely restricted; that this goal of our knowledge of God (i.e., its veracity) also means in fact its limit to forward progress (corresponding to and in fact coinciding with the incomprehensibility of God). If our knowledge of God is true, our words stand in a correspondence and agreement with the being of God. But we have already seen that this cannot be a correspondence and agreement which mean parity, because that would mean the annulment either of the deity of God or of the manhood of man.[61]

God, even as we suspect of the natural world, is both inexhaustible and irreducibly complex. Thus, the correspondence of *our* words to God inherits all the limitations discussed in section 4.3.1. Direction is important, for the correspondence of God to our words in the grace of revelation can be spoken of with all the positiveness that Torrance desires. But the correspondence of our words to God can only be spoken of dialectically.

As I pointed out in section 6.2, Torrance is probably the first person to call Barth a critical realist. He recognizes and describes Barth's critical realism in a manner that *almost* captures its character. But because he accepts and adopts von Balthasar's thesis about the turn from dialectic to analogy in Barth's work he continually speaks as though being a critical realist entitled Barth to be a positive realist without further dialectical reservation.[62] He speaks of "Barth's breakthrough to a profound objectivity and a new realism."[63] He treats dialectic as a temporary expedient,[64] and says that "it would now be a misnomer to speak of his theology as 'dialectical.'"[65] The transition to *Church Dogmatics* meant that he "threw out the old dialectic . . . and interpreted the Word of God in the most concrete and positive way."[66] But though Barth speaks in the *Church Dogmatics* of "the undialectical certainty of the realization of the true knowledge of God," he is speaking of the certainty of faith, which is a gift of grace that takes place in "the dialectic of certainty and uncertainty which is our part in this event." The certainty arises because

61. Ibid., 233.

62. Torrance, *Karl Barth*, 139–40, 174. See McCormack, *Barth's Critically Realistic Dialectical Theology*, 4–5, 438.

63. Torrance, "Transformation and Convergence in the Frame of Knowledge," 287.

64. Torrance, *Karl Barth*, 85.

65. Ibid., 89.

66. Ibid., 139, 142.

"the dialectic is directed and controlled from the side of the event which is God's part." But that certainty inheres in revelation, and not in our theology. Theology is on our side of the event and "the dialectic still remains on our part."[67]

As an example of Torrance getting Barth almost, but not quite right: "Christology, therefore, has for Barth a supreme *critical* significance, for it is through Christology that theology is enabled to break through subjectivism, in its romantic-idealist or its existentialist forms, to the sheer reality of God. And it is through radically Christo-centric thinking that pure *theology* can arise and be preserved from all corruption from the side of anthropocentric thinking."[68]

It is true that Christology has for Barth a critical significance and is a part of how theology breaks through subjectivism. It is part, with the doctrine of revelation, of an attempt at a critical theory for a critically realistic dialectical theology. But it is revelation itself that is the source of our self-criticism; doctrines are only an attempt to theorize that critique. Moreover, the continuing presence of dialectic in Barth's thinking means that theology *never* breaks through to the sheer reality of God. God breaks through to us. Our theology is *not* pure and is *not* preserved from all corruption. Anthropocentric corruption, especially in the form of natural theology, is endemic to us as human beings.[69] Theology that is an adequate witness to revelation only arises actualistically by grace, and no more becomes the embodied true theology than the words of Scripture become the revealedness of God.

This is a point Torrance seems to miss when he says: "Of course, when our statements are simply and formally identical with statements of the text of Scripture in which Christ speaks his Word to us, they are directly authoritative."[70] Barth's own statement is: "But it is also not true that there is a 'simple' thinking and speaking which, in its 'child-likeness,' does not stand under the crisis of the hiddenness of God. Even the language of ecclesiastical dogma and that of the Bible is not exempt from this crisis. It is not the case, then, that we have only, say, to rediscover the world of

---

67. Barth, *Church Dogmatics II/1*, 75.

68. Torrance, *Karl Barth*, 143.

69. Barth, *Church Dogmatics II/1*, 165–66. Torrance, *Transformation and Convergence*, 289–91, takes note of this, but still manages to speak as above.

70. Torrance, *Karl Barth*, 188.

the biblical view and concept or to adopt the biblical language, in order to make the viewing and conceiving and language of truth our own."[71]

Torrance also examines closely the essay "Fate and Idea."[72] In his exposition of the first two sections on realism and idealism his judgments are very close to those I have made in 6.2.1 and 6.2.2. He correctly identifies the dialectical appropriation of the tension between realism and idealism as the clearest statement of Barth's critical realism. However, he treats dialectic as a way of synthesizing realism and idealism, instead of a reservation to be held against all human thinking about God. In his exposition of the third section on the relation between philosophy and theology he neglects the dialectical reservation that is to be held against dialectical theology itself. In this way he is able to mute the dialectic in Barth's critical realism and treat it as a method for producing a positive (and positivist) realism.

> The dialectic between realism and idealism has undoubtedly helped him to grasp more profoundly the objectivity of the Word and contributed to his movement into a fundamentally realist theology[73] . . .
>
> The immense significance of Barth's theology is that in it we have a Herculean undertaking to *expound within the more dynamic and critico-idealist style of modernity a fundamentally realist theology.*[74]

I have defended the realism of Barth's theology, but without muting the element of dialectic or the critical element. If any of the three elements in Barth's critically realistic dialectical theology is fundamental it is dialectic, not realism, but it is best to hold all three in careful balance.

Torrance's defining work was done from the late 1950s to the early 1970s when the philosophy of science still had a positivistic cast. He speaks as though critical realism meant the critical discounting of the human ingredients in our knowledge so that it is solely determined by its object, even in his writings on the philosophy of science.[75] Given

71. Barth, *Church Dogmatics II/1*, 195. See also 242 where Barth says that "we cannot adopt and repeat the orthodox doctrine of analogy," in speaking of seventeenth-century Protestant orthodoxy.

72. Torrance, *Karl Barth*, 151–71. Emphasis Torrance.

73. Ibid., 171.

74. Ibid., 176.

75. See "The Place of Michael Polanyi in the Modern Philosophy of Science" in Torrance, *Transformation and Convergence*, 107–73.

Torrance's pronounced interest in the science-theology dialogue and his interpretation of Barth using scientific analogies, it should be no surprise that this reading of Barth tends to give his doctrine of revelation a positivistic flavor.[76] Torrance forms his idea of critical realism before the most radical discussions in the philosophy of science. It still has a positivistic cast.

With all this in mind, I think that we should understand van Huyssteen's criticisms as supporting a critically realistic reading of Barth's dialectical theology and impugning the Neo-Orthodox reading of Barth. It is the Neo-Orthodox reading of Barth that is naïve realism, with a positivistic model of rationality, a phenomenalistic treatment of the text of Scripture, and an immunization strategy built into its doctrine of revelation. Van Huyssteen is utterly correct when he says that "the assumed axiomatic datum of God and His revelation offers no escape from this dispute [whether theological discourse is meaningful]." Barth does indeed take the act of God in revelation, the Word of God, as an axiomatic datum. But it is an axiom for hermeneutics,[77] for the right interpretation of the Word of God written, not an axiom to be used as an immunization strategy. Moreover, it is, even there, an axiom, freely chosen in an attempt to respond faithfully to the event of the Word of God, and not self-evident absolute truth.

Critically realistic dialectical theology does not attempt to escape from the dispute over the meaningfulness of theological discourse by means of this axiom; Neo-Orthodoxy does. Barth does not enter into the dispute by producing philosophical argumentation for the meaningfulness of theological language, nor by attempting to refute philosophical argumentation denying the meaningfulness of theological language. He enters into the dispute rather by using the axiom in an attempt to give

76. It would be easy, and largely true, to see my work in this book as a mere updating of Torrance. But though I go where Torrance has already gone, I do so with two brighter and clearer lights that make it possible to go deeper into the cave and see more clearly. First, I use the critically realistic interpretation of Barth's dialectical theology, rather than the Neo-Orthodox. Second, I use a much more flexible postfoundational critical realism, formed in the crucible of the more sophisticated and nuanced philosophy of science from the 1970s on. This means that I affirm the multidimensionality of human knowledge. Without surrendering its realism I decline to affirm that in its pure form it is determined solely by its conformity to its object.

77. See Burnett, *Karl Barth's Theological Exegesis*, an examination of the unpublished drafts for the preface of the first edition of *Romans*, on this point.

a witness to revelation that demonstrates its meaningfulness by success in being meaningful (not by its own power, but by God's faithfulness).

Van Huyssteen does critically realistic dialectical theology a service by 1) describing carefully a fault often considered to be present in its thought, 2) confirming its judgment about the inadequacy of the Neo-Orthodox interpretation of Barth, and 3) warning it of an error into which it may yet fall. The refusal of Neo-Orthodoxy to enter into dialogue with its critics was harmful to both sides. The critically realistic interpretation of Barth's dialectical theology should be able to listen to, learn from, and speak with its critics.

Barth is a dialectical critical realist with a strong Kantian background. It is in theology and with respect to God's self-revelation that Barth is critically realistic. Van Huyssteen's critical realism has its immediate background in the philosophy of science and its ultimate background in faith. Faith is to be interpreted in both men as trust, not fideism. As a result, van Huyssteen is critically realistic about all human knowledge, not just the knowledge of God. Since Barth is a critical realist only in anticipation, critical realism not being a developed and available option to him at the time he was doing most of his theological work, it is very much to be hoped that Barthian interpretation can benefit from encounter with modern critical realism, once the Neo-Orthodox misreading has been set aside.

For one thing, Barth's theological epistemology is postfoundational only by holding the dialectical reservation against Kant's foundational epistemology. It should now be possible, while still working in the school with Barth, to develop a more flexible and helpful theological epistemology. It will achieve greater theological and theoretical clarity by holding the dialectical reservation against a fallibilist critical realist epistemology. The more adequate an epistemology is as an understanding of the human act of knowing the more adequate it is, when used under the dialectical reservation, for giving witness to both the transcendence and the immanence of God in revelation.

It is in dialogue with van Huyssteen and his postfoundational model of critically realistic rationality that critically realistic dialectical theology has its best hope of becoming not only an interpretation of Barth, but also, as Barth would clearly have wished, a continuing creative theological endeavor in its own right.

7.2 IRRATIONALITY

7.2.1 Bartley's Pancritical Rationalism

In 1962 W. W. Bartley III published *The Retreat to Commitment*, an argument in support of rationalism in philosophy in general and the philosophy of science in particular. In it he advances a very important modification of Karl Popper's program.[78] One of the consequences of his position is a criticism of much Protestant theology, and Karl Barth's theology in particular, for making ultimate commitments that render their theology specifically and pathologically irrational.

Bartley calls his position pancritical rationalism, and we should understand it in the terms used here as a rationalist critical realism. It has three key features. The first is the divorce of justification from criticism. The second is the emphasis upon rationality as a characteristic of persons and the way in which persons hold their beliefs. The third is the universality that rationality acquires from the first two features and by which (1) a pathological infinite regress is avoided, (2) irrational commitments as the logically necessary foundations of rationality are rendered unnecessary, and (3) the field of applicability of rationality is not artificially limited.

The recognition that rationality in general and criticism in particular need not be justificational (the modification in Popper's program) was the original insight from which Bartley developed his position.[79] The insight arose in response to an anomaly in the problem of criticism or justification, to wit, how is a position, or a belief, or a practice, or indeed, anything that may come under consideration, to be judged rationally? "Criticism" is derived from the Greek word for judgment, and that root meaning must be kept in mind in this context, for what is desired is not merely a complaint against a position, belief, or practice, but a judgment

---

78. Bartley, *Retreat to Commitment*, 105: "Thus in 1960 I discussed these matters with him [Popper] and suggested how the problem could be dealt with within the general framework of his own approach, in terms of my distinction between justification and criticism . . . In response Popper altered the terminology of chapter 24 of *The Open Society and Its Enemies* (4th and subsequent English editions) to mute its fideism, and introduced a polemical addendum on relativism. In *Conjectures and Refutations*, chapter 10, and in his *Realism and the Aim of Science*, part 1, section 2, he introduces my distinction between justification and criticism, and this distinction is now routinely presented as a feature of Popperian thought."

79. Ibid., 103–6.

about its truth formulated in response to a question. All the standard theories of rationality before Popper, and before Bartley's modification of Popper, gave the same answer to this question. A position, belief, or practice was to be judged rational if it could be justified on rational grounds; that is justified from another position, belief, or practice already known to be rational. The procedure for making this judgment must also be known to be rational and is treated as rationality itself.[80]

The anomaly in this procedure is that when a position, belief, or practice is judged to be rational on the basis of another already known to be rational by a procedure known to be rational the question irresistibly arises, How are the other position and the procedure of derivation judged to be rational? It is this anomaly that gives rise to Fries' trilemma, that such a procedure of rational justification must lead in the end either to a dogmatically held starting point, or to an infinite regress, or to something, most commonly sense experience, that is not itself justified rationally.[81]

Bartley considers that the history of the philosophical discussion of the problem of rationality constitutes sufficient evidence that no theory of rationality in which positions are criticized by reference to rational *justification* can possibly avoid this trilemma. The most common modern [1984] reaction to the anomaly is to accept that an ultimately non-rational starting point forms the ground of every scheme of rational justification.[82] Bartley calls this non-rational ultimate starting point an ultimate commitment and regards it as not merely non-rational, but irrational.

Now, as Kuhn describes them, anomalies are the ultimate incitements to paradigm changes.[83] Bartley's response to the anomaly of the trilemma is a change of paradigm. The paradigm of criticism by demand for rational justification is abandoned entirely.

80. Ibid., 222.

81. Ibid., 211–13; see also Brown, *Rationality*, 59, 69.

82. Bartley, *Retreat to Commitment*, 117.

83. Kuhn's description makes it clear that he considers that it is paradigms themselves that make possible the discovery, isolation, and focusing of attention upon anomalies. Without the uniformity and co-operativity fostered in a field by the sharing of a paradigm, there would be no anomalies, only things we did not happen yet to know, none of which were any more significant to the ultimate task of understanding the world and our knowledge of it than any other. This historically observed effect of paradigms is of significance for anyone who wishes, as Kuhn himself apparently wishes, to judge that what Kuhn has discovered about scientific revolutions does not render science totally relativistic. Kuhn, *The Structure of Scientific Revolutions*, 52–110.

> The authoritarian structuring of philosophy's fundamental epistemological questions can be remedied by making a shift . . . We may not only reject (as did the critical rationalists) the demand for rational proofs of our rational standards. We may go further and *also* abandon the demand that everything else *except* the standards be proved or justified by appealing to the authority of the standards, or by some other means. *Nothing gets justified.* Instead of following the critical rationalists in replacing philosophical *justification* by philosophical *description*, we may urge the philosophical *criticism* of standards as the main task of the philosopher. *Nothing gets justified; everything gets criticized.* Instead of positing infallible intellectual authorities to justify and guarantee positions, one may build a philosophical program for counteracting intellectual error.[84]

What this means is that criticism is no longer taken as a demand for rational justification. Instead, submission to criticism is the standard of rationality. Some attention needs to be given at this point to what criticism is and what constitutes a rational response to criticism.

Bartley's understanding of criticism is descended from Popper's recognition that scientific theories cannot be justified inductively, but can be falsified deductively by the rule of *modus tollens*.[85] But, as Harold Brown points out, Popper's understanding of how theories are to be falsified leaves a great deal unspecified about what justifies a falsifier.[86] A falsifier must be something that is not itself questionable, what Popper calls a basic statement; that is, an empirical statement that is not burdened by the suppositions of any given theory. But a falsifier must also be sufficiently strong to falsify the theory in question. Many theories tolerate many potential falsifiers for some time before they are adequately explained in a way that nullifies their potential for falsification.

Bartley's understanding of criticism is much more flexible than Popper's understanding of falsification. For Bartley criticism consists in making explicit an understanding of what would serve to falsify *or* render inadequate a position, belief, or practice. Popper's understanding seems limited to a logical evaluation of the connections between a theory and its potential *empirical* falsifiers. Bartley recognizes criticisms in four major areas. These are (1) logic, interpreted primarily as logical

---

84. Bartley, *Retreat to Commitment*, 112.

85. Ibid., 195.

86. Brown, *Rationality*, 50–70.

consistency, (2) sense observation, the empirical check for refutation that Popper required, (3) scientific theory, which is the possibility that a position, though consistent logically and conformable to sense observation, is nonetheless in conflict with currently unproblematical scientific hypotheses, and (4) problem, which is the possibility that a position, though not refuted by any of the preceding checks, is nonetheless an inappropriate answer to the problem to which it is addressed.[87]

The flexibility of Bartley's understanding of what it means to criticize a position, belief, or practice is dependent upon a clear understanding that "everything gets criticized." The potential falsifiers of a position—whether logical, empirical, scientific, or philosophical—are also open to criticism, and Bartley's specifications, or anyone else's, of what amounts to a criticism also get criticized. Bartley makes it clear that if a position must specify its potential falsifiers in advance in order to be held rationally, then we would have reverted to a justificational judgment.[88] Bartley does not intend this. Openness to *unspecified* criticism is essential to holding a position rationally. Moreover, criticism is not strictly limited to possible falsifiers. Bartley refers to Lakatos's work on the history of mathematics to show how statements of necessary truth, valid under all possible interpretations, nonetheless get criticized and revised.[89] This is a point at which Bartley has gone beyond Popper. Another is his recognition that even the criticisms of a position are themselves to be held open to criticism. This means that the criticism of a theory or position does not *prove* the theory to be false, for this would then be an attempt to justify the disproof of the theory.[90]

> The test statements are intended to be hypothetical, and criticizable and revisable, just like everything else in the system; there is no justification, no proof, no fixed point anywhere. There is nothing "basic" about basic statements. And hence no possibility of dogmatism with respect to them.
>
> If such basic statements happen to be incompatible with a theory, then the theory is false *relative to them*; and they are false *relative to the theory*. There is no question of theory proving

---

87. Bartley, *Retreat to Commitment*, 127.

88. Ibid., 234–35.

89. Ibid., 239–41.

90. Ibid., 213–16.

reports wrong, or reports proving theory wrong. *Both* could be . wrong; neither is "basic."[91]

It is this recognition of the hypothetical and criticizable character of the criticisms of positions that are held open to criticism which prevents Bartley's position from falling back into a justificational mode which would subject it to Fries' trilemma.

Bartley does not claim that the inability to give a rational justification for a position makes it *ipso facto* irrational. On the contrary, he admits that many positions are held, even by pancritical rationalists, that cannot be justified rationally. But the positions are considered to be held in a rational manner (not to be confused with being a rational position) if they are held open to criticism and subject to revision under the impact of criticism.[92]

Of course, the obvious question now is, how do we tell when a criticism is such that we should abandon the position that it criticizes, and when is a position strong enough to endure such criticisms as have, to that point, been brought to bear upon it. This is the point at which Bartley's work is the least developed. Bartley speaks of building "a philosophical program for counteracting intellectual error," and creating "an ecological niche for rationality."[93] He seems to be well aware that there is a great deal of work to be done on the idea of criticism if his program is to be adopted. He says that, "in terms of the new theory of criticism to be outlined here, the notion of criticism, far from being trite, becomes one of the most *unexplored*, puzzling, and rewarding areas of philosophy."[94]

Bartley does give some clues, not amounting to a fully worked out position, to how we should treat criticisms of positions.

> When one belief is subjected to criticism, many others, of course, have to be taken for granted—including those with which the criticism is being carried out. The latter are used as the basis of criticism not because they are themselves justified or beyond criticism, but because they are *unproblematical at present*. These are, *in that sense alone and during that time alone*, beyond criticism.
>   We stop criticizing—temporarily—not when we reach uncriticizable authorities, but when we reach positions against which

91. Ibid., 215.
92. Ibid., 121.
93. Ibid., 112–13.
94. Ibid., 114. Emphasis mine.

we can find no criticisms. If criticisms of these are raised later, the critical process then continues. This is another way of saying that there is no theoretical limit to criticizability—and to rationality.[95]

This means that any decision to accept a position for the time being, or to accept a criticism as sufficient reason to reject a position for the time being, entails a judgment that either the presuppositions and consequences of the position or the presuppositions and consequences of the criticism are more problematic relative to whatever context the position and the criticism share.[96] Note though that the standards of judging what amounts to more or less problematic, including standards for what is a shared context between a position and a criticism, are themselves criticizable, and up for grabs.

The "up for grabs" character of everything, even the standards for judging what is "up for grabs," gives Bartley's pancritical rationalism its comprehensive character, but it also renders it indefinite in a way that needs to be filled out by further work. What is called for here is an understanding of the role of judgment in the sense that Harold Brown gives it. "Judgment is the ability to evaluate a situation, assess evidence, and come to a reasonable decision without following rules."[97] It is judgment of this sort that is necessary for making the decisions between positions and criticisms of them mentioned above. The question of what would make such a decision reasonable in the absence of rules to follow can be answered exactly and precisely in a Bartleyan sense. The decision of judgment is reasonable if it is considered to be criticizable and held open to revision in the light of criticisms that may be made against it. Bartley and Brown complement one another at this point.

There are two primary reasons for supporting Bartley's inversion of the standard for rationality from justification to submission to and survival of criticism. The first is that it is a possible understanding of rationality that complements a fallibilist epistemology. Fallibilist epistemology is necessary in any critical realism, as I have described it in this

---

95. Ibid., 122. Emphasis Bartley.

96. Ibid., 169–77. This appendix, added to the second edition, on contexts and metacontexts is very helpful for fleshing out some of the bones that were left a little bare in the original work.

97. Brown, *Rationality*, 137. The whole chapter on judgment is the kind of thing that can be understood in a way that is consonant with Bartley's position.

work. Not to be complementary to a fallibilist epistemology would be a severe criticism of Bartley's understanding of rationality.

The second reason for supporting Bartley's inversion is that it gives full and proper respect to the semantic distance between the sign and the thing signified, between the symbol and the referent. Even a true statement that is as complete and unproblematic as possible (at this time) is not identical with that which it is true about. It is a correspondence, not an identity. In most cases this is obvious because the statement is a syntactical arrangement of language, or a thought, or, most abstractly considered, a proposition, while that to which the statement refers is something in the world and outside the mind. But even where the thing referred to by a statement is itself a statement, the semantic distance remains. Even the interesting Gödelian statement that refers to itself does not refer to its direct and identical self, but rather to the natural number that is the unique Gödel code number for itself.

Any system of understanding rationality that supposed that there were a class of statements, observation statements perhaps, that were capable of reducing the semantic distance between the sign and the thing signified to an irreducible minimum, would be failing to take that semantic distance seriously. It would be criticizable on that account. But Bartley regards all statements, even observation statements and "basic" statements as criticizable. This implies that a statement cannot be such as to reduce the semantic distance between itself and its referent to zero, and that if there is a minimum semantic distance, then that minimum can only be approached asymptotically. A justified statement would have to assert that it was at the minimum possible semantic distance from its referent. A criticizable statement need only assert that in the present context it has reduced the semantic distance to its referent more than any other available statement about that referent in that context.

In appendix four Bartley makes explicit something that is implicit in his main presentation, but is easy to miss. The rationality that Bartley is describing in his abandonment of justification for criticizability is to be understood as a characteristic of persons, and not of statements, claims, positions, or beliefs. The characteristic that is appropriate to statements, claims, and beliefs is truth. Rationality is a characteristic of how these statements, claims, and beliefs are held by people.[98] Without this distinction Bartley's position on rationality, misunderstood as a way

98. Bartley, *Retreat to Commitment*, 233–34.

of judging the rationality of positions, statements, beliefs, claims, practices, and such, does not escape from infinite regress.

The value of accounting for rationality as a predicate of people in how they hold their positions or beliefs is this: Infinite regress is stemmed because in holding a position open to criticism, both criticism by those who hold different presuppositions and criticism that cannot yet be formulated because of the present state of human knowledge, it is *not* the case that the rationality of holding the position cannot be established until after all the relevant criticisms appear and are examined. Such a requirement, to acquire and examine all relevant criticisms before making a judgment as to whether a position is being held rationally, *would* lead to an infinite regress. The position is held rationally in the first place by being held open to criticism, even if all the criticisms have not yet been formulated and examined. There is no regress because nothing further is required. An infinite regress might be required before a position could be revised into perfect conformity with truth, but at every stage along the way the fact that the position was being held open to criticism and further revision would be sufficient for the position to be held rationally. Notice how beautifully this fits with the critically realistic idea that even fallible knowledge can nonetheless be properly considered to be true knowledge if it is held in such a way as to lead to further knowledge.

This emphasis on rationality as a characteristic of persons, and how they hold positions, and only derivatively, if at all, a characteristic of positions is another respect in which Bartley's work fits well into Harold Brown's work. Brown cites Bartley's response as a comparable position to his own.[99]

Bartley's position avoids the infinite regress. It avoids irrational commitments as logically necessary foundations for systems of formal rationality, where rationality here means formal systems of rules for making connections in thought, in that the choice of axioms is now considered to be irrational only if it is held to be immune to criticism. The work that mathematicians have done investigating the relationships among the axioms in various foundational systems of mathematics, as well as in formulating mathematical theories with alternate sets of axioms, is a sufficient demonstration that even the most formal and rigorous systems of rational rules can be held to be criticizable and revisable in the light of criticism. Bartley calls this kind of commitment to a revisable set

---

99. Brown, *Rationality*, 184.

of axioms in formal systems where axiomatic foundations are necessary "conviction," rather than "commitment."[100]

7.2.2 Bartley's Critique of Barth

Bartley's charge against Barth, and indeed, against most modern Protestant theology, is that it makes an ultimate and irrational commitment to a position that is not defended because it ignores criticism. Bartley admits that the making of such a commitment seemed, for some time, to be at least compatible with rationalism, because when rationality was conceived in terms of justification the making of arbitrary commitments to designated stopping points in the regress of justifications was regarded as a rational action. He says that, "the only serious argument for Christian commitment today concerns the problem of the limits of rationality."[101] It seems to Bartley that Protestant theology, and Barth's in particular, takes advantage of a legitimate philosophical concern for the limits of reason and rationality to defend its irrational choice of religious commitment by means of a *tu quoque* argument. "Just what is the powerful *tu quoque* argument? It argues that (1) for certain logical reasons, rationality is so limited that *everyone* must make a dogmatic irrational commitment; (2) therefore, the Christian has the right to make whatever commitment he pleases; and (3) therefore no one has a right to criticize him (or anyone else) for making such a commitment."[102] This argument provided a rational excuse for irrational commitment.

Bartley considers that liberal Christianity was attempting to maintain its religious beliefs in the manner that he calls conviction, holding those beliefs to be responsible for coherent conformity with the best science and philosophy available, and criticizable by them. Liberal Christianity took its responsibility for remaining rational seriously enough to permit the results of scientific investigations to criticize its understanding of who God is and who we are in consequence of who God is. Unfortunately, ongoing scientific investigation, especially in the form of the search for the historical Jesus, brought liberal Christianity to the point where it was very much at issue whether what remained after being reinterpreted in terms of philosophical and scientific criticisms had any reasonable claim

---

100. Bartley, *Retreat to Commitment*, 121.

101. Ibid., 72.

102. Ibid.

to being truly Christian. This, however, constitutes evidence that liberal Christianity was attempting to remain rational in Bartley's terms, in as much as it was willing to be rationally argued out of even its own most deeply held convictions.[103]

Barth's accomplishment, according to Bartley, was to recognize that the gap in the justificational model of rationality made it possible to recover a substantially orthodox understanding of the content of the Christian faith by founding it upon the absolute assumption that the revelation of God has occurred in Jesus Christ.[104] Since presuppositions are chosen arbitrarily by convention, this one has as much right to serve as the foundation of an intellectual discipline as any other. Moreover, Bartley admires the skill and judgment with which Barth chose this assumption, because it permits Barth to be as rational as possible while maintaining an irrational position.[105]

> Barth wove into a web of amazing complexity of detail, yet beautiful simplicity of structure, an acute denunciation of the basic errors of liberalism and an elegantly appealing alternative approach. Given his intentions and his commitments, it is hard to imagine a more skillful intellectual solution. He is one of the most interesting, as well as one of the most learned, self-critical, and bold writers in the history of Christian thought[106] . . .
>
> For anyone who begins with the assumption—or the commitment—that final revelation happened in a particular historical event, Barth's is the best theory I know about how to approach the task of determining the content of that revelation.[107]

It is important to understand why Bartley objects to an ultimate commitment. It is not because he considers commitment itself to be illegitimate or irrational. He has himself a commitment, which he would call conviction, to the core of logic, which can be derived from the very idea of deducibility.[108] But he does not consider this to be an *ultimate*

---

103. Ibid., 15–33.

104. "Beginning with the assumption or commitment that revelation 'happened' in Jesus, Barth resolves to take the assumption seriously in order to trace its implications." Ibid., 44.

105. Ibid., 38. Richard H. Roberts, *A Theology on Its Way?*, 61, also calls the rational attempt to develop Christian theology in this way "an intellectual monstrosity."

106. Bartley, *Retreat to Commitment*, 39.

107. Ibid., 47.

108. Ibid., 254–56.

commitment, even though he admits that it is the last thing he would surrender before discourse breaks down into mere un-ordered conversation, because it is not held to be beyond criticism and revision. An ultimate commitment is one that is held *beyond all criticism and revision*; an immunization strategy. Since Bartley has redefined rationality in terms of criticizability and openness to revision an ultimate commitment is, by its very ultimacy, irrational. I suspect that Bartley considers that, as making or having an ultimate commitment is opposed to rationality itself, having or holding an ultimate commitment when pursuing a rational task is to begin by assuming a contradiction. This would account for the flexibility and comprehensiveness with which those who have ultimate commitments are able to give religious explanations for any possible state of affairs. It is because anything follows from a contradiction.

7.2.3 The Dialectical Conviction about Commitment

Bartley asserts that Barth recognized that the gap in the theory of rationality made it possible to do substantially orthodox theology upon the absolute assumption that the revelation of God has occurred in Jesus Christ. Putting the matter this way implies that the choice of assumption was, in large part, a consequence of recognizing the gap and of being in need of such a gap. McCormack and the scholars upon whose work he built, as well as those like Burnett who have followed down the path that McCormack opened, demonstrate that there is no historical evidence that these considerations contributed anything to Barth's choice of axioms. It was the Neo-Orthodox interpreters of Barth who recognized that his axiom could be used in that gap. Of course, Barth's axiom might still be culpable of Bartley's accusation, even if he did not formulate it for that reason and in that way.

But it is clear throughout his discussion of Barth that Bartley understands Barth to be a Neo-Orthodox theologian.[109] Bartley writes this book in 1962 on the basis of work he has been doing since 1956 and offers a second edition with appendices in 1984. This whole period is

---

109. Ibid., 10: "The new idol that was to replace liberalism is referred to by names like 'Neo-Orthodoxy' and 'new Reformation theology.' Although the emphases of this new theology have changed considerably since its birth, its main themes remain largely the same, and its leading names are still Barth, Brunner, Niebuhr and Tillich." See also 25, 37, 102. It is to be noted that Bartley spends almost as much space talking about Tillich and Niebuhr as he does about Barth.

one in which the Neo-Orthodox reading of Barth was dominant in the English speaking world. Because Bartley understands Barth as a Neo-Orthodox theologian he fails to recognize and understand that Barth's dialectical theology is meant to be critically realistic. This means that he misunderstands Barth's self-criticism in such a way that he is unable to give it credit for being the kind of openness to criticism and revision that he regards as the essence of rationality.

At several points Bartley suggests that the strategy of making a commitment to Jesus Christ as the revelation of God means making a commitment that is not firmly attached to any particular content. "Barth's formula was of course not without its own dangers, ones with which he never satisfactorily dealt: if the character of the Jesus or the Word of God to whom assent was required was indefinite, and if such commitment was required *no matter what* Jesus was and did, at best the subjective commitment itself would be definite. Its object would be an 'I know not what and I care not what'—perhaps a less than satisfactory object for worship."[110]

Now Barth does indeed regard the assumption of revelation in Jesus Christ as identity-making for Christian theology, as can be seen in his often repeated theme that "every concept used in dogmatic theology is to be defined on the basis of a particular event called Jesus Christ."[111] But if the critically realistic reading of Barth is correct, then the particular event called Jesus Christ is not a contentless concept.[112] Jesus Christ is always for Barth the particular, concrete, and specific Jesus Christ as witnessed to in the testimony of the prophets and the apostles.[113] Barth specifically denies the charge that his doctrine of revelation was derived in an idealistic fashion from the concept of revelation.[114] Moreover, he denies that his understanding of the concept of the Trinity was derived idealistically from the concept of revelation.[115] Instead these things are determined *a posteriori* from the content of the revelation. It is on this

---

110. Ibid., 48.

111. Hunsinger, *How to Read Karl Barth*, 4; see Barth, *Church Dogmatics II/1*, 162.

112. Ibid., 7.

113. "Jesus Christ, *as he is attested for us in Holy Scripture*, is the one Word of God." Emphasis mine. PCUSA, *The Book of Confessions*, 249. Barth's role in writing the Barmen Declaration is well known.

114. Barth, *Church Dogmatics I/1*, 338.

115. Ibid., 314.

account that theology moves from the particular to the general, like all the sciences, with the generalizations which we use, such as the doctrine of revelation or the doctrine of the trinity, remaining always criticizable by reference to the particular actual event of revelation of which they are abstractions and to which they refer.[116]

Barth makes it clear that he does not mean the assumption of revelation to be an empty concept into which *any* content can be poured when he speaks of Scripture as having the power to throw off false interpretations.[117] If the assumption of revelation were to be held as an ultimate commitment, if it were to be held no matter what the content of revelation might be, then it would be tautological. But in being tautological it would thereby surrender any claim to be speaking about what God might actually be. It would no longer be a presupposition whose truth is semantic and referential.

For Barth revelation is not first and foremost an assumption that we must make in order to be Christians and do Christian theology. It is first of all an event, an action that God does.[118] It is our *doctrine* of revelation that is an assumption, and as such it is not merely criticizable and revisable, but it is criticized continually by the actual and ongoing event of revelation.[119] If the critically realistic reading of Barth is correct, then in making this distinction Barth is precisely holding his own position open to criticism and revision, as Bartley demands that rationally held positions should be. That which Barth does not criticize, the actual event of the Word of God, is not a position, presupposition, theory, statement, or any other thing to which we normally apply rational criticism. It is *the reality itself* to which we address the question of the truth of our positions, statements, theories, and presuppositions by asking whether the statements our positions make are actually the case. But Barth would understand that even the statement that "God has spoken and we must test all our speaking about him against his own speech about himself" is a position, a theoretical construct, to which criticism is legitimately addressed. Again: "I was and am a regular theologian at whose disposal

---

116. Barth, *Church Dogmatics I/2*, 602.

117. Ibid., 681. See also the discussion of this topic in 6.1.1 of this book.

118. This is the theme or motif that Hunsinger refers to as actualism. See Hunsinger, *How to Read Karl Barth*, 4, 30–32.

119. See the quote from Barth, *Church Dogmatics I/2*, 530 explicated in 6.1.2 of this book.

stands not the Word of God, but at best a doctrine of the Word of God, . . . whereas the Word of God spoke for himself or did not speak where and when it pleased God."[120]

This means that it is a legitimate question whether the Word of God has actually spoken or not, and that the possibility that God has not spoken is a part of the critical background against which we make the assertion that God has indeed spoken in Jesus Christ. It is certainly true that we do not even begin to do Christian theology until we have made this assertion, but because Barth's critically realistic dialectical theology is dialectical even about itself this assertion is not to be held beyond all criticism and revision. The possibility that God might not speak, indeed, might not ever have spoken, remains and the awareness of it is a crucial element in the dialectical reservation. But for Barth the legitimate question as to whether the Word of God has actually spoken is not to be answered by arguments in the field of the philosophy of religion prior to an examination of the Scripture. It is to be addressed by the witness to revelation that the theologian gives in faithful exposition of the meaning of the Scripture under the presupposition that God has spoken. It can only be answered positively by God's own act in fulfilling the truth conditions of such witness. The presupposition does not answer the question. It only enables us to interpret Scripture with sufficient theological and theoretical clarity that the presupposition can only be held as true if God actually speaks. It cannot be held no matter what.

Barth admits that theologies with philosophical presuppositions other than those that he has chosen are not only possible but legitimate.[121] He has a regular habit of conducting his theology in conversation with past theology, including with great prominence those theologians with whose presuppositions he disagrees rather strongly, both in the small print sections of the *Church Dogmatics* and in his books on *Protestant Theology in the Nineteenth Century* and *The Theology of Schleiermacher*. This is evidence that he is holding his own position open to criticism and revision. The fact that Barth continues to hold his position, even in the face of these criticisms, is not to be taken as evidence that Barth holds it *beyond* and *despite* all possible criticism, but only that he judges

---

120. Karl Barth, *Die Christliche Dogmatik im Entwurf*, 8, translated by McCormack, *Barth's Critically Realistic Dialectical Theology*, 325.

121. See the quote from Barth, *Church Dogmatics* I/2, 731 explicated in 6.1.3 of this book.

that the criticisms that such positions address to his theology are, for the moment, more problematical than his own. But this is what Bartley expects of a rationally held position, which he calls "conviction," a term with more than a little Christian history.

Even when Bartley correctly understands why Barth is self-critical he still misunderstands Barth's self-criticism as not amounting to rationality because he reads Barth as Neo-Orthodox rather than critically realistic. Bartley characterizes Barth's theology:

> All theological statements are forever *conjectures* about the Word of God . . . Thus the theologian must commit himself to the Word of God. But the theologian ought not to commit himself to any particular interpretation of the Word of God, to any particular cultural morality or ideology . . . It may be helpful to explain it by mapping these expressions approximately into ordinary secular language. Take the case of the natural scientist: he is presumably committed to the truth about the natural world, but is not committed to the truth of any particular hypothesis about the nature of that natural world. Substitute "theologian" for "natural scientist," "Word of God" for "natural world," and "interpretation" for "hypothesis," and you have the crux of Barth's position.[122]

This is actually a very good characterization of Barth's critically realistic dialectical theology. Yet Bartley makes this characterization to demonstrate that Barth is only imitating rational behavior, not behaving rationally. The key lies in the first sentence. "All theological statements are forever *conjectures* about the Word of God." For Bartley the problem with this sentence is that it does not have a period after the word "conjectures." If it did, then the theological statements that assert that there is such a thing as the Word of God, that it is a reality, an event, would also themselves be conjectures. Then it might be possible to consider theology rational in Bartley's terms. But Bartley is convinced that what Barth really means and does is treat all theological statements as conjectures *except* the statements that assert that the Word of God is a real event to which our theological statements refer and about which they are conjectures.[123]

122. Bartley, *Retreat to Commitment*, 45–46. Notice that this is the kind of mapping of which Torrance was so fond, as noted by Hunsinger in *How to Read Karl Barth*, 11, and that such a reading of Barth tended to err in the direction of revelational objectivism. As argued in 7.1.4 of this chapter, an error in this direction tends to support a positivistic Neo-Orthodox reading of Barth.

123. Ibid., 45, 47: "Argument about the truth of the Word of God is, however, for-

If the critically realistic reading of Barth's dialectical theology is correct then this is a misreading of Barth, and it *is* possible to put a period after the word "conjectures." Even the critically realistic dialectical theology of the Word of God is itself only a conjecture, and it is held with what Bartley would call conviction, rather than an ultimate commitment.

In Barthian terms, the difficulty with Bartley's description is the idea of ultimate commitment. If an ultimate commitment is one that is held beyond all criticism and revision, then Barth's response would be, first, that human beings are not capable of ultimate commitments. Second, even if they were, ultimate commitments would be illegitimate and actually blasphemous in theology because God is God and is not bound by our commitments, however ultimate they may seem to us. An ultimate commitment in theology, even one to the Word of God as the foundation of all possible theology, would still constitute a philosophical *a priori* determination of who God might and might not be, and thus illegitimate.

If theology is to be a critically realistic response to who God actually is and what God actually does then even the apparently necessary presuppositions of any human thought about God cannot determine who God might or might not be, and must be held as conjectures whose truth is dependent upon that to which they refer. Therefore they cannot be understood as ultimate commitments but only as convictions.

If there is any such thing as an ultimate commitment, if such language can be used to speak rationally about God at all, then it cannot be any commitment we have to any of our speaking about God. It cannot even be our commitment to revelation itself, for it is not by our power that we apprehend the veracity of God in revelation.[124] It can only refer to God's commitment to us, to God's determination before all creation to be our God and take us to be God's people; it can only be God's self-election in Jesus Christ to be the mediator and to suffer on our behalf, and God's free choice of self-revelation. That commitment does not belong to us as human beings, as Christians, and as theologians in such a way that we can use it to justify our theological positions and statements as rational. Ultimate commitment is not our commitment to the Word of God, but God's commitment to us in the Word, a commitment proved to be ultimate upon the cross.

---

bidden." "'Those people who interpret the Word of God . . . do not ask whether it is true, but only whether any statement about it is a statement about the Word of God.'"

124. Barth, *Church Dogmatics II/1*, 184, 197, 210, 212.

Our theology is rational because it submits to criticism, just as Bartley demands, although Barth understands this as theology submitting to the criticism of the Word of God. When Barth is understood as a critically realistic dialectical theologian, rather than as Neo-Orthodox, then the mapping onto scientific process that Bartley outlined is a good analogy. It is the actual behavior of the world that ultimately criticizes all our hypotheses about what it might actually be, although usually through the medium of people's statements about it. It is the actual event of revelation that criticizes all our theology about it, although usually in the form of other interpretations of it.

Of course, it remains the case that if there is no God, or if God has not chosen to reveal himself in Jesus Christ, then all our theology is false and we are still in our sins. But in that case it is *false*, and *not irrational*, as Bartley claims. Falsehood is a much different matter than irrationality.

Bartley wants to claim that rationality is not limited, despite the work that has been done since the time of Kant on the limits of rationality. A geometric plane is unbounded, it extends infinitely in all directions *in the two dimensions in which it exists*. But it is limited to being two-dimensional, rather than three-dimensional. Even so rationality might be unbounded, so that Bartley might rightly expect that rationality can legitimately criticize anything and everything that it can address at all, anything and everything that can be spoken in human language. Yet it could still be limited to those dimensions necessary to contain the minds concerning whose rationality we are debating. God could still be beyond the limits of rationality, even though all possible human knowledge of God, even that which we have in revelation, is still subject to the criticisms of rationality. It is possible for an object to be unbounded and yet limited, and I think that this is the correct way to understand rationality in such a way as to honor both Bartley's contention that rationality must be unlimited (translate unbounded) and Barth's Reformed contention that the finite is not capable of the infinite (translate God). But in this case Barth's contention about God being beyond finite (or denumerably infinite) grasp is to be interpreted not as an immunization strategy that will guarantee to theology a place to work which is immune from rational criticism, but rather as a conjecture about the actual character of the reality to which we refer when we speak of the Word of God.

It is hard to escape the impression that Bartley considers that the assumption of the Word of God, the presupposition that God is revealed in Jesus Christ, can *only* be held as an ultimate commitment because if it were truly an honest conjecture then it would also be necessary to admit that it is a conjecture that has already been refuted by the rest of our scientific and historical knowledge.[125] If this is how Bartley understands the matter, it would explain why he is unable to recognize the critically realistic character of Barth's dialectical theology.[126]

7.2.4 The Sermon on the Mount

At the very end of his book (bar the appendices) Bartley argues at length that the Sermon on the Mount constitutes very valuable and "highly realistic" advice on how to conduct dialogue and dispute. He then uses it to criticize theologians who use the *tu quoque* argument as an excuse to refuse to listen to their critics. He has understood the Sermon on the Mount and applied it in interpretation with beautiful correctness. For this theologians owe him great thanks, and to the extent that we have been guilty of this sin we should be ashamed of ourselves.[127] This is not to grant Bartley's thesis about Barth's theology, but only to confess that using the *tu quoque* argument to cut off conversation is a sin. Neither is this to admit that we should be doing apologetics, in the sense to which Barth denies legitimacy. It is often justifiable to put a dialogue on hold, for we are entitled not to be trapped in endless prolegomena. Indeed, it is often necessary to turn to the exposition of our theology in order to bring substance, rather than presupposition, back to dialogue. But it is not justifiable to cut the dialogue off, not only on Bartley's terms, which we might not admit bind us, but on the grounds of the command of God to give witness to the Gospel.

There is also a critical measure of humility necessary here, and Bartley has correctly pointed to where theologians sometimes fail of it. If God exists, if God does speak, if the presupposition of the knowledge

---

125. Bartley, *Retreat to Commitment*, 14, 72.

126. Nielsen, *Die Rationalität der Offenbarungstheologie* deals with many of the same issues that I have addressed in this work and appears to have an understanding of Barth's theology that is compatible with the critically realistic interpretation. He also spends a section dealing with Bartley's charge of irrationalism. Since leaving the academic world to enter church work my German has deteriorated to the point where I have been unable, within a reasonable time, to consult this work (there is no translation). It is probable that he has anticipated at least some of my results. My attention was called to this work by Zijlstra, "Barth und der (Pan-)Kritische Rationalismus".

127. However, I can find no instance, nor even a hint, of Barth using a *tu quoque* argument.

of God is a reflex of an encounter with God in revelation rather than a substitute for it, then God does not need us to make excuses. God must speak for himself, for we cannot speak for God. The most we can do is give witness to what we understood when we heard God speak. But the arguments that we give when we undertake to do theology in obedience to the Word of God depend for their veracity (not validity, for that is a matter of logic, as Bartley demands) upon the event of the Word of God. The only proper grounds for accepting our witness is an encounter with that Word.

I have argued in various places that Barth's careful listening to his opponents, in Christian theology at least, shows that he is attempting to hear and obey this word from the Sermon on the Mount. It remains to consider whether he is using an immunization strategy.

The crux of the issue between Barth and Bartley lies here. A critically realistic interpretation of Barth's dialectical theology indicates that it depends upon the reality of the event of the Word of God. That presupposition is necessary to do Christian theology at all. But the presupposition depends upon the reality. If God does speak, then the presupposition is a sound starting point for our explication of what we have heard God say. But if God does not speak, then it is exactly as has been described, merely a postulate of our subjective religious consciousness, an immunization strategy.

> The conclusion that God is known only through God (we speak of the God who has revealed Himself in His Word) does not have either its basis or its origin in any understanding of the human capacity for knowledge. For that reason it cannot be assailed from that quarter. Its basis is not in the subject, but in the object of the knowledge concerned. It is grounded in the God revealed in His Word. It is because He is who He is and does what He does that we have made that assumption and reckoned and worked with it all along. But now we must show how far this basis, which is so clearly distinct from a human theory of knowledge, does actually compel us to make that assumption.[128]

When Barth says that the conclusion cannot be assailed, it sounds like an immunization strategy. But he says only that it cannot be assailed

---

128. Barth, *Church Dogmatics II/1*, 44 See also 4, "Knowledge of God within the Christian Church is very well aware that it is established in its reality and to that extent also called in question by God's Word, through which alone it can be and have reality, and on the basis of which alone it can be fulfilled."

from a prior determination in epistemology. By going on to say that we must show why the reality of revelation compels us to make the assumption he is back on critically realistic ground. That reality is the reason for the assumption and it is with regard to the reality that the assumption is to be criticized. This passage shows the ambiguity in Barth's position. Other passages seem unambiguously immunizational: "For in the Word of God it is decided that the knowledge of God cannot let itself be called in question, or call itself in question, from any position outside itself . . . True knowledge of God is not and cannot be attacked."[129]

If the argument I have been making throughout this book is correct, then passages like this should be mitigated by the realization that Barth distinguishes clearly and dialectically the *event* of the Word of God and the *reality* of the knowledge of God from our *doctrines* of revelation and of God.[130] But this is very close to the whole point that Bartley is arguing: that Barth is willing to revise any doctrine, but holds the assumption of the Word of God itself beyond argument and revision. Bartley says, "We wish to question the truth of the Word of God."[131]

The difference here is very delicate. It is the Word of God *itself*, God's self-revealing *act*, that is beyond argument and revision. It would be both daring and dangerous to argue with God and attempt to revise God's Word. (Though there are certainly stories in the Scripture about those who have attempted it. And not all of them came to grief.) But not only are our doctrines of revelation and of God revisable, but even the assumption that God speaks. For as an assumption it is a human assertion.

> The first step should have made it clear that when we delimited the bound knowledge of God from other ostensible or real knowledge of God by rejecting any other understanding of its reality and possibility than that which proceeds from within outwards, we were not guilty of an arbitrary absolutizing of any human position. Of course, this bound knowledge of God is also formally a human position, and materially a human affirmation. It is a human thesis

---

129. Ibid., 4, 7.

130. "It follows from this that theological statements can be made with only scientific certainty, which, on account of its relativity, has to be distinguished from the certainty of faith. Theological statements as such are contested statements—challenged by the sheer incomparability of their object." Barth, *Anselm*, 30.

131. Bartley, *Retreat to Commitment*, 47.

like any other, to which the question coming from without seems to be not only permissible but even necessary.[132]

Theology is bound to the knowledge of God in revelation and can only give witness to that revelation and make explication of that knowledge from within its own boundaries, where the assumption of the Word of God holds and its own response to revelation is one of obedience. But the assumption is itself a thesis that can and must be questioned from without. The question from without is recognized to include the question of the truth of the Word of God that Bartley raises. The assumption of the Word of God is a human position which is not to be absolutized, and ought not to be guilty of an ultimate commitment nor taken as an immunization against question. Theology's beginning from the event of the Word of God arises from a refusal to be trapped in prolegomena, not an immunization strategy. Its continuous and permanent exposure to the question that comes from without, whether or no the event of the Word of God actually occurs, is carried in the dialectical reservation under which theology is conducted.

Theologians must take Bartley's criticism as a kindness, being warned by it against the possibility that we may make the mistake of absolutizing our foundations. Theology only differs from Bartley in reminding itself that this is not a mistake primarily for the reasons he has given, but because of who God is in revelation and what the responsibilities of theology are. In the case of Barth, as was just said, the difference is delicate and many passages can be read as refusals to entertain the question of the truth of the Word of God. By Bartley's criticism we are pushed back from a Neo-Orthodox to a critically realistic interpretation of Barth's dialectical theology.

Barth is not attempting that of which Bartley complains in Protestant theology because he is not Neo-Orthodox.

> A theology of revelation and grace is obviously not protected as such (i.e., by the fact that it has made these concepts its leading concepts) from the possibility that it may have set itself an impossible theme. May it not be that this possibility is so threatening that we must now affirm that we have not attained an understanding of the veracity of the knowledge of God . . . And in the face of this question in the narrower and wider context, it is not sufficient simply to maintain that we have thought and said

132. Barth, *Church Dogmatics* II/1, 30.

all this in faith and for this very reason in veracious knowledge of God. This may well be just an empty phrase, which does not protect us at all against the menace of the question . . . If our continual appeal to God's grace and revelation—whatever else may be thought of it—was not at any rate for us subjectively a mere playing with words or operating with a systematic *Deus ex machina*, if we at least thought we knew what we were saying with these words, we cannot wish to have it otherwise than that we cannot in fact protect ourselves against this question. If we can, what are we doing to put our whole deliberation under the leading concepts of revelation and grace? In the same way we only need to take ourselves at our word—that we pursued this way in faith—to see at once that we cannot really wish to protect ourselves against this question.[133]

This is the quote that demonstrates in the strongest possible way that Barth's theology is not an immunization strategy. He has not put aside the question of the truth or even the reality of the Word of God. The theme of a theology of revelation and grace may be impossible. It might be a mere playing with words. It might be simply appealing to the Word of God as a protection against question and doubt. We cannot protect ourselves against the question, nor even wish to protect ourselves against the question, because doing so would be to abandon our total dependence upon God's grace in revelation and reduce revelation from an act of God to a necessary axiom of our subjective religious consciousness.

Barth may not have succeeded in what he has attempted. It is always a legitimate question whether he has chosen an appropriate axiom for his theology. But Barth believes that theology does not address this question by a retreat into prolegomena or natural theology, and does not address it from before or outside its own obedient response to the Word of God. Theology addresses this question by a clear exposition of the content of revelation as interpreted under this presupposition. But a faithful attempt at such exposition "can not wish to have it otherwise" than that it is open at all times to the question as to whether that which it interprets is even real.

It is impossible for theology to retreat outside itself to defend its presupposition, because it cannot be defended on any other grounds than that it is necessary in order to understand and interpret this reality

133. Ibid., 245–46.

that it has encountered. But this is also the only way to defend many scientific and philosophical assumptions as well. Even though Barth eschews an apologetics that attempts to defend the faith on common ground with unbelief, he nonetheless believes that appropriate communication with unbelievers can be practiced. It consists not in the defense, but rather in the explication of the content of revelation under the conviction of faith.[134] Since the veracity of revelation can only be confirmed by a further act of revelation the only rational way that theologians can apologize for it is to give witness to where they encountered it and what they heard and understood when they did. It remains for God to speak or not when those to whom witness is given look where theologians are pointing to see whether there is anything there. Were they to accept that witness on any other grounds than hearing the Word of God themselves they would be acting irresponsibly.

Barth is not defending his theology by an appeal to what Bartley calls an ultimate commitment. Faith is not an irrational commitment. Barth would regard that as the worship of an idol. Neither is faith unquestioning fidelity to a chosen position. Even if the position was once the veil in which God unveiled himself in revelation, it does not remain so. To avoid questions in this matter is to abandon the hope that revelation not only did occur but does and will occur again. Faith is trust; trust in God. If God does not honor that trust by continuing revelation, if God is not trustworthy, then faith is in vain and even a theology of grace and revelation is but dust and ashes. Theology is an hypothesis, ventured in faith and hope. Were it not so, it would not be an hypothesis about the Word of God. But as a venture, an hypothesis, it cannot escape question without ceasing to be faith. Barth is not the most rational irrationalist, but rather a rational believer in something that may yet turn out to be false. As Bartley himself points out, the possible falsity of a truth claim does not make the assertion of it irrational.

7.3 PANNENBERG, SCHOLZ AND THE CHARGE OF SUBJECTIVITY

Wolfhart Pannenberg is aware of the charge of revelational positivism against Barth and he shares it.[135] He also shows his awareness of Bartley's

134. Ibid., 93–96.

135. Pannenberg, *Basic Questions in Theology, Volume I*, 3, 13.

criticisms, and to some extent he shares them as well.[136] For that reason I will deal in this section only with what is particular to him. He adds a focus upon the questions put to Barth by Heinrich Scholz in the 1930s and concludes that no matter what it is that Barth intends, he only succeeds in adopting a subjectivistic viewpoint for his theology that makes it to be no more than an intricate, detailed, artistic explanation of personal faith.[137] The crux of the issue lies in the matter of rational standards.

Pannenberg is not compromised by the misunderstanding of Barth as Neo-Orthodox as were so many in the English-speaking world. He understands clearly and deeply what Barth is trying to do.

> Barth's idea of the scientific nature of theology to which he would like to hold in spite of his stress upon the theology of revelation fits quite naturally into this [the dialectical] conception. According to Barth, theology is scientific in its "proper treatment of its object," "its conformity with its object or its appropriate treatment of it." But the subject matter of theology is God in his revelation, that is, the Word of God (see above). Theology's proper treatment of its object is determined by whether it corresponds to the word of God through the obedience of faith.[138]

Pannenberg shows in the ensuing discussion that he understands that Barth intends all this in a critically realistic manner. He cites the background for Barth's understanding of what makes a position scientific.[139] Barth believes that in theology we are investigating an unknown object, a truly other, but one which nonetheless gives itself to be known, else there would be no investigation. This is not the same as the situation of the physical sciences, because the object is different, but there is sufficient similarity in the way the two investigations stand before their respective objects to make it reasonable to call them both scientific. In this investigation we grant the object priority over method, and hold all our methods, along with their presuppositions, however necessary and universal they may seem to be, variable with respect to our object.

---

136. Pannenberg, *Theology and the Philosophy of Science*, 29, 44–46.

137. "But the critical question by which to judge Barth's theological foundation is whether he has succeeded in making God and his revelation anything but the postulate of our (or his) consciousness. If it were possible, this would be the only proper way of conducting a theology as a science of God, with God himself and his revelation as the starting point." Ibid., 266.

138. Ibid., 267–68.

139. Ibid., 268–69.

The standard with which we are concerned is how well the model that we construct by our various methods as knowledge of the object fits the object itself.[140] We make rational judgments about rules for our methods on the basis of the (anticipated) success of those rules in crafting models as knowledge of the object. Since we do not have direct knowledge of the object, and since the model is still and always only a model, an ongoing process of comparison of the models with their objects is necessary. This is not always easy, and the rules for this also become part of the rules for our methods. But scientific objectivity means that whenever we can, with all the critical awareness of the implications of our own presuppositions that we can muster, we change the rules to improve the fit. This attitude towards the relationship between the rules of our thinking and the objects of our inquiry is common to critical realism in both the sciences and in Barth's dialectical theology. The quality of the fit of the model to the reality determines the rules.

For Barth objectivity does not mean the universal rational rules by which we determine what the object truly is. Objectivity means, in the rest of human knowledge as well as in theology, that we enter into a "uniting and distinguishing relationship to an object," an interactive relationship, in which "our subjectivity is opened up" to the object and we are "grounded and determined anew."[141] This is why theology is different than other fields even though the human apparatus of knowing is the same as in them. The object is different. This definition of objectivity means that the act of knowledge is necessarily an act of changing our minds. This is the meaning of Barth's insistence that the "knowledge of God is obedience to God."[142] This understanding of objectivity and the

140. Barth, *The Göttingen Dogmatics*, 8. Barth's emphasis upon the power of the object to determine knowledge of it was not taken as an excuse to return to a simpler theology. From an article in *Christliche Welt* in 1923: "It is my private view that the exercise of repristinating a classical theological train of thought, which in the days of medieval and Protestant scholasticism was known as 'theology,' is probably more instructive than the chaotic business of today's faculties for which the idea of a determinative *object* has become strange and monstrous in the face of the determinative character of the *method*. But I also think I know that this same kind of thing can and should not return and that we must think *in* and *for* our time. Actually the point is not to keep historical-critical method of biblical and historical research developed in the last centuries away from the work of theology, but rather to fit that method, and its refinement of the way questions are asked, into that work in a meaningful way." Cited in Rumscheidt, *Revelation and Theology*, 41–42.

141. Barth, *Church Dogmatics II/1*, 14–15.

142. Ibid., 26.

character of knowledge is entirely congruent with all that was said about critical realism in chapters 3 and 4 of this work.

Pannenberg wishes to argue that the opposite attitude is required. The rules should determine the quality of the fit.

> Scholz gave his reason for this, "I have not yet found a criterion by means of which any given idea can be judged appropriate to its subject, even in cases of serious disagreement." At least such a verdict—and in this case we must agree with Scholz—cannot be reached independently of formal criteria of scientific validity, in particular the demand for control of its propositions. These demands make it possible to decide whether an assertion suits its subject matter or not. This is the crux of the controversy between Barth and Scholz.[143]

But we have seen, and specifically in the area of the philosophy of science, and in Brown's theory of rational judgment in a situation in which formal criteria are not yet present, that such verdicts can be reached. They may be mistaken, may be falsified, but they are not impossible. Pannenberg is opting here for a strongly classical understanding of rationality in which there are universal and necessary rational standards. Pannenberg has correctly identified the crux of the problem here, for if there are universal and necessary rational standards, then Barth, and almost all critical realism in the philosophy of science as well, is wrong to hold rational standards variable relative to the object of discourse. If there are necessary and universal rational standards then it is impossible without them to even touch the object of discourse, much less judge the quality of the fit of the construction that is our knowledge.

Barth, as a Kantian in ordinary matters, might possibly agree with Pannenberg with respect to the rationality which is appropriate to the knowledge of the world in which we have our being, but with respect to the particular and peculiar object God, Barth must differ. It cannot be known in advance whether even universal and necessary rational standards will be appropriate to such an object as God. We use what we have as best as we can, but we hold even our methods variable relative to this object. What we can now add to Barth that he would only have been able to affirm anachronistically is that this attitude about the relationship of our theoretical structures to the realities to which they refer is also found in a critically realistic philosophy of the physical sciences and is probably

---

143. Pannenberg, *Theology and the Philosophy of Science*, 269.

characteristic of all human knowledge. But what we must immediately add, lest we do attribute anachronistic judgments to him, is that he does not adopt this critically realistic attitude as a method for getting at the problem of who or what God really is, but rather as a description of the consequences and implications of adopting the presuppositions and methods that turn out to be actually and contingently necessary to give an account of who God claims to be when encountered in revelation. For Barth, being critically realistic, just as being dialectical, is a methodological reflex of his doctrines of revelation and of God.

I am certain that Pannenberg intends to be critically realistic as well, but it is a form of critical realism that is, like Bartley's, strongly rationalistic. We are faced here with a choice of postulates in a situation in which there is a long history of controversy. The postulates in question are that the quality of fit of knowledge to its object is to be judged by universal and necessary rational standards, or that rational standards and methods are to be held variable relative to the object of inquiry and judged by the relative improvement in the quality of the modeled knowledge of the object which those standards and methods produce. Improvements in quality are rational judgments in Brown's sense, not rational calculations. They have the character of hypotheses. By the standards of the first postulate the holders of the second, which in this case include Barth, must seem either irrational or hopelessly subjective. In fact does it appear so to Pannenberg.

> Barth's unmediated starting from God and his revealing word turns out to be no more than an unfounded postulate of theological consciousness. Barth rightly rejects the reduction of the subject matter of theology to human religious consciousness, but his use of God and his revelation as an unmediated premise provides no escape from these problems. Barth's description of the obedience of faith as a venture shows, and his dispute with Scholz confirms, that a positive theory of revelation not only is not an alternative to subjectivism in theology, but is in fact the furthest extreme of subjectivism made into a theological position. Whereas other attempts to give theology a foundation in human terms sought support from common arguments, Barth's apparently so lofty objectivity about God and God's word turns out to rest on no more than the irrational subjectivity of a venture of faith with no justification outside itself.[144]

144. Ibid., 272–73.

On the basis of a critically realistic reading of Barth we can answer this criticism at several points. First, it is not clear what criticism Pannenberg means to make by calling Barth's starting point unmediated. If he means that it is not justified or mediated philosophically, then he is correct. But then it does not amount to a criticism in a critically realistic view. Barth's starting point is an hypothesis, not antecedently justified, but held open to criticism and correction in the course of the inquiry for which it serves as a starting point.

It is actually mediated in two ways, both historical. Barth began as a traditional liberal theologian. It was the experience of difficulty in interpreting the Scripture and of anomalies in the liberal position that moved him towards a new starting point. Barth's disappointment over the signatures of his teachers on the declaration of support for the war policy of the Kaiser during the First World War is one such anomaly. Another was his growing awareness, as he became involved in the socialist movement, that liberal theology was supporting the socio-economic status quo despite much prophetic condemnation of social injustice.[145] Another mediation is to be found in the confessions of the church which Barth takes to be a preliminary agreement of the church, fallible and revisable, but mediating the choice of starting points for a church dogmatics.[146]

Second, Barth's postulate may be incorrect, inappropriate, or even false, but it is wrong to call it unfounded. It is only unfounded with respect to the rationalist rules which Pannenberg is using. With respect to the critically realistic rules that Barth is using it is reasonably founded as a conjectural postulate for a dialectical theology. It does not arise out of thin air, although bold hypotheses may sometimes appear to do so, and yet be counted as rational. It arises, as Brown requires of a judgment that chooses postulates prior to rules, from meaningful knowledge of a body of relevant information. Third, Barth's doctrine of revelation is misunderstood when it is understood as a positivistic theory, as already argued in the previous sections. Fourth, to the extent that it is legitimate to seek outside justification, Barth is doing so in designing his doctrine of revelation to depend upon the actuality of what God does. At the same time, precisely because the justification in question is outside the idea being justified, it is impossible to give a justification in classical

---

145. McCormack, *Barth's Critically Realistic Dialectical Theology*, 78–125.

146. Barth, *Church Dogmatics I/2*, 589–96.

terms. Instead the rationality of acting this way towards postulates is justified by holding them open to criticism and correction.

Barth may well be mistaken in choosing the postulates he does; they may be false or inadequate. But Pannenberg is certainly mistaken in calling Barth's choice of postulates *irrational*. It is correct to identify that Barth has chosen different postulates than those Pannenberg thinks best. But it is wrong to call that choice "the furthest extreme of subjectivism" when it simply springs from a different conception of the nature and use of rationality. Pannenberg's insistence upon universal and necessary rational standards by which to judge the quality of a fit must seem dangerously close to subjectivism itself, as it asserts the relevance of a certain set of standards to an object about which it is entirely in question what standards, if any, apply, on the question begging grounds that those standards have to apply to everything. The rational standards in question are necessary to the subject, as it is subjects and not objects that are rational or not. Their universality lies in the determination of the subject that all objects must submit to them. Thus, from Barth's standpoint, Pannenberg's position seems hopelessly subjective.

Bartley, Pannenberg, and Scholz all have a great deal of difficulty with Barth's refusal of necessary and universal rational standards, even to the point of rejecting the requirement of the freedom from contradiction. Barth's dialectical theology has always used contradictory and paradoxical language, and Barth is not about to give it up as it often seems to be the only way to give witness to the free activity of God in revelation. Barth has opted for the advantages of natural language, with rigor supplied in a more formal language that exhibits a three-valued logic that eschews the principle of bivalence. So we are now in a position to give a critically realistic explanation of what Barth means when he says:

> And theology can only say point blank that this conception is unacceptable to it. Even the minimum postulate of freedom from contradiction is acceptable to theology only when it is given a particular interpretation which the scientific theorist can hardly tolerate, namely that theology does not affirm in principle that the "contradictions" which it makes cannot be resolved. But the statements in which it maintains their resolution will be statements about the free activity of God, and not therefore statements which dismiss contradictions from the world.[147]

147. Barth, *Church Dogmatics I/1*, 9.

First of all, theology employs contradictions because it is attempting to speak about God, conceived of as different than and other than the world and different than and other than the necessary presuppositions of our own consciousness. Theology does not insist that the contradictions cannot possibly be resolved, but does doubt that the ultimate resolution will be forthcoming soon enough to make it unnecessary to use contradictions.[148] Barth refuses to abandon the right to use contradictory locutions because God is not known in advance of revelation. The advantage of natural language is that it does tolerate contradictions and can, thereby, say anything. The ability to say anything is an advantage in the investigation of an unknown object. Feyerabend's claim that "anything goes" is as legitimate in theology as in the sciences. Rigorous formulation of propositions and the resolution of the paradoxes that arise in our first response to our encounter with revelation are matters for further work.[149] Given the attempt to conceive God as transcendent, it may be that such resolutions will only be forthcoming eschatologically. In the meantime the contradictions serve as a witness that God may turn out to be other than what we may think that God must be even in the knowledge of God that we have in revelation. This is considered to be appropriate because of the particular and peculiar kind of object that God is.

When Barth abandons *standard* logic in order to permit such contradictions in his dialectical theology Pannenberg, Bartley, and Scholz talk as if he had thereby abandoned *all* logic of any sort whatsoever. But we have seen that even standard logic can be modeled in several slightly different ways, despite the hope or belief that down at bottom they are all somehow the same. We have noted also that non-standard models of logic have been invented, and some of them have been given interesting and valuable interpretations. Barth is rejecting this standard model of logic, *not* all logic whatsoever; not all rationality. Standard logic is usually

148. It is always theoretically possible to demonstrate the assertions of three-valued or multi-valued logic in two-valued logic. But it usually requires such a difficult and complex restatement of our propositions in a form laden with conditions and modifications that it would have made it very difficult to have conceived of them in the first place. It is easier to work with straightforward statements in a multi-valued logic. Afterwards they can be reified, if that is necessary or helpful.

149. "We can lay down that the Biblical witness does not say one thing in one way, but in many ways, not one line only, but on several converging lines, and therefore not without difference or contrast, but yet without contradiction. It is on the 'without contradiction' that we must insist." Barth, *Church Dogmatics II*/1, 106.

composed of a group of four to six initial postulates. The kind of non-standard logic towards which Barth is working here is probably the same as standard logic in all but one or two postulates.

In mathematics one of the variations on standard logic is the model that L. E. J. Brouwer created in response to the paradoxes and counterintuitive results attendant upon Cantor's set theory. Its primary feature is that the law of the excluded middle is modified. This modification is made specifically with respect to the difficulty of describing the properties of infinite sets, because it is with respect to infinite sets that paradoxes and counterintuitive results appear.[150]

In physics Niels Bohr introduced the complimentarity principle, which is actually less a principle than the observation of an anomaly. In quantum physics it happens that some realities, such as light, must be conceived in different and apparently contradictory ways (as a wave phenomenon and as a particle phenomenon), in order to account for the entire range of their actual behavior. This is not meant as an affirmation of a contradiction at the level of logic, but rather as an admission that the reality in question is such that none of the available ways of describing it are sufficient for a complete description.[151] The contradiction lies in the model where complimentarity applies. It is assumed that the contradiction does not lie in reality. The contradiction is also assumed not to lie in the theory, for if it did the theory would then be invalid and in need of revision. This means that we need, not two different theories, but two different models for the same theory, to map the behavior of reality in those cases where complimentarity applies.

I think that we must understand Barth as intending something similar, particularly as he is not merely attempting to refer to an infinite object, but more especially as he is attempting to refer to the problem of describing an infinite object in finite speech. When he rejects the standard logic that was readily available, even though it was sometimes thought to be the only possible logic, he is only opting for a *non-standard* logic, not no logic or no rationality at all. He makes this postulate choice in a critically realistic way, using rational judgment in a situation in which only some of the rules are known, and not all of those certainly,

150. Bartley, *Retreat to Commitment*, 252–56; Boyer and Merzbach, *A History of Mathematics*, 612, 623.

151. For a discussion of possible applications of the complementarity principle to theological matters, see Loder and Neidhardt, *The Knight's Move*, 2–3 for a basic definition and then throughout the book.

with respect rather to the fit achieved thereby in knowledge of the object of inquiry, and not by mere arbitrary and subjective choice. Though he refuses the demand not to use contradictory language, he does affirm that the contradiction does not lie in reality and is, in fact, ultimately resolvable (although that ultimately may lie in the eschaton). Either the contradiction lies in the theory, our doctrine of revelation, or our doctrine of God, perhaps. In this case our doctrines (theories) must be altered. Or else the contradiction lies in the model and we must recognize it as signaling a shift. Either two different models of the theory must be used to map the same reality, or the present model is inadequate and a new one must be sought and used.

Scholtz's assertion that there is no criterion by means of which a model can be evaluated as appropriate to its subject or as a better fit than another model would not be accepted even in a modern postfoundational philosophy of science. Most modern philosophers of science would agree that there is no universally necessary rational standard that can make this determination, but not that there is no method for doing so. The method is to bring the theory and its model into interaction with the reality that it models. In the sciences this means experimentation that tests the specifications of the model, or tests extensions of the accuracy of the model, or tests the application of the model to behaviors of the world assumed to fall under the model but previously untested, or to test the application of the model to apparent anomalies. It is not universal rational standards that validate the tests, but rather the possibility of other explanations, other theories and other models, as espoused by other knowledgeable practitioners in the field that validate the tests in the provisional manner proposed by Bartley and Brown.

This is Barth's method. He tests the fit of his model of the Word of God against the problem of interpreting passages of Scripture other than those that stimulated the formation of his hypothesis. He tests it by comparison with the results of interpretation conducted with different models than that which he currently has in hand. He tests it by continuing to listen and respond to theologians with whom he disagrees. Even though he refuses to be trapped in prolegomena by endless arguments with those theologians, he nonetheless regularly comes back to them at particular points of interpretation, comparing the fit of their model to that of his. It is not in prolegomena, in the discussion of rational standards and theological presuppositions, but rather in active interaction with the object of discourse, that rational judgments without universal and necessary rational standards are made about the fit of a model to its object are made.

The point between Barth and Pannenberg and Scholz here can be settled by a simple appeal to the current belief that the attempt to use and apply universal rational standards is illegitimate. This does not justify Barth's theology, it only prevents it from being disqualified at the beginning of the inquiry. The inquiry must be made, as I have attempted in this book, as to what rational standards are appropriate to Barth's work and whether he is due criticism on those grounds.

8

Conclusions

If the reader is convinced by my arguments, then I have furthered the critically realistic interpretation of Barth's dialectical theology by showing, as Feynman suggested, that "it makes something else come out right as well"; something other than the purpose for which it was first hypothesized. It originally served, primarily, to distinguish Barth from the other dialectical theologians and to help correct the periodization of his development by making it possible to see clearly that he never ceased to be a dialectical theologian. In this study it is seen how this interpretation further answers the criticisms of revelation positivism, irrationality, and subjectivity. It has also led to an increased awareness of just how deeply ingrained the Neo-Orthodox reading of Barth is among scholars and the degree to which it is responsible for critiques of Barth. Clearing away misunderstandings in those critiques leaves open the possibility of reformulating criticism accordingly.

Once concerns about the model of rationality implicit in Barth's theology have been answered and it seen that his theology cannot simply be swept aside by evaluating it as positivist, irrational, or subjectivist, then it can be seen where the real issue lies. The true issue, about which the critics of Barth may still wish to criticize him, is the doctrine of revelation. Barth's dialectical conception of the task of theology, and in particular its *strongly* actualistic and particular doctrine of revelation, is where the conversation should be taking place and where critics should attempt to lay their axe to the root of the tree. The interpretation of Barth's dialectical theology as critically realistic in character only answers those criticisms insofar as they are formulated and confined to criticisms of the model of rationality that Barth is using. The issue with Barth's doctrine of revelation is not whether it is positivistic or rational or subjectivist, but whether it is a faithful explication of what revelation is.

Barth's use of philosophy is always instrumental. It is a tool chosen and used for the sake of its convenience and for the skillful help that it gives in explicating our theology. No philosophy, whether perennial or universal and necessary, can determine what revelation must be. In God's freedom and transcendence revelation must always be miracle. Therefore, no philosophy can be permitted to dictate terms to theology. The presuppositions of any philosophy used as a tool of explication do certainly condition, but they cannot determine what we must say when we address the revelation of God.

Because revelation is always miracle, any philosophy may be used to address the revelation so long as it is held with conviction rather than commitment. This postfoundational abandonment of universal and necessary rational standards opens the art of interpreting the revelation to anyone who may care to address it with whatever presuppositions they may have in hand. They cannot be dismissed merely because they do not share our presuppositions. Barth acknowledges this freedom out of trust that revelation is capable of adopting and adapting any and every philosophy to acknowledge, accept, and confess that Jesus Christ is the revelation of God so long as that philosophy is a servant rather than a master.

Barth uses philosophy the way a physicist uses mathematics. He needs it, and he uses the best tools that he can understand. But mathematicians are often frustrated at the way physicists use mathematics as a tool without concern for the true mathematics, the warp and woof of argumentation and proof out of which it is woven. So it is with Barth's use of philosophy. It is a tool. If material decisions in theology demanded it, he would seek out and use another. And he refuses to abandon his own task and take up the examination of philosophical first principles or to determine which is the right philosophy to use in explicating the gospel. As he is convinced that *no* philosophy can, in its pure form, be the right tool for the explication of all that is communicated in revelation, he finds it easier to use the one he has to hand (Kant's) and simply violate its precepts from time to time. From our vantage point in intellectual history we may be able to do better.

The critically realistic interpretation of Barth's dialectical theology is directed against misunderstandings on both the right and the left. On the right the misunderstanding is to see Barth's theology as too positive, failing to understand that he has come to traditional orthodox conclusions about the material content of theology under the conditions of modernity. The temptation is always to assimilate Barth's method to the classical reason that so often accompanied classical orthodox theology. The postfoundational way he sits loose to assumptions about the nature of reason has not always been taken seriously. On the left the misunderstanding is that Barth is merely aping modern critical and self-critical rational practices. The fact that he comes to traditional orthodox conclusions about the material content of theology gives rise to the suspicion that his commitments control his conclusions regardless of evidence, or that he is merely explicating as rationally as possible his own subjective faith.

Both sides fail to see how truly radical Barth's theology is. It is rooted in revelation. If there is no revelation, then his doctrine of revelation fails. But if there is revelation, then the first thing that his doctrine of revelation affirms is that it cannot capture, cannot tame, cannot control revelation. The most it can do is give faithful witness. That witness will require both flexible rationality and realistic commitment. Interpreting Barth's theology in terms of a postfoundational critical realism implicit in it is an attempt to be faithful to both the realism and the dialectical reservation that are explicit in it.

One of the burdens of this work has been to demonstrate that modern mathematics in its free and abstract exploration of the consequences of possible axioms has shown us just how wide open the possible choice of axioms is. When logic itself is recognized as an axiomatized field, when the incredible range and variety of even rigorous thinking is recognized, then reason can exercise itself in an infinite number of different rationalities. This does not mean that any and every way of thinking is right and justifiable. As I said earlier, those forms of thinking that are truly rational may be as rare among all possible ways of thinking as the prime numbers are among the counting numbers. But it is still the case that almost any form of thought, even the strangest, will be able to find a rational expression. This means that it is almost always useless to criticize an intelligent, informed, and thoughtful position by criticizing its rationality or its lack thereof. It will almost always be necessary to deal with the matter rather than the method.

It must be kept in mind that the critically realistic reading of Barth's dialectical theology is a model of his theology, not that theology itself. It incorporates some anachronistic judgments not as properties of Barth's own theological work, but as properties of this model. Its quality is to be judged by how well it fits Barth's theology. The distinction that must be kept in mind in evaluating nonfoundational readings of Barth is one that was made at the beginning of this study: Barth would probably have agreed with nonfoundationalism, in theology at least, about the status of foundations. But he would also probably have disagreed about realism in the human knowledge of God. This relation to nonfoundationalism was the position that was distinguished as postfoundational, following van Huyssteen.

Because Barth was a Kantian in ordinary matters he would probably have disagreed with nonfoundationalism about the status of foundations in the realm of human knowledge outside of theology. But that need not be a serious concern. Barth does not need to have a strongly foundational epistemology, such as Kant's, for ordinary human knowledge in order to distinguish the knowledge of God from it. Because Barth holds the dialectical reservation even against his own dialectical theology, a postfoundational option, he would have been able to hold it against a postfoundational fallibilist epistemology just as easily. The knowledge of God is distinguished from ordinary human knowledge by its *object*, not by its method, its epistemology, or the epistemic capacity of human beings.

Because Barth was a Kantian in ordinary matters he might have been willing to accept antirealism in the realm of human knowledge outside of theology. But that may be questionable if he reads Kant as a sort of proto-pragmatic critical realist, as I argued in chapter 6. This also need be of no great concern. Barth does not need an antirealist epistemology on ordinary matters in order that the knowledge of God can be contrasted to it by its realism. The dialectical reservation is held just as firmly against positive knowledge as against negative.

If this caution is kept in mind, that neither positively nor negatively must we fall into natural theology, and this distinction, that the acceptance of nonfoundational critique and adoption of postfoundational standards does not embrace antirealism, then we will be equipped to make a reasonable judgment about modern and postmodern readings of Barth. As I pointed out while arguing that Barth can correctly, but anachronistically, be called a postfoundationalist, he is just barely one, and that only in theology with reference to the knowledge of God in revelation. This is because he is, in ordinary matters, still a Kantian—a realistically flavored Kantian, but still basically an idealist.

But scientific realism in our time has come to a postfoundational and fallibilist epistemology about the knowledge that is gained in scientific investigation, and a larger critical realism holds such an epistemology about all human knowledge. Perhaps this will be no surprise, as one of the most basic attitudes of scientific investigation is compatible with the name of God. The world is what it *is*; not what you wish it was, not even what you think it is. But it is what it is, and we have to conform our theories to the world because the world is independent of our theorizing. God is the one who declares "I am Who I am," or "I will be Who I will be." Theology must conform to revelation because revelation is independent of our theologizing.

This common attitude in the sciences must not be taken as a *vestigium trinitatis* lest we fall once more into the trap of natural theology. It is probably, rather, evidence that science originally learned this attitude from Christian faith. But that is a matter for historical investigation. But if care is taken to avoid the pitfalls that beset a traveler on this path, it should then be possible for those who work in the school with Barth to enter with joy and enthusiasm into the dialogue between science and theology. Both have something to gain in this conversation.

A theology that works in the school with Barth will be able maintain a largely orthodox understanding of traditional Christian dogma without insisting upon the magisterial right to tell the sciences what they may and may not do, what they may and may not say. Barth was comfortable with the results of critical historical investigation of the texts which are included in the Bible, without surrendering his right to criticize them for stopping at the end of prolegomena rather than proceeding to exegesis and interpretation, and without surrendering his right to interpret them according to the subject matter of the texts, God in self-revelation. So also can theology relate the physical sciences without fear, and yet without surrendering its own field of discourse and its own necessity to speak what it finds there.

In the course of time this should produce a critique of the intelligent design movement on the theological grounds that it has neglected the Reformed observation that the sovereign providence of God operates in such a way as to respect the integrity of secondary causes. Science is the field of secondary causes, as it does not (usually) even try to address the question as to why there is something rather than nothing, or what the ultimate purpose of the universe is. Good theology should, for *theological* reasons (and not as a matter of compromise) recognize the appropriate independence of the sciences in their own fields of inquiry. Good theology should also, in those areas where the fields of inquiry of the sciences and theology overlap, be able to join the conversations with reasons for the dialogue to be conducted in good fellowship.

I have not attempted to bring Barth's theology into conversation with the philosophy of science because the philosophy of science bears the rational standards that all fields must adopt. Even while adopting different standards, Barth nonetheless claims to be acting in a scientific and rational way. His theology is rational precisely because it adopts and adapts the critically realistic standard of holding method and presupposition variable relative to the object of inquiry and judging among methods and presuppositions by the quality of fit to the object of inquiry of the knowledge gained by those methods under those presuppositions. He believes that the particular character of the object of his inquiry makes it necessary for him to hold his standards in this way.

To claim scientific character is to announce one's entry into the arena of public discussion. Public discussion does not mean the mutual adoption of common presuppositions. It means rather, in a Bartleyan sense, submission to mutual examination and criticism. In as much as God is not directly identical with any of our theological formulations, not even the methodological ones that tell us how to go about doing theology, one of the standard ways of protecting theology from making the error of direct identification is to submit to the criticism of people who do not share theological presuppositions. Theology does not lay its own presuppositions aside when it engages in this task; it maintains them clearly and plainly. But submitting to this criticism has the same function for dialectical theology that dialectical theology's use of contradictions and paradoxical statements has for other positions: it serves as a reminder that God is not directly identical with any human knowledge of him.

Barth's theological epistemology can be updated by elaborating it anew with a postfoundational fallibilist epistemology as a description of the ordinary process and character of human epistemic faculties. Doing so in no way justifies Barth's theology, but will make it more easily understood by those who do not share its axioms. Theology will benefit by developing a better understanding of how the human knowing apparatus is and is not adopted and adapted by God in revelation, can and can not serve as the instrument which God uses for the knowledge of God, is and is not the veil with which God veils himself when he unveils himself in revelation. Jesus Christ himself is first of all that revelation, that veil, and that unveiling. But he is also fully human, and this constitutes the *theological* reason for using the best understanding of epistemology that we are able to find or construct.

Bibliography

Anderson, Clifford Blake. "The Crisis of Theological Science: A Contextual Study of the Development of Karl Barth's Concept of Theology as Science from 1901–1923." PhD diss., Princeton Theological Seminary, 2005.

Asimov, Isaac. *The Secret of the Universe: Essays from the Magazine of Fantasy and Science Fiction*. New York: Windsor, 1990.

Barbour, Ian. *Religion in an Age of Science: The Gifford Lectures, 1989–1991, Volume One*. New York: Harper Collins, 1990.

Barrow, John D. *Pi in the Sky: Counting, Thinking, and Being*. New York: Little, Brown & Co., 1992.

Barth, Karl. *Anselm: Fides Quaerens Intellectum, Anselm's Proof of the Existence of God in the Context of His Theological Scheme*. Translated by Ian W. Robertson. London: SCM, 1960.

———. *Church Dogmatics*. Vol. I. Part 1. *The Doctrine of the Word of God*. Translated by G. W. Bromiley. Edinburgh: T. & T. Clark, 1975.

———. *Church Dogmatics*. Vol. I. Part 2. *The Doctrine of the Word of God*. Translated by G. T. Thompson and Harold Knight. Edinburgh: T. & T. Clark, 1956.

———. *Church Dogmatics*. Vol. II. Part 1. *The Doctrine of God*. Translated by T. H. L. Parker, W. B. Johnston, Harold Knight, and J. L. M. Haire. Edinburgh: T. & T. Clark, 1957.

———. *Church Dogmatics*. Vol. IV. Part 1. *The Doctrine of Reconciliation*. Edited and translated by G. W. Bromiley. Edinburgh: T. & T. Clark, 1956.

———. *The Epistle to the Romans*. Translated by Edwin C. Hoskyns. London: Oxford University Press, 1933.

———. "Fate and Idea in Theology." Translated by George Hunsinger. In *The Way of Theology in Karl Barth: Essays and Comments*, edited by H. Martin Rumscheidt, 25–61. Alison Park, PA: Pickwick, 1986.

———. "The First Commandment as an Axiom of Theology." Translated by David Lockhead. In *The Way of Theology in Karl Barth: Essays and Comments*, edited by H. Martin Rumscheidt, 63–95. Alison Park, PA: Pickwick, 1986.

———. "From a Letter of Karl Barth to Landessuperintendent P. W. Herrenbrück, 21 December 1952." In *World Come of Age: A Symposium on Dietrich Bonhoeffer*, edited and translated by Ronald Gregor Smith, 89–92. Philadelphia: Fortress, 1967.

————. *The Göttingen Dogmatics: Instruction in the Christian Religion, Volume One.* Translated by G. W. Bromiley. Grand Rapids: Eerdmans, 1991.

————. *Protestant Thought: From Rousseau to Ritschl.* Translated by Brian Cozens, revised by H. H. Hartwell. Salem, NH: Ayer, 1959.

————. *The Word of God and the Word of Man.* Translated by Douglas Horton. Gloucester, MA: Smith, 1978.

Bartley, W. W. *The Retreat to Commitment.* London: Open Court, 1984.

Bonhoeffer, Dietrich. *Letters and Papers from Prison.* Translated by Reginald Fuller, revised by Frank Clarke. New York: Macmillan, 1967.

Boulos, George S., and Richard C. Jeffrey. *Computability and Logic.* 2nd ed. Cambridge: Cambridge University Press, 1980.

Boyd, Richard N. "The Current Status of Scientific Realism." In *Scientific Realism*, edited by Jarrett Leplin, 41–82. Berkeley: University of California Press, 1984.

Boyer, Carl B. *The History of the Calculus and Its Conceptual Development.* New York: Dover, 1949.

Boyer, Carl B., and Uta C. Merzbach. *A History of Mathematics, Second Edition.* New York: Wiley & Sons, 1991.

Bradshaw, Timothy. *Trinity and Ontology: A Comparative Study of the Theologies of Karl Barth and Wolfhart Pannenberg.* Rutherford Studies in Contemporary Theology. Lewiston, NY: Mellon, 1988.

Brown, Harold I. *Rationality.* London: Routledge, 1990.

Buchdahl, Gerd. *Kant and the Dynamics of Reason: Essays on the Structure of Kant's Philosophy.* Oxford: Blackwell, 1992.

Burnett, Richard E. *Karl Barth's Theological Exegesis: The Hermeneutical Principles of the Römerbrief Period.* Tübingen: Siebeck, 2001.

Cassirer, Ernst. *Kant's Life and Thought.* Translated by James Haden. New Haven, CT: Yale University Press, 1981.

Chia, Roland. *Revelation and Theology: The Knowledge of God in Balthasar and Barth.* Berne: Lang, 1999.

Copleston, Frederick. *Modern Philosophy, Part I: Fichte to Hegel.* A History of Philosophy. Garden City, NY: Image Books, Doubleday, 1963.

————. *Modern Philosophy, Part II: Kant.* A History of Philosophy. Garden City, NY: Image Books, Doubleday, 1960.

————. *Modern Philosophy, Part III: Schopenhauer to Nietzsche.* A History of Philosophy. Garden City, NY: Image Books, Doubleday, 1963.

Couvalis, George. *The Philosophy of Science: Science and Objectivity.* London: SAGE, 1997.

Crowe, Michael J. "Ten Misconceptions About Mathematics and Its History." In *History and Philosophy of Modern Mathematics*, edited by William Aspray and Phillip Kitcher, 260–77. Minneapolis: University of Minnesota Press, 1988.

Daston, Lorraine J. "Fitting Numbers to the World: The Case of Probability Theory." In *History and Philosophy of Modern Mathematics*, edited by William Aspray and Phillip Kitcher, 221–37. Minneapolis: University of Minnesota Press, 1988.

Detlefson, Michael. *Hilbert's Program.* Dordrecht, Holland: Reidel, 1986.

Devitt, Michael. *Realism and Truth.* Cambridge, MA: Blackwell, 1991.

Drake, Durant, Arthur O Lovejoy, James Bisset Pratt, Arthur K Rogers, George Sanayana, Roy Wood Sellars, and C. A. Strong. *Essays in Critical Realism: A Co-Operative Study of the Problem of Knowledge.* New York: Macmillan, 1920.

Einstein, Albert. *Albert Einstein, Philosopher Scientist.* Edited by Paul A. Schlipp. La Salle, IL: Open Court, 1970.

————. *Relativity: The Special and the General Theory.* Translated by Robert W. Lawson. New York: Three Rivers, 1961.

Eves, Howard. *An Introduction to the History of Mathematics.* New York: Holt, Rinehart and Winston, 1976.

Feyerabend, Paul. *Against Method. Revised Edition.* London: Verso, 1984.

Feynman, Richard P. *The Pleasure of Finding Things Out.* Edited by Jeffrey Robbins. Cambridge, MA: Perseus, 1999.

Fichte, Johann Gottlieb. *Foundations of Transcendental Philosophy.* Translated and edited by Daniel Breazeale. Ithaca, NY: Cornell University Press, 1992.

————. *The Science of Knowledge.* Translated by A. E. Kroeger. London: Trübner, 1889.

Fisher, Simon. *Revelatory Positivism?: Barth's Earliest Theology and the Marburg School.* Oxford: Oxford University Press, 1988.

Friedman, Michael. *Kant and the Exact Sciences.* Cambridge, Massachusetts: Harvard University Press, 1992.

————. "Logical Truth and Analycity in Carnap's 'Logical Syntax of Language.'" In *History and Philosophy of Modern Mathematics*, edited by William Aspray and Phillip Kitcher, 82–94. Minneapolis: University of Minnesota Press, 1988.

Gadamer, Hans-Georg. *Hegel's Dialectic.* Translated by Christopher Smith. New Haven, CT: Yale University Press, 1976.

Goldfarb, Warren. "Poincaré Against the Logicists." In *History and Philosophy of Modern Mathematics*, edited by William Aspray and Phillip Kitcher, 61–81. Minneapolis: University of Minnesota Press, 1988.

Gunton, Colin. "Bruce McCormack's Karl Barth's Critically Realistic Dialectical Theology: Its Genesis and Development 1909–1036." *Scottish Journal of Theology* 49.4 (1996) 483–91.

Hegel, G. W. F. *The Difference Between Fichte's and Schelling's System of Philosophy.* Translated by H. S. Harris and Walter Cerf. Albany, NY: State University of New York Press, 1977.

————. *The Encyclopedia Logic.* Translated by T. F. Geraets, W. A. Suchting, and H. S. Harris. Indianapolis: Hackett, 1991.

————. *Hegel's Philosophy of Mind: A Translation from the Encyclopaedia of the Philosophical Sciences.* Translated by William Wallace. Oxford: Clarendon, 1894.

Hicks, G. Dawes. *Critical Realism: Studies in the Philosophy of Mind and Nature.* London: MacMillan, 1938.

Hofstadter, Douglas R. *Gödel, Escher, Bach: An Eternal Golden Braid.* New York: Basic, 1979.

Hooker, C. A. *A Realistic Theory of Science.* Albany: State University of New York Press, 1987.

Hrbacek, Karel, and Thomas Jech. *Introduction to Set Theory.* 2nd ed. Basel: Dekker, 1984.

Hunsinger, George. *How to Read Karl Barth: The Shape of His Theology.* New York: Oxford University Press, 1991.

Johnson, Roger A. *The Origins of Demythologizing.* Leiden: Brill, 1974.

Kant, Immanuel. *Critique of Practical Reason.* Translated by Lewis White Beck. New York: Liberal Arts, 1956.

————. *Critique of Pure Reason.* Translated by Norman Kemp Smith. New York: St Martin's, 1929.

————. *Foundations of the Metaphysics of Morals.* Translated and edited by Lewis White Beck. New York: Bobbs-Merrill, 1959.

———. *Logic.* Edited and translated by Robert S. Hartman and Wolfgang Schwarz. New York: Dover, 1974.

———. *Prolegomena to any Future Metaphysics.* In *Philosophy of Material Nature*, translated by Paul Carus and James W. Ellington, 1–122. Indianapolis: Hackett, Inc, 1985.

Kitcher, Phillip, and William Aspray. "An Opinionated Introduction." In *History and Philosophy of Modern Mathematics*, edited by William Aspray and Phillip Kitcher, 3–60. Minneapolis: University of Minnesota Press, 1988.

Kolakowski, Leszek. *The Alienation of Reason.* Translated by Norbert Guterman. Garden City, NY: Doubleday, 1968.

Kolman, Bernard. *Elementary Linear Algebra.* New York: Macmillan, 1986.

Korzybski, Alfred. *Science and Sanity: An Introduction to Non-Aristotelian Systems and General Semantics.* Lancaster, PA: Science, 1941.

Köhnke, Klaus Christian. *The Rise of Neo-Kantianism: German Academic Philosophy between Idealism and Positivism.* Translated by R. J. Hollingdale. Cambridge: Cambridge University Press, 1991.

Kuhn, Thomas S. *The Essential Tension: Selected Studies in Scientific Tradition and Change.* Chicago: The University of Chicago Press, 1977.

———. *The Structure of Scientific Revolutions.* Chicago: The University of Chicago Press, 1970.

Laudan, Larry. "A Confutation of Convergent Realism." In *Scientific Realism*, edited by Jarrett Leplin, 218–49. Berkeley: University of California Press, 1984.

Leplin, Jarrett, ed. *Scientific Realism.* Berkeley: University of California Press, 1984.

Levin, Michael. "What Kind of an Explanation is Truth?" In *Scientific Realism*, edited by Jarrett Leplin, 124–39. Berkeley: University of California Press, 1984.

Loder, James E., and W. Jim Neidhardt. *The Knight's Move: The Relational Logic of the Spirit in Theology and Science.* Colorado Springs: Helmers & Howard, 1992.

Lohmann, Johann Friedrich. *Karl Barth und der Neukantianismus: Die Rezeption des Neukantianismus im Römerbrief und ihre Bedeutung für die weitere Ausarbeitung der Theologie Karl Barths.* New York: de Gruyter, 1995.

Lonergan, Bernard J. F. *Insight: A Study of Human Understanding.* New York: Philosophical Library, 1970.

Lukasiewicz, Jan. *Elements of Mathematical Logic.* Translated by Olgierd Wojtasiewicz. New York: Macmillan, 1963.

McCormack, Bruce L. "Barth in Context: A Response to Professor Gunton." *Scottish Journal of Theology* 49.4 (1996) 491–8.

———. "Beyond Nonfoundational and Postmodern Readings of Barth: Critically Realistic Dialectical Theology." *Zeitschrift Für Dialektische Theologie* 13.1 and 13.2 (1997) 67–95, 170–94.

———. *Karl Barth's Critically Realistic Dialectical Theology: Its Genesis and Development 1909–1936.* Oxford: Clarendon, 1996.

———. *Orthodox and Modern: Studies in the Theology of Karl Barth.* Grand Rapids: Baker Academic, 2008.

———. "A Scholastic of a Higher Order: The Development of Karl Barth's Theology, 1921–1931." PhD diss., Princeton Theological Seminary, 1989.

McFague, Sallie. *Metaphoric Theology: Models of God in Religious Language.* Philadelphia: Fortress, 1982.

McMullin, Ernan. "A Case for Scientific Realism." In *Scientific Realism*, edited by Jarrett Leplin, 8–40. Berkeley: University of California Press, 1984.

———, ed. *Construction and Constraint: The Shaping of Scientific Rationality*. Notre Dame, IN: The University of Notre Dame Press, 1988.

———. *The Inference That Makes Science*. Milwaukee, WI: Marquette University Press, 1992.

———. "The Shaping of Scientific Rationality." In *Construction and Constraint: The Shaping of Scientific Rationality*, edited by Ernan McMullin, 1–47. Notre Dame, IN: University of Notre Dame Press, 1988.

Momsa, Peter Halman. *Karl Barth's Idea of Revelation*. Somerville, NJ: Somerset, 1937.

La Montagne, D. Paul. "Hans-Georg Gadamer's Ontological Hermeneutics and Karl Barth's Biblical Hermeneutics." *Koinonia* 8.1 (1996) 57–84.

Moore, Gregory H. "The Emergence of First Order Logic." In *History and Philosophy of Modern Mathematics*, edited by William Aspray and Phillip Kitcher, 95–135. Minneapolis: University of Minnesota Press, 1988.

Murphey, Nancey. "The Limits of Pragmatism and the Limits of Realism." *Zygon* 28 (1993) 351–59.

Nielsen, Bent Fleming. *Die Rationalität der Offenbarungstheologie: Die Struktur Des Theologieverständnisses von Karl Barth*. Aarhus, Denmark: Aarhus University Press, 1988.

Niiniluoto, Ilkka. *Critical Scientific Realism*. The Clarendon Library of Logic and Philosophy. Oxford: Oxford University Press, 1999.

Pannenberg, Wolfhart. *Basic Questions in Theology, Volume I*. Translated by George H. Kehm. Philadelphia: Westminster, 1970.

———. *Theology and the Philosophy of Science*. Translated by Francis McDonaugh. Philadelphia: Fortress, 1976.

PCUSA. *The Book of Confessions: Presbyterian Church (USA)*. Louisville, KY: The Office of the General Assembly, 1999.

Peacocke, Arthur. *Intimations of Reality: Critical Realism in Science and Religion*. Notre Dame, IN: University of Notre Dame Press, 1984.

Pedersen, Olaf. "Christian Belief and the Fascination of Science." In *Physics, Philosophy and Theology: A Common Quest for Understanding*, edited by Robert J. Russel, William R. Stoeger, and George V. Coyne, 125–40. Vatican City State: Vatican Observatory, 1988.

Penrose, Roger. *The Emperor's New Mind: Concerning Computers, Minds, and the Laws of Physics*. Oxford: Oxford University Press, 1989.

Pirsig, Robert. *Zen and the Art of Motorcycle Maintenance*. New York: Bantam, 1974.

Poincaré, Henri. *The Foundations of Science*. Translated by George Bruce Halstead. Lancaster, PA: Science, 1946.

Popper, Karl. *The Logic of Scientific Discovery*. London: Routledge, 1980.

Prenter, Regin. "Dietrich Bonhoeffer and Karl Barth's Positivism of Revelation." In *World Come of Age: A Symposium on Dietrich Bonhoeffer*, edited by Ronald Gregor Smith, translated by Martin Rumscheidt, 93–130. Philadelphia: Fortress, 1967.

Putnam, Hilary. "What is Realism?" In *Scientific Realism*, edited by Jarrett Leplin, 140–53. Berkeley: University of California Press, 1984.

Rescher, Nicholas. *Kant and the Reach of Reason: Studies in Kant's Theory of Rational Systematization*. Cambridge: Cambridge University Press, 2000.

Roberts, Richard H. *A Theology on Its Way?: Essays on Karl Barth*. Edinburgh: T. & T. Clark, 1991.

Roberts, Richard. "The Reception of the Theology of Karl Barth in the Anglo-Saxon World: History, Typology and Prospect." In *Karl Barth: Centenary Essays*, edited by S. W. Sykes, 115–71. Cambridge: Cambridge University Press, 1989.

Rorty, Richard. *Philosophy and the Mirror of Nature*. Princeton, NJ: Princeton University Press, 1979.

Royce, Josiah. "Introduction." In *The Foundations of Science*, by Henri Poincaré, translated by George Bruce Halstead, 9–26. Lancaster, PA: Science, 1946.

Rumscheidt, H. Martin. *Revelation and Theology: An Analysis of the Barth–Harnack Correspondence of 1923*. Cambridge: Cambridge University Press, 1972.

Scott-Taggart, M. J. "Recent Work on the Philosophy of Kant." In *Kant Studies Today*, edited by Lewis W. Beck, 1–71. LaSalle, IL: Open Court, 1969.

Sellars, Roy Wood. *Critical Realism: A Study of the Nature and Conditions of Knowledge*. New York: Russell & Russell, 1916.

Sellars, Wilfrid. *Philosophical Perspectives*. Springfield, IL: Thomas, 1967.

Silber, J. R. "The Metaphysical Importance of the Highest Good as the Canon of Pure Reason in Kant's Philosophy." *Texas Studies in Literature and Language* 1 (1959) 232–44.

Stein, Howard. "Logos, Logic, and Logistiké: Some Philosophical Remarks on Nineteenth Century Transformation of Mathematics." In *History and Philosophy of Modern Mathematics*, edited by William Aspray and Phillip Kitcher, 238–59. Minneapolis: University of Minnesota Press, 1988.

Sykes, S. W. "Introduction." In *The Way of Theology in Karl Barth*, edited by Martin Rumscheidt, 1–24. Alison Park, PA: Pickwick, 1986.

Thiel, John E. *Nonfoundationalism*. Minneapolis: Fortress, 1994.

Thompson, John. *The Holy Spirit in the Theology of Karl Barth*. Allison Park, PA: Pickwick, 1991.

Torrance, Thomas F. *Karl Barth: An Introduction to His Early Theology*. London: SCM, 1962.

———. *Karl Barth: Biblical and Evangelical Theologian*. Edinburgh: T. & T. Clark, 1990.

———. *Transformation and Convergence in the Frame of Knowledge*. Belfast: Christian Journals, 1984.

Trigg, Roger. *Rationality and Science: Can Science Explain Everything?* Oxford: Blackwell, 1993.

———. *Reality at Risk: A Defense of Realism in Philosophy and the Sciences*. Brighton, UK: Harvester, 1980.

van Fraasen, Bas C. *The Scientific Image*. Oxford: Clarendon, 1990.

van Heijenoort, Jean, ed. and trans. *A Sourcebook in Mathematical Logic, 1879–1931*. Boston: Harvard University Press, 1967.

van Huyssteen, J. Wentzel. *Essays in Postfoundational Theology*. Grand Rapids: Eerdmans, 1997.

———. "Postfoundationalism in Theology and Science." In *Rethinking Theology and Science: Six Models for the Current Dialogue*, edited by Niels Hendrik Gregerson and J. Wentzel van Huyssteen, 13–50. Grand Rapids: Eerdmans, 1998.

———. *The Shaping of Rationality: Toward Interdisciplinarity in Theology and Science*. Grand Rapids: Eerdmans, 1999.

———. *Theology and the Justification of Faith: Constructing Theories in Systematic Theology*. Grand Rapids: Eerdmans, 1989.

van Kooten Niekerk, Kees. "A Critical Realist Perspective on the Dialogue Between Theology and Science." In *Rethinking Theology and Science: Six Models for the Current Dialogue*, edited by Niels Hendrik Gregerson and J. Wentzel van Huyssteen, 51–86. Grand Rapids: Eerdmans, 1998.

von Rintelen, Fritz Joachim. *Contemporary German Philosophy and Its Background.* Bonn: Bouvier, 1973.

Wang, Hao. *Reflections on Kurt Gödel.* Cambridge: MIT Press, 1987.

Warnke, Georgia. *Gadamer: Hermeneutics, Tradition and Reason.* Stanford, CA: Stanford University Press, 1987.

Wigner, Eugene P. "The Unreasonable Effectiveness of Mathematics." *Communications in Pure and Applied Mathematics* 13 (1960) 1–14.

Zijlstra, Onno. "Essay: Barth und der (Pan-)Kritische Rationalismus." Übersetzung von Siegfried Arends. *Zeitschrift für Dialektische Theologie* 5.2 (1989) 269–77.

Zinov'ev, A. A. *Philosophical Problems of Many Valued Logic.* Translated by Guido Küng and David Dinsmore Comey. Dordrecht, Holland: Reidel, 1963.

Names Index

Subjects Index

232